Behind Deep Blue

Behind Deep Blue

BUILDING THE COMPUTER THAT DEFEATED
THE WORLD CHESS CHAMPION

FENG-HSIUNG HSU

Princeton University Press
Princeton and Oxford

Published by Princeton University Press,
41 William Street, Princeton, New Jersey 08540

In the United Kingdom: Princeton University Press,
3 Market Place, Woodstock, Oxfordshire OX20 1SY

ISBN 0-691-09065-3 (cloth : alk. paper)

Library of Congress Cataloging-in-Publication Data
has been applied for

This book has been composed in Stone Serif and Stone Sans
by Stephen I Pargeter, Banbury, Oxfordshire, UK

Printed on acid-free paper. ∞

www.pupress.princeton.edu

Printed in the United States of America

10 9 8 7 6 5 4 3 2 1

Contents

Preface

This book recounts my view of the adventure to create Deep Blue, the first computer to defeat the World Chess Champion in a serious match. I started the project in 1985. Twelve years later, the adventure ended with Deep Blue setting a major milestone in human history and forever altering our view of how we would live with the computer.

Chess machines like Deep Blue have a long history. The Turk, a "chess machine" built by Hungarian engineer Baron Wolfgang von Kempelen, first appeared at the Austrian court in 1769. Its most famous victim was probably Napoleon Bonaparte. The Turk, however, was a fake—a hidden human chess player made the moves for it.

In the 1830s, Charles Babbage dreamed of building a chess machine to attract funding for his Analytic Engine (the first *mechanical* programmable computer, but never completed). He built a tic-tac-toe machine instead. A real chess machine was too hard, especially if you had to build it with only mechanical parts.

The first *electronic* programmable computer, ENIAC, was completed in 1946. Shortly after, in 1949, Claude Shannon gave a lecture that laid the foundation for modern chess computers. At that time, many renowned computer scientists believed that the Computer Chess Problem—creating a chess computer that could beat the World Champion—would be solved within a few years, but their predictions turned out to be overly optimistic. As time went on, and with no solution in sight, solving the Computer Chess Problem became a holy grail for computer scientists. By the early 1980s, over thirty years after Shannon's seminal work, the best chess computers were playing at US national master level, still a long way from challenging the World Champion.

My involvement with computer chess was by accident. In the spring of 1985, Professor H T Kung, my faculty advisor at Carnegie Mellon, informed me that my survival in graduate school was in doubt. A couple of weeks earlier, as a favor, I looked into a technical problem for a leading computer chess expert in our department. He, the expert, did not like the solution that I came up with. Neither did I. After some thinking, I reached the conclusion that the real issue was with his approach. A radical new design, in part based on his competitors' ideas, was far superior. After he rejected my new solution, I told him bluntly that his approach was inferior and I had lost interest. Professor Kung explained that I should have been more tactful. He then urged me to write up a technical report and give a presentation to back up my assertion. I already had enough trouble from an earlier indiscretion that almost got me kicked out of the school ...

Thus began the strange and unexpected journey to create the most powerful chess-playing entity in the world, Deep Blue.

Initially, I planned to retrace this journey along the same route as that taken in a favorite book of mine, *The Double Helix: A Personal Account of the Discovery of the Structure of DNA* by Nobel Laureate Dr James D Watson. As I was writing, however, I realized that the two books would be quite different in scope and nature. Dr Watson's book tells of one of the greatest scientific discoveries in the twentieth century. This book is more about an engineering quest than a scientific discovery. By nature, an engineering quest covers a richer fabric of life. The technical ideas behind the quest have first to be discovered and then carried to their logical completion. The discovery may come from luck or inspiration, but the rest of the quest is a matter of perspiration and perseverance. The scope of the book, therefore, is closer to, say, Chuck Yeager's *The Quest for Mach One*, his account of breaking the sound barrier. This book depicts the quest to exceed, even if only briefly, the chess-playing ability of the best human chess player on the planet.

Comparatively, this book is perhaps more light-hearted than either of those mentioned above. One reason for this is the seemingly frivolous nature of the very idea of creating a computer that can defeat the World Chess Champion. Computer scientists are humans too, and they do like to have fun. The other reason is that I, and my writing, were greatly influenced by another favorite book of mine, *Surely You're Joking, Mr Feynman: Adventures of a Curious Character* by Nobel Laureate Dr Richard P Feynman. From Dr Feynman's book, I learned of his peculiar sense of humor, irrepressible passion for life, and no-nonsense way of looking at things. But, more importantly, I learned of the value of being able to laugh at myself. Computer chess was a highly competitive research field—scientific rivalry was as strong and heated as in the DNA research area. The final competition with Garry Kasparov, the World Chess Champion, was also an extremely serious affair. The ability to laugh at myself and not to take myself too seriously kept me sane during some very tense situations, arising first from the scientific rivalry and then from the two matches with Garry. If you can take a step back and see the larger picture, the most serious moments in life can also be the funniest.

Many books cover the matches between World Chess Champion Garry Kasparov and Deep Blue, but most of them dwell on the "man versus machine" aspect. These books also tend to be instant chess books. The "man versus machine" angle apparently sells well for chess books, but it does not capture the true essence of the contest. The contest was really between men in two different roles: man as a performer and man as a toolmaker. Two matches were played between Garry and Deep Blue, with different results. In the 1996 match, man won as a performer, and in the 1997 rematch, man won as a toolmaker.

This book records the stories of the toolmakers, the people who built the machines. Chapter two, the early part of Chapter three and Appendix A are, however, about my life prior to the launching of the project. The stories in Chapter two and the early part of Chapter three have direct relevance to the project. The project existed only because events in these stories took place. Appendix A contains stories of my early life in Taiwan, and can be read as background material. I put this material in for two reasons. One is to answer the question of what kind of chess imbecile would decide to take on the world's greatest chess mind. The other reason is to provide you with clues about why things ended up the way they did.

The stories in the book span two socially and culturally different organizations, the Carnegie Mellon Computer Science Department and IBM Research. The first half of the book focuses on the project at Carnegie Mellon. During this period the basic technical ideas took shape, a new computer chess team was formed as a lark, and an intense scientific rivalry erupted. The rest of the book documents the evolution of the project at IBM: adjustment to the new environments, painful personnel changes, development of new chess machines and, of course, two intense and controversial matches between Garry and Deep Blue. The epilogue of the book covers post-match events, including Garry's apparent avoidance of a replay even though for two years after his defeat by Deep Blue, he had continuously thrown out a challenge for such a match. Garry lost the World Championship to Vladimir Kramnik in November 2000. Will this make a match against Kramnik a possibility? It is not clear at this time of writing.

A frequently-asked question about Deep Blue is, "Is it intelligent?" Garry's accusations of cheating both during and after the 1997 match confirmed that Deep Blue passed the chess version of the Turing Test (a blind test to tell whether you are interacting with a human or a computer). But Deep Blue is not intelligent. It is only a finely-crafted tool that exhibits intelligent behavior in a limited domain. Garry lost the match, but he was the player with the real intelligence—Deep Blue would never be able to come up with the imaginative accusations.

One final note: Deep Blue was a team effort. One of the dangers of writing a first-person account of a team effort is that the time and the energy put in by other members of the team can be under-represented. To reduce this problem, I have sought out team members' feedback on early drafts. If I still fail to credit someone's contribution properly, the fault is all mine.

Acknowledgments

The pioneering work of Joe Condon and Ken Thompson at Bell Labs, on the chess machine Belle, was the direct inspiration for the project. Ken also provided some of the endgame databases used by Deep Blue in both matches against Garry Kasparov. Lewis Stiller provided the other endgame databases.

The Computer Science Department at Carnegie Mellon University and IBM Research were the two organizations that made the project possible. There are many other people from both organizations to whom I want to give special thanks:

At Carnegie Mellon,
- Deep Thought team members Thomas Anantharaman, Mike Browne, Murray Campbell, Peter Jansen, and Andreas Nowatzyk for their contributions and tolerance of my sometimes irrational behavior.
- My advisor, Professor H T Kung, for his understanding and encouragement and for providing the funding to build Deep Thought.
- Professor Raj Reddy and Professor Randy Bryant, for providing additional financial assistance in the later phases of the Deep Thought project.
- Lawrence Butcher and John Zsarnay, for providing much-needed technical support.
- Various members of the Hitech team, but in particular Carl Ebeling and Gordon Goetsch, for valuable hints and interesting discussions. Dr Hans Berliner, who was more the royal opposition, provided the spur that kept us running forward.

- Other people who provided help and encouragement include Professor Roberto Bisiani, Kai-Fu Lee, Professor Tom Mitchell, Professor Danny Sleator, Professor Bob Sproull, and Professor Hide Tokuda.

At IBM Research,

- Deep Blue team members Murray Campbell and Joe Hoane, for their contribution and commitment to the project. In passing, I want to thank Murray's wife Gina and Joe's wife Elizabeth for their tolerance and understanding of the long work hours and the lost weekends. Several times, Murray and Joe had to bail me out of some technical troubles associated with the bringing up of the Deep Blue chess chips, at the cost of their family lives.
- The entire management chain, but especially our two managers, Randy Moulic and C J Tan, for their support and encouragement.
- Jerry Brody, for providing the technical support for the team.

Many outsiders have helped. Back in Deep Thought days, Larry Kaufman, Stuart Cracraft, Jim Gillogly, Frederic Friedel, Don Maddox and Dap Hartmann all provided help. Numerous IBMers, both in and outside IBM Research, were involved in hosting or providing technical support for the two Deep Blue matches, as did people from ACM and TSI. I thank them all.

Deep Blue would not be where it is without the help of many Grandmasters and other chess players who either played games against or trained with Deep Blue and its predecessors. Among the Grandmasters who had direct responsibilities at one time or another were Maxim Dlugy, Joel Benjamin, Miguel Illescas, Nick DeFirmian, and John Fedorowicz. Joel, of course, was also our chess advisor for both Deep Blue matches. Grandmaster Robert Byrne, the *New York Times* chess columnist, has been a good personal friend who dropped in occasionally for a few games. Besides the Grandmasters who worked on the project, Robert was the one who provided the most input. Finally, without the participation of Garry Kasparov, the World Chess Champion, we would never have found out Deep Blue's real strength.

Many people have reviewed earlier drafts of this book and made suggestions for improvements. Dennis Allison, Thomas

Anantharaman, Mike Browne, Robert Byrne, Murray Campbell, Yih-Farn Robin Chen, Joe Hoane, Robert Hyatt, Howard Landman, Jim Loy, Timothy Mann, Andreas Nowatzyk, George Paul, Jonathan Schaeffer, Danny Sleator, C J Tan, Ken Thompson, and an anonymous reviewer all provided valuable feedback. My agent, William Clark, contributed an alternative view from his unique perspective.

Some of the photos in the book are from my private collection. Many of the match photos come from the IBM collection. Monty Newborn, Andreas Nowatzyk, and Danny Sleator provided the balance.

Last but not least, I would like to thank David Ireland, my editor, for refining and polishing my writing. In the end, however, any mistakes and omissions are solely my responsibility.

Chess Notation

This is not a chess book—there is no real chess analysis here. I have tried to avoid using chess notations or chess diagrams as much as possible. However, some of the controversies, especially those from the second Deep Blue match, centered on the chess moves played by Deep Blue. In theory, you could follow the controversies simply by treating the chess moves as labels, but it does no harm to know what the moves really mean. The chapters on the two Deep Blue matches contain chess diagrams to make it easier for you to visualize the game situations—you can treat them as though they are photos of the chessboard. Overleaf is a short description of the algebraic chess notation used in the book.

The diagram shows the names for the eight rows (also known as ranks) and the eight columns (also known as files) of the chessboard. The rows are labeled 1 to 8 from the bottom row to the top. The columns are labeled a to h from the leftmost column to the rightmost. The name of each square of the chessboard is based on the column and the row that it is on. Therefore, the lower right corner square of the chessboard is known as h1, and the upper left corner square is known as a8. The chessboard itself can be divided vertically into two equal halves: the queenside (a, b, c, and d file) and the kingside (e, f, g, and h file). The names for the two halves come from the position of kings and queens on the starting chessboard.

Not counting the pawn, there are five types of pieces: knight, bishop, rook, queen, and king. The pieces can be colored white or black. On the starting chessboard, white pawns are on the second rank and black pawns are on the seventh rank. The pieces on the first and the eighth rank are, from a file to h file, rook, knight, bishop, queen, king, bishop, knight, and rook. The first rank pieces are white and the eighth rank pieces are black. The player with the white pieces is referred to as White, and the player with the black pieces, Black.

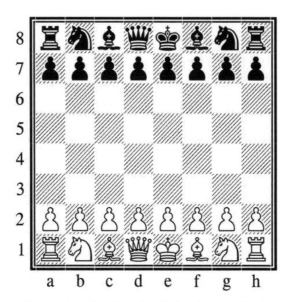

The starting chessboard, with labeled coordinates.

Pawn moves are represented by the destination square of the pawn move. The move e4 is a pawn move to the e4 square. Pawn captures are represented by the name of the file that the pawn came from, followed by the destination square. An optional symbol 'x' can be placed between the file name and square name. Thus, the pawn capture axb4 uses an a-file pawn to capture a piece on the b4 square.

Knight moves are represented by the piece symbol 'N' followed by the destination square. The move Nf3 is a move that places a knight on the f3 square. When there is more than one knight that can move to the same destination square, the name of the from-file or the name of the from-rank might be added before the name of the destination square. The move N2f3 would mean moving the knight on the second rank to the f3 square. If the knight move is a capture, then the optional capture symbol 'x' could be added before the destination square. The move Nxg5 therefore is a knight move that captures a piece on the g5 square.

Bishop moves, rook moves, queen moves, and king moves follow the same format as the knight moves but with the piece symbol replaced by 'B', 'R', 'Q' and 'K' respectively. The move Qa4 therefore means moving the queen to the a4 square.

The symbol '+' following a move means the move is a check; Rc4+ means rook to c4 and giving a check.

Pawn promotions are represented by the pawn's move followed by the symbol for the piece to which the pawn is promoted. Therefore g8Q means pawn to g8 and promoted to a queen.

Castling moves are represented by O-O and O-O-O, which mean castling kingside and castling queenside respectively.

The move annotation symbols '!', '!!', '?', '??' mean "a good move", "an excellent move", "a questionable move" and "a dubious move" respectively. So h5! means "pawn to h5, a good move".

Prologue

 CHAPTER 1

Show Time!

In late April 1997, posters for an unusual chess event were appearing on the streets of New York. They showed a somber and pondering gentleman in his early 30s peering over a chess set at the viewers. The small caption under his chin said, "How do you make a computer blink?" The gentleman on the poster was the World Chess Champion Garry Kasparov, possibly the strongest chess player who has ever lived.

Off the street, in the basement of the Equitable Building, I was staring at the blank screens in an empty auditorium. In a few days, the auditorium would be filled with an overflowing crowd; TV cameras would be entrenched at vantage locations and the three huge projection screens at the front would come to life. The left screen would be showing a live image from a TV studio on the 35th floor of the building, serving as the game room. The live image would usually show the two contestants sitting across a specially designed playing table. The contestant on the left would be Garry Kasparov. The contestant on the other side would be one of my two colleagues, Murray Campbell and Joe Hoane, or me. Garry's real opponent was the chess computer, Deep Blue, that the three of us had designed and programmed. During the games we acted merely as extensions of Deep Blue and made moves for it on the physical chessboard. In the auditorium itself, three chess commentators, sometimes with a guest commentator or two, would be using the center screen to show their analysis of the ongoing game. The right screen would be displaying the overhead shot of the chessboard. This way, the audience in the auditorium would have a clear view of the present game position.

It had taken me almost twelve years to reach this point. When

I started, Garry was not the World Champion; it was a few months yet before he was crowned. For the past eleven years, since 1986, my partners and I had been building successively more powerful chess computers. Our eventual goal was to beat the World Chess Champion, whoever he or she was.

Before us, many pioneers, some famous and some not so famous, had made their contributions to the "Computer Chess Problem". In 1949, Claude Shannon made his proposal on how to program a computer to play chess. Since then, thousands of computer scientists, engineers, hobbyists, chess players, and even commercial organizations had worked on the problem. Some wanted to use chess as an experimental tool to find out how human intelligence worked. "If one could devise a successful chess machine, one would seem to have penetrated to the core of human intellectual endeavor," said Allen Newell, Cliff Shaw and Herbert Simon in one of the early computer chess papers. Other people viewed chess as a clear-cut, well-defined example of a complex problem. "Solving" chess could conceivably provide new techniques to solve other complex problems. The commercial entities did it for profit, of course, and some people, especially the hobbyists, did it just for fun.

We approached the problem from a different direction. We, or at least I, viewed the problem as a purely engineering one. Since the late 1970s, it had been established that chess computers became stronger as their hardware speed increased. By 1985, when I started my small project that eventually become Deep Blue, the extrapolation from the experimental data indicated that a one thousandfold increase in hardware speed might be sufficient to produce a World Champion-class chess machine. Our project began with a simple goal, namely, to find out whether a massive increase in hardware speed would be sufficient to "solve" the Computer Chess Problem. Building this "Mother of all Chess Machines" was an interesting problem by itself. Of course, it would be an added bonus if our machine could indeed defeat the World Champion.

The previous version of Deep Blue, lost a match to Garry Kasparov in Philadelphia in 1996. But two-thirds of the way into that match, we had played to a tie with Kasparov. That old version of Deep Blue was already faster than the machine that I conjectured in 1985, and yet it was not enough. There was more to solving the Computer Chess Problem than just increasing the hardware speed. Since that match, we rebuilt Deep Blue from scratch, going through every match problem we had and engaging Grandmasters extensively in our preparations. Somehow, all the work caused Grandmaster Joel Benjamin, our chess advisor, and one of the best chess players in the US, to say, "You know, sometimes Deep Blue plays chess." Joel could no longer distinguish with certainty Deep Blue's moves from the moves played by the top Grandmasters.

The press covered this new match with much anticipation. If the new Deep Blue won the match, then it would be a momentous occasion in the long history of men as toolmakers. It would also be the completion of a long-sought-after milestone for computer scientists and artificial intelligence researchers. It was almost certain that this match would be bigger than any World Chess Championship match, with possibly the sole exception of the Fischer vs. Spassky match in 1972. If we did win, perhaps not even that Fischer vs. Spassky match would compare.

The new Deep Blue was much improved, but would it be enough? Would the journey begun by my partners and me so many years ago finally be over?

Carnegie Mellon

 CHAPTER 2

An Office of Troublemakers

"Your office is an office of troublemakers!" Kung exclaimed, with a resigned look. Kung was Professor H T Kung, my faculty advisor at Carnegie Mellon University in Pittsburgh. He was a tall, well-built man in his 40s. I was a graduate student in the Computer Science (CS) Department. We had just had a long private conversation in his office.

It was the autumn of 1987. Professor Kung had been my advisor during my entire stay at Carnegie Mellon. I had a great deal of respect for him, not just because he was a good advisor to me, but also because of the deeds that he did in private. Professor Kung was a direct descendent of Confucius and took great pride in doing whatever he could to assist the technical and economic developments of Chinese societies around the world. I was not having trouble with Professor Kung. My troubles were with another faculty member in the department.

At the time of the conversation, there were two computer chess teams at Carnegie Mellon. Dr Hans Berliner headed the Hitech team. The competing ChipTest team was a group of free-willed, mostly unsupervised graduate students, of which I was one. I had some light faculty supervision from Professor Kung, while my team members worked on ChipTest almost purely for fun. The competition between the two teams had been friendly, but it was about to turn into an intense rivalry.

In hindsight, the rivalry was inevitable. There had been some friction between the two teams. The ChipTest team was not happy with the frequent and incorrect public portrayal that Dr Berliner was supervising us or that we were his students. To a great extent this portrayal was the result of Dr Berliner's existing fame in computer chess, which led reporters automatically to assume [1] that he led all computer chess efforts at Carnegie Mellon. This characterization was somewhat insulting to the ChipTest team, but it alone would not have caused the immediate escalation of the contention.

The escalation was triggered by, of all things, an invitation for the ChipTest team to play in a chess tournament. The Hitech team happened to be going to the same tournament and Berliner had made his case to Kung on why ChipTest should skip the event [2].

My conversation with Professor Kung was precisely on what to do with the chess invitation. Kung was supportive of the ChipTest team and saw no reason why we should not play. However, to avoid further problems, the ChipTest team had already decided to honor Dr Berliner's suggestion prior to the conversation.

Professor Kung was relieved that the issue seemed to be resolved, but when he made his remark about the "troublemakers", he must have had a sense of déjà vu. Two years before, in 1985, we had had another conversation, also on an issue related to Dr Berliner. That other conversation was a critical part of the chain of events that led to the creation of ChipTest and, eventually, Deep Blue.

The real seed of the Deep Blue project can be traced back even further. It all began with Professor Kung's "troublemakers" ...

First Year Graduate Students

The Computer Science (CS) Department at Carnegie Mellon was *the* Department of the university. Several others ranked among the top ten in their disciplines, but CS was ranked among the top three, the other two being the ones at MIT and Stanford. Depending on personal preferences, some would even say that the CS Department at Carnegie Mellon was *the* best. The Department had its own unique atmosphere, and the graduate students had a great deal more say in their own research directions than at other schools. The fact that the Department offered only a PhD program

---

[1] This incorrect assumption persists to this day. Almost all the chess books on the Deep Blue matches state wrongly that Berliner was the faculty advisor of the ChipTest/Deep Thought team.

[2] The section *An Invitation from California* in Chapter 4 details how this whole incident played out.

(no BS or MS program) probably gave the faculty the chance to experiment and come up with the unique system.

In part because of the unusual system and in part because of the diverse background of the incoming students, the entire first month of each fall semester was designated the "Immigration Course". For the incoming students, it was a time to learn about the environments, tools, projects, and people, and generally to have a good time. The older students would spend time demonstrating their projects, helping the new students to adapt, and of course, generally having a good time themselves. Near the end of the Immigration Course, the annual Department "Reception" would be held, usually at some fancy location in Pittsburgh. I have a fond memory of pigging out at the Reception as a starving graduate student. The Immigration Course was also the time the "Marriage" process took place. During the Immigration Course, the new students sought out the faculty whose research interested them, and decided whom they wanted as their faculty advisors. The faculty, of course, also observed the new students, deciding whether they wanted a particular student. As in real life, the Marriages were not final, and "divorces" between faculty members and students did occur sometimes, made possible partly by the fact that the funding sources for the students were not necessarily tied to specific projects. Faculty members controlled their advisees mainly through the respect that their advisees had for them. Other than course work, faculty members had very little hold over non-advisee students.

In 1982, the year I "immigrated" into the Department, the acceptance rate of the admitted students was higher than expected, and there was a space crunch. Normally when offices were assigned, it was considered preferable to mingle the incoming students with older students. As a result of the space crunch I ended up in an empty office together with three other incoming students, Mike Browne, Andreas Nowatzyk and Tony Stentz. In the end, the four of us came out all right, but along the way the faculty probably wished that they had done otherwise. The next year, Tony moved to another office, and for several years only Mike, Andreas and I occupied the office, becoming close friends. Professor Kung's remark on troublemakers probably did not include Tony.

Mike was probably the first American with whom I had a real conversation, which took place on my first day on the Carnegie Mellon campus. It was also only my third day in the United States.

When I opened the door to my newly-assigned office, I found a bearded man inside. This was Mike. Because of his beard, I could not tell quite how old he was, but he turned out to be one of the younger students in the incoming class. Born in New Jersey, but growing up in Allentown, Pennsylvania, Mike finished his undergraduate degree at Lehigh University in just three years. In our conversation Mike described himself as a "hacker", which he defined as someone who could churn out computer programs. That is, someone who creates, although in a specialized domain. This definition is still in use today, although the more common definition used by the media is someone who damages or exploits computer systems through virtual means. The newer definition describes a destructive person. Mike was obviously very smart, but he was also surprisingly self-effacing. He attributed his accelerated college schooling entirely to his ability to do well in multiple-choice tests. "I just happened to be good at taking multiple-choice tests," he said, suggesting that he had no other useful talent.

While Mike was one of the younger incoming students, Andreas and I were among the older ones. In my case, this was because in Taiwan, where I came from, boys were required to serve two years in the military after college [3]. Andreas was older because he had spent one extra year to get *two* tough undergraduate degrees: physics and computer science. He hailed from Germany, was a graduate of the University of Hamburg, and had been one year into his PhD program in Germany before he decided to make the move to Carnegie Mellon. Mike was an extremely good programmer, and Andreas was not too shabby either. Besides being a top-notch programmer, Andreas turned out to be a man with many technical skills. He never ceased to amaze me while we were at Carnegie Mellon. I had a dogged belief that I could be good at anything technical if I put my mind to it. Andreas seemed to be already good at everything technical.

Both Mike and I were somewhat playful in our early years at Carnegie Mellon, while Andreas was all business from day one. Andreas and I did not really become close friends until much later when we found that we shared many common technical interests. The friendship, however, was not really symmetrical. I can remember many instances of Andreas helping me in areas where I was

---

[3] See *Sidestepping Authorities* in *A Lad in Taiwan*, Appendix A, for a discussion on the military service in Taiwan.

lacking. But he was so self-sufficient that I don't recall ever doing anything to in any way help him.

Andreas, Mike, and I all had some prior contact with chess, or computer chess, before arriving in Carnegie Mellon. Mike used to be a serious tournament chess player when he was in high school. Andreas did not play chess seriously, but he had been keenly interested in computer chess. He had once helped to referee a World Microcomputer Chess Championship tournament in Germany while an undergraduate student. My earlier contacts with computer chess were mainly from reading technical journals and books. During our immigration both Andreas and I checked out the existing computer chess research in the Department. We were both interested in Very Large Scale Integration (VLSI) chip design and Carl Ebeling, a graduate student in the VLSI group, was designing a VLSI-based chess machine. Neither Andreas nor I were sufficiently interested to do anything with computer chess. At the time I thought computer chess still had a long way to go and I did not see how it would end. Moreover, I was really interested in doing something *practical*.

Professor Kung was the leading faculty member in the VLSI group and the obvious choice for both Andreas and me. Mike decided to work with a professor in Artificial Intelligence (AI).

Andreas had a very low opinion of AI research in general. Mike did not share the same opinion at first but, after he split with his first advisor, both he and Andreas referred to AI as bullshit. I did not go to the same extreme, but I had seen some so-called research in AI that really deserved the bullshit label. The largest group by far in the Department was the AI group, including almost half of the students. The majority view toward AI in our office was clearly the minority view in the Department.

Despite our mutual low opinion of AI, over the years Mike, Andreas and I had several conversations about computer chess. One of the conversations was about Belle, the top chess machine from the early 1980s. While Andreas was still at the University of Hamburg he had attended a talk by Ken Thompson, one of the Belle designers. In the talk, Ken described experiments that showed Belle playing more strongly when given more time. I posed the question of what would happen if a Belle-like machine were, say, one thousand times faster. None of us believed that such a machine would be sufficient to beat the World Champion, but it might be close. Anyway, when we had the conversation, none of us realized that I would drag both Andreas and Mike into a computer chess project trying to answer that very question.

Professor Kung's remark about troublemakers perhaps included Andreas as, after a couple of years, Andreas and he had a falling-out. I don't know how bad Mike's split was, but it might have been bad enough for Professor Kung to have noticed at the "Black Friday" faculty meeting held at the end of each semester. Andreas could well have been high on Professor Kung's list of "troublemakers", but I probably took the top slot since I was the source of a lot of other troubles. Some of the troubles I caused resulted from immature pranks. Other troubles were not entirely my doing, as you will see in the next few chapters.

The pranks that I pulled in the early years had two profound effects. The first was that I gained a reputation of a questionable nature among the students. This reputation ironically was helpful in recruiting other students to work on the chess project. (Of course, recruiting others was just the first step. In the end, the project had to be interesting in its own right and I had to treat my friends properly.)

The second effect was to place me on the endangered species list at the Department. My first prank, mentioned in the next section, did not win me any friends at the Black Friday faculty meeting. My second prank almost got me kicked out of the school and could have landed me in jail if it had taken place a few years later.

A License to Make Mischief

Taiwanese students were supposed to pay strict attention to school rules and, while I was still in Taiwan, I was always fascinated by stories of students pulling ingenious April Fool's pranks on US college campuses.

During the Immigration Course, one of the sessions attended by everyone was the Department Introduction where we all squeezed into a large classroom and introduced ourselves to the rest of the Department. After introducing herself to the incoming students, Sharon Burks, who was the Department Administration Assistant at the time [4], jokingly advised whoever had forged an

---

[4] Sharon is now the Associate Department Head of the Computer Science Department and the Assistant Dean for Academic Affairs of the School of Computer Science at Carnegie Mellon.

electronic post from her on April 1 to watch out. Surprised to hear of such insubordination from the older students, I said to myself, "This is neat. So we have a license to make mischief."

My first year at Carnegie Mellon was a busy one. I wanted to pass all the core qualifiers as fast as I could. The two years spent in military service in Taiwan had made me rusty so I also had a lot of ground to catch up. After the first semester, I was in decent shape school-wise, and my first April Fool's day at Carnegie Mellon was coming up.

Back in the early 1980s, even in a top CS graduate school like Carnegie Mellon, the graduate students were only guaranteed access to text-only terminals in their offices. Some of us had office workstations that could display black-and-white graphics, and there were a few other workstations for public use in the Terminal Room. But most of our work was still done on terminals connected to then state-of-the-art minicomputers. The minicomputers were less powerful than the personal microcomputers that we can buy today for less than $300 (which, by the way, was not enough to buy even one of the terminals that we used). Most of the minicomputers ran the UNIX operating system [5]. UNIX is widely used today in areas where computer crashes caused by the operating system are not tolerable.

UNIX allows you to "talk" to another user on the same computer, assuming that the other user grants the privilege. Most users grant this privilege by default. When you "talk" to the other user, UNIX writes your typed characters directly onto the other user's terminal. Normally this would be harmless, other than possibly annoying the hell out of the other user if you get obnoxious. There is, however, a way to wreak havoc when the computer terminal used by the other user is somewhat "intelligent". The smarter computer terminals usually will accept command strings that the computer can use to move the cursor (the indicator on the screen which highlights where the new character is to appear) and to read back the (x, y) location of the cursor. By sending appropriate command strings, you can move the cursor to a particular screen location and then cause the terminal to send out the location of the cursor back to your victim's computer. Since the computer is

---

[5] The operating system can be viewed as the basic program controlling all hardware aspects of a computer. Normal programs indirectly access the system hardware through the operating system.

very likely expecting a user command, it usually appears as if the victim has entered the cursor location as a command. Presto, you have caused your victim to execute a command of your own choosing. This was the basic idea behind my April Fool's prank in 1983.

On March 31, I had a conversation with a colleague who then got involved. Our plan was the following: I was to write two programs. The first program would randomly select victims and send out appropriate strings to their terminals. The strings would then cause the victim's terminal to send out a command that executed my second program. The second program would post a random, possibly inappropriate, message on the Department electronic bulletin board from the victim's account. My colleague was to come up with the collection of random messages for the posts, and he did a great job. The hardest technical part of the whole thing was to figure out a way that the victims would not know what had happened, even when they were in front of their terminals. The cursor had to be moved to the appropriate locations to build up the computer command to execute the second program, and it then had to get back to its original location. After the whole process, the screen should look exactly the same as before the attack. It was tricky, but doable. Even sitting in front of the terminal, the victim would only see something similar to a power flicker with the cursor flashing around for about a second. The programs were not ready until the evening of April 1, and we let them loose for the remaining few hours of the day.

The next morning we saw several unusual messages showing up on the electronic bulletin board, with most of the victims being faculty members [6]. An interesting message had a faculty member at the time, asking who was the owner of a pair of panty hose that he found in the ladies' room. Another faculty member "posted" a message saying that he managed to log on to the computer, but did not know how to log off and needed help. He was not amused, and not realizing what day it was, he posted, for real, a message demanding that whoever posted the logging-off message confess. I resurrected my programs, but this time with only one allowed victim, namely me, and the message file was modified to contain only one message. The message first pointed out that professors were

---

[6] Students working late tended to be hackers. Hackers were more likely to disable the writing privilege to their terminals.

sometimes forgetful and that the previous day was April 1. Furthermore, there were clear indications that the messages were not real. All of the message titles were enclosed in quotation marks and, technically, the message was indeed posted from the professor's own account, just as my message was posted from my account through the same mechanism.

I suffered no direct consequence from this incident. But this, and my next far more serious prank, probably affected my standing in the eyes of some faculty members.

After this episode, my colleague disabled the writing privilege to his terminal permanently. Nobody was ever going to do the trick to him! Another friend got interested in playing with the cursor control and eventually created a "psychedelic command prompt". Every time he typed in a command a cowboy-like figure would be displayed on his terminal screen, and an arrow would shoot out from the left side of the screen and hit the cowboy who then disintegrated into nothing.

Mister Rogers' Neighborhood

UNIX is a relatively secure operating system. Ken Thompson, one of its creators, mentioned several ways to compromise it in his Turing Award Lecture. But generally, a well-maintained UNIX system is almost immune to amateurish attacks. The problem is that most UNIX systems are not necessarily well maintained.

In the early 1980s, almost all of the newer computers in universities ran UNIX. Many of these systems were connected to the DARPA (Defense Advanced Research Project Agency) Net, the precursor to today's Internet. The DARPA net was frequently shortened to the Arpanet. The CS Department, with a lot of research projects sponsored by DARPA, was on the Arpanet.

The Department had a dedicated and capable staff maintaining the computer systems, and I never could figure out a way to break the main departmental machines. Out there on the Arpanet, however, there were lots of less secure machines.

In the Department, all computer accounts accessible from the Arpanet had passwords that had to be entered before logging on. This was not true for many computers on the Net. I stumbled [7] onto a machine at UC Berkeley that had a guest account

---

7 Well, not precisely. I had friends studying at Berkeley. Another thing was that I was curious about some of the peculiar bugs in the computer game Rogue, which was authored by students at Berkeley.

without any password. Someone left the door ajar. Now this act alone does not necessarily mean there was a problem. The UNIX operating system allows you to lock up your own private property so that other users cannot access your on-line love letters. (Although why you would leave your love letters on line is beyond me.) The guest account, by definition, had limited rights, therefore a guest should not be able to unlock the locks. So everything's OK, right?

In real life, the building managers usually have master keys that they can use to open any door in the building. On a UNIX system, the system manager can become a so-called "superuser" who can do anything to the system. Certain trusted programs that are needed to maintain the system are usually also given the superuser privilege so that the programs can function properly. Occasionally, the trust placed in these superuser programs is misplaced. The programs themselves may be OK, but the files that they rely on to function might be insecure. Any competent system manager would make sure that the superuser programs themselves cannot be compromised, but the files referenced by the superuser programs can, and do, get neglected by less experienced system managers. On the Berkeley machine, for whatever reason, some of the files were not properly secured, and there was a backdoor where a guest could get in and help himself to a master key.

So I became the superuser, a virtual god, on the Berkeley machine. What should I do with the power? Obviously, I did not want to do anything damaging. A friend made the suggestion that a computer account be created for Fred Rogers, the preacher and host of the Public Broadcasting System's "*Mister Rogers' Neighborhood*" TV show for children. Fred Rogers lives in Pittsburgh, and the show itself is recorded in Pittsburgh, within walking distance from Carnegie Mellon. The suggestion seemed very appropriate. Soon Mister Rogers got possibly his first computer account on the Berkeley machine without realizing it. We made one mistake in naming Mister Rogers' account: my friend thought Fred's middle initial was S, and the account name was given as *fsr*. Mister Rogers' middle name is McFeely. The account name should have been *fmr*.

One of the regular users on the Berkeley machine was apparently working on a network project for DARPA, and he had a file that contained passwords for machines all over the Arpanet. The file was protected, but not against a superuser. The passwords were also in plain text. Suddenly, I had keys to a lot of normally locked front doors all over the Arpanet.

For the next two weeks, during my free time, Mister Rogers' Neighborhood started to expand over the Arpanet. During this period, I was constantly hearing in my mind Mister Rogers' song from the show, "It is a beautiful day in this neighborhood. A beautiful day for a neighbor. Would you be mine? Could you be mine? ..."

Creating new accounts for Mister Rogers was slow going as each system had a different weakness. I also did not have a lot of free time—it was close to the finals for three of the courses that I was taking. But at the peak, Mister Rogers had almost ten computer accounts at top US universities.

Then I received a summons from our Department Head, Nico Habermann.

The system manager at Purdue University had noticed an account created for Fred Rogers and he followed the trail back to Carnegie Mellon. The staff at Carnegie Mellon then found me out.

Nico gave me a short lecture and I was ordered to write what amounted to a confession about how it was done, and to show my remorse. It was a slap on the hand. There was no real damage, and possibly the systems involved became safer as a result. Mister Rogers, of course, lost all his accounts. This was before Congress passed the law about computer privacy. I would be in deep trouble if my misdeed were done today. It is also unethical to look at protected files without permission, and even unprotected files of a personal nature should not be looked at without permission. I was treating it as a game when in fact it was a serious matter. On the other hand, one should never leave a plain text file containing passwords lying around, protected or not, and definitely, definitely, not on a system with guest accounts that do not require passwords. The world is a big place, and there are some bad people out there.

I must have been dangerously close to being shown the way out in the Black Friday meeting that year. As it was, I was probably one more incident away from being asked to leave the Department.

♚ CHAPTER 3

Taking the Plunge

Japanese Work Ethic

I can work hard when I choose to, but basically I am a lazy person. By the time I was in my second year at Carnegie Mellon, I had only worked hard *once* for an extended period of time, and that was to prepare for my College Entrance Exam in Taiwan [1]. But studying for exams cannot really be considered work. In that sense, until my second year at Carnegie Mellon, I had never worked hard in my life. Andreas Nowatzyk, my German office mate, was a hard worker, but he worked mostly at night and his work attitude did not rub off on me. This changed when I started to work with a Japanese visitor on one of Professor Kung's projects.

Teiji Nishizawa was a visitor from Matsushita Electric in Japan. (Matsushita is probably better known in the US as the company behind the Panasonic brand of consumer electronic products.) At that time the Computer Science Department had deals with big Japanese companies that allowed them, for a fee, to send representatives to work temporarily at the Department under the professors. Teiji was one of these representatives.

In my experience, there are two types of hard worker. The first tends to work in short bursts. Many software programmers fall into this type, although not all of the good programmers do. Hard workers of this type might work for, say, 48 hours in a row while their creative juices are flowing. I can never work in this way; I get cranky if I don't have enough sleep. Teiji was a good example of the second type of hard worker. He was highly motivated and self-

---

[1] For a discussion of the Taiwanese educational systems, see *An Early Riser* in *A Lad from Taiwan*, Appendix A.

disciplined. He might not work long hours, but he would put in solid days of work for long periods of time. This type of hard worker is more suitable for chip design work, where being able to provide sustained, high-quality output is more important than sudden flashes of brilliance. Working closely with Teiji for the next year or so turned out to be quite an educational experience for me, especially in terms of work ethic.

Teiji, Alan Sussman (another of Professor Kung's advisees), and I worked together on Professor Kung's joint project with General Electric (GE). For both Alan and me, this project counted as the *area qualifier*, a required element in getting our PhD degrees. The area qualifier was usually some task given by the faculty advisor to the students to demonstrate adequate grounding in the research area. In reality, it was also a way for the faculty to extract useful work from the students. I got my first contact with the Japanese work ethic during this project.

Our project was to design a chip to act as the programmable communication channels between several of the commercially-available floating-point arithmetic chips [2]. One of the possible applications was computer tomography for medical diagnosis, which happened to be important business for GE. In the early phase of the project, Kung and the three of us had weekly meetings to go over the design. We were still at the stage of specifying what the chip would do when Teiji came to a meeting with hand-drawn, complete top-level schematics, along with the basic timing information. Having never seen anyone working this way, I made a personal note, "Wow, this guy works fast."

GE was responsible for the back end of the chip design, which included the physical layout and the chip fabrication, while Carnegie Mellon was responsible for the logic design. Teiji, Alan and I split the logic design into three sections, with each one of us

---

[2]   There are two types of arithmetic used in computers: fixed point and floating point. The simplest example of fixed-point arithmetic is integer arithmetic, where the fixed *binary* point is after the least significant bit (binary digit) of the integer. Floating point arithmetic uses two numbers, *magnitude* and *mantissa*, to represent a single quantity. The magnitude part holds the significant bits; the mantissa is a number indicating where the *binary* point is located and can be viewed as a scaling factor. Floating point arithmetic is typically used in engineering applications. In the early 1980s, it became possible to do floating-point arithmetic on a single chip by itself. Today, the floating-point arithmetic unit is only a small part of a general-purpose microprocessor.

responsible for a section. In the beginning, only Teiji was putting in the hours, but both Alan and I soon caught the spirit and learned from his example. Andreas Nowatzyk actually helped quite a bit as well. We were using a new set of Computer Aided Engineering (CAE) tools, of which Andreas happened to be the first user.

The Carnegie Mellon portion of the joint project was completed in early 1985. At this point, I had finished all the other requirements for the PhD degree, with only the small matters of proposing, researching, writing, and defending my thesis left to do.

The joint project had taken over a year by then. I could not use it as a thesis topic, since there was no significant research content. Still, the project experience had made me better disciplined and, for the first time in my life, I had gone through the entire logic design process for a chip. Without going through the project and without the subtle influence of our Japanese visitor, I don't think I would be ready for my next step.

Brownie Points

In 1984 or thereabouts, the Japanese office equipment manufacturer Canon announced a low cost laser printer engine that potentially could be used to produce laser printers priced under $3000. Within a year, both Hewlett Packard and Apple announced the first personal laser printers based on the Canon engine, and a new market segment was created. Before Canon's announcement, laser printers were mostly used in large departments, and cost more than $10,000. The personal laser printer business turned out to be very important for both Hewlett Packard and Apple. For Hewlett Packard, this development was the beginning of their highly successful computer printer business. For Apple, the personal laser printer provided the killer application—desktop publishing—that allowed Apple's Macintosh computer to penetrate the business market.

With the proliferation of these new laser printers, it became increasingly important to be able to send electronic documents from one user to another. To communicate with another user, the format of the electronic documents would have to be standardized in some way. Xerox pioneered the laser printer business and had what was close to an existing standard, but the company was slow in getting its standard adopted widely. Adobe, a small software startup in California, seized the opportunity and quickly made its own new page description language, Postscript, the accepted standard. Today, Adobe has a thriving business and a market capitalization greater than Xerox itself [3].

I had been following the printer business since I was an undergraduate, and I found the chain of events started by Canon's announcement quite interesting. Canon's engine could print up to eight pages per minute, but the printer controller in use in 1985 had problems printing at the maximum speed even for simple pages. If one wanted to print complicated Chinese characters at high speed, one would be out of luck. Furthermore, neither Xerox's nor Adobe's standard handled Chinese characters. There was a window of opportunity to produce a custom VLSI printer controller that could print more complicated pages at high speed. There was also an opportunity to either create a new standard or extend one of the two potential standards to handle Chinese, Japanese, and other East Asian languages. The business opportunities seemed to be there and the ideas probably would make a decent PhD thesis topic. I told Professor Kung about my ideas and, in early 1985, I started to collect literature on printers, computer fonts, and so on.

It was hard to collect the relevant Chinese literature in the United States. However, a paper on the chip we designed with GE was accepted for a conference in Taiwan in May 1985, and I had a free [4] trip back to Taiwan to collect Chinese literature. Everything was looking good.

Then something unexpected happened. Dr Hans Berliner, who was an AI faculty member, asked me to help with the design of Hitech, a chess machine that he and a group of graduate students were building.

I had learned about the Hitech chess-move generator, which was used to generate the chess moves directly in hardware for Hitech, at the very first seminar that I attended at Carnegie Mellon. The seminar was a VLSI group seminar; Carl Ebeling was the speaker. The move generator was a 64-chip design, one chip per square of the 8x8 chessboard. It was neat stuff, but even on first

---

3 As of July 2000, Adobe is worth over $16 billion, while Xerox is worth just over $13 billion.

4 Being a poor graduate student at the time, I found the "free" part important.

glance, there was a lingering question at the back of my mind. Was it really necessary to use 64 chips?

At the time that Dr Berliner approached me, an early version of Hitech had just been designed and built. I was not the first graduate student with chip design experience that Berliner had approached. Well before I arrived at Carnegie Mellon, Berliner had persuaded Carl Ebeling to design the Hitech move generator. Carl later became the chief architect of Hitech after agreeing to build the whole chess machine.

A chess machine has three main components: the *move generator* which finds the chess moves, the *evaluation function* which assesses the quality of the positions reached when the chess machine looks ahead, and the *search control* which guides analysis of move sequences examined by the chess machine. Typical chess programs have the same basic structure, except that the move generator, the evaluation function, and the search control are all in software. This is also the case for commercial "chess machines" that you can buy in a store, as they are really just chess programs encapsulated in a stand-alone microcomputer. When a computer chess researcher talks about a chess machine, they are usually talking about a machine that has at least a hardware move generator and a hardware evaluation function. You can expect a hardware chess machine to be at least a hundred times faster than chess programs running on microprocessors manufactured in the same semiconductor technology. When Dr Berliner talked to me, Hitech had the 64-chip move generator and a very simple-minded hardware evaluation function.

Dr Berliner wanted to improve Hitech's evaluation function. He asked me whether I would be interested in designing a 64-chip system to compute how well the squares of the chessboard were controlled by the chess pieces. I told Dr Berliner that I had a thesis topic that I wanted to work on, but if his problem was something that could be done in a summer, I might be willing to look into it. I did not mind doing Dr Berliner a favor, but I did not want to give him the impression that he could just grab hold of my time. I have to admit that I was also looking forward to the chance of working with Carl who was putting together a real system, and I had never done anything like that. And, of course, the whole idea seemed like a good temporary escape from thesis work.

I had a meeting with Dr Berliner to find out what he had in mind. Near the end of the conversation, he mentioned that I would not be getting anything more than "brownie points" from this work. That was a new term for me. Berliner explained that it meant I would not get anything tangible other than appreciation for the work done. I was not expecting anything to begin with, and that should have been quite clear from the fact that I was only willing to work on it for the summer. The conversation gave me an odd feeling.

I spent about a week on Dr Berliner's project, entering the top few levels of the circuit schematics. I then had a meeting with the Hitech group and presented some of my findings. The good news was "yes, it could be done". The bad news was "the 64-chip partitioning makes it necessary to add a lot of external circuits and the system would be quite slow". A year later, I discovered that my definition of "quite slow" would have been more than adequately fast for Hitech, but nobody realized this at the time of the meeting. Dr Berliner seemed unhappy and asked me to fit the external circuits onto the chip anyway. I explained that the system would get even slower as the chip input/output delays went up when the slower on-chip FET (Field Effect Transistor) drivers replaced the faster off-chip bipolar drivers [5]. The meeting was adjourned without any decision.

I was not a happy camper. The root of the problems appeared to be the 64-chip partitioning. The question at the back of my mind when I first heard about the Hitech project came back. Was the partitioning necessary?

In the early 1980s, Ken Thompson and Joe Condon, both from Bell Laboratories, built Belle, a special purpose chess machine, from small and medium scale integrated circuits. Belle became the first chess automaton to play at the US National Master level in 1983. It had replaced the Chess 4.X as the new top chess automaton while I was still carrying out my military service in Taiwan. I only learned of Belle's existence after arriving at Carnegie Mellon.

They had written a paper about Belle, describing its basic architecture, and I had a reprint at home. That night, after the meeting with the Hitech group, I picked up the reprint and reread

---

[5] Drivers in IC use relatively large transistors, usually of two types: bipolar and FET. Bipolar transistors are generally faster due to their higher current driving capability. To fully explain what bipolar and FET transistors are would take up too much space.

it. Yes, the move generator described in the Belle paper indeed could not be fitted into a single chip. But was it possible to modify the design so that it would fit?

The way I saw it, there were two major problems.

The first was that the Belle chess move generator had too many transistors. The circuit size was simply too big.

In a chess program, the move generator literally generates the chess moves that the program examines. But to work properly, the move generator needs to do more than just generate moves. It also needs to *only* generate *unexamined*, or not yet searched, moves by the program. In the Belle design, this second task—of generating only unexamined moves—is the job for the *disable-stack*. The disable-stack in Belle is a 64-bit[6] wide memory, one bit for each square of the chessboard.

The disable-stack has two entries for every move searched. A normal chess move has a from-square (attacker) and a to-square (victim). Each entry on the disable-stack corresponds to one of the two types of squares.

Move generation in Belle has two phases. In the first phase (find-victim), a new to-square (victim) is generated. For instance, the first phase might generate "rook on h8" as the victim. The first entry on the disable-stack is used to mask off all the to-squares already searched for this phase. If "rook on a8" is a victim already searched, then the a8 square is masked off.

After a victim has been found, Belle enters the second phase of move generation. In this second phase (find-attacker), a new from-square (or attacker) is found for the given victim. Say we might find that "knight on g6" is an attacker for "rook on h8". The second entry on the disable-stack is used to mask off all the from-squares (attackers) that are already searched for the given victim. If no attacker is left, then Belle returns to the first phase to find new victims.

In all the chess machines that I later designed, I allowed the program to look up to 128 plies[7] ahead. With two entries per move, the disable-stack would need to be 256 words deep to han-

---

6 A bit is a binary digit, either 1 or 0.

7 "Ply" is computer chess jargon. It means a move made by one of the two players. The word "move" might have been more appropriate were it not for the fact that in chess literature a "move" could mean a pair of *plies,* with both White and Black making one move each.

dle up to 128 plies of looking ahead. Let us assume that we need six transistors for every bit of memory. The number of transistors used by the disable-stack alone would be at least 1500 for each square of the chessboard, or about 100,000 transistors for the whole board. Not a lot by today's standards. But back in 1985, after adding in all the other circuits, it was nearly impossible to fit the Belle move generator into a single chip.

What possible ways were there to reduce the number of transistors? I had had the reprint of the Belle paper in my apartment for more than two years, but had never thought about this question for two reasons. One was that I did not believe that a solution to the Computer Chess Problem was within reach. Therefore, I had no motivation to probe further. The second was that I had made a wrong assumption. I assumed that the Belle designers, as well as the Hitech group, must have explored ways to reduce the number of transistors. I forgot that the Belle designers, able though they were, were not trying to fit their design onto a single chip. They designed Belle with discrete off-the-shelf chips, and chips used for the disable-stack were fairly easy to come by. For them, the disable-stack was perhaps the most elegant solution. It just was not the best solution for a single chip design. The fact that the Hitech group had adopted the 64-chip design for their chess move generator also clouded my judgment. If the Hitech group needed 64 chips to complete their move generator, how likely was it for anyone to create a single chip chess move generator?

There I was, lying on my bed, thinking about the question of the disable-stack seriously for the first time. Once I started thinking about the question, I realized there might indeed be a solution. The Belle designers were not looking for an alternative solution and Dr Berliner was probably quite happy that the Hitech design was different from the Belle design. When Carl Ebeling took the job of creating the Hitech move generator, the Hitech group was already set with the idea of using 64 chips, one chip per square of the chessboard. Consequently, Carl concentrated all his efforts on perfecting the 64-chip design. So, even though all the people involved were highly capable, they did not have strong reasons to look for alternatives. There may very well be an alternative to the disable-stack!

The most radical answer would be simply to get rid of the disable-stack from the move generator chip completely. The easiest way to do this was to take the disable-stack out of a move generator chip and connect 64 wires, one wire for each square of the chessboard, from the move generator chip to the external disable-stack. It was a possible solution but I did not like it. Ideally, I preferred to keep the number of pins [8] for any chip below 40. Higher pin-count packages back in those days could cost over twenty-five dollars. At that price, the package might cost more than the chip itself. A more personal reason for wanting to keep the pin count under forty was to see how far I could push the idea. The Hitech move generator chips were using 40-pin packages. It would be quite a coup if not only a one-chip design was possible, but also the new design could use the same package used by the Hitech chips. Another reason why I did not like the external disable-stack solution was that it was really a nine-chip design. Eight memory chips would be needed for the 64-bit wide external disable-stack. The widest memory chip in those days was only 8-bit wide.

At this point, an idea hit me. The new idea rid the whole design of the disable-stack, not just the chip itself.

The idea hinged on what information the disable-stack was really carrying. The disable-stack was keeping track of the history of the moves searched so far. In a chess machine, the "move stack" contains the very same information, albeit in a different form. The 64-bit patterns stored in the disable-stack could, in theory, be computed from the last move searched and currently stored on the move stack. The from-square and the to-square of the last moving piece contain all the information needed to compute the 64-bit disable-mask. I sat up, grabbed a pen and paper, and started working out the details. Every one of the sixty-four squares of the chessboard is assigned a unique priority number. For a given from-square or to-square, we disable all squares with higher square priorities. We can compute the 64-bit disable-mask from the 6-bit square number by using a six to sixty-four priority decoder [9] circuit. The priority decoder circuit used about ten transistors on

---

[8] Silicon chips usually communicate with the outside world through the *pins* of their packages. With some of the newer IC packages, *pads* might be used instead.

[9] Here is a simple explanation of a priority decoder. A six to sixty-four priority decoder computes a function with a 6-bit input and a 64-bit output. The 6-bit input N can be viewed as an integer from 0 to 63. If the 64 output bits are numbered from 0 to 63, then all the output bits numbered below N should be 0s and all the other output bits should be 1s.

average for each square instead of the fifteen-hundred transistors used by the disable-stack. This was a 150 to 1 reduction. How significant was this reduction? My final implementation of the complete move generator used about five-hundred and fifty transistors on average for each square. Without the design change, the number would have been over two-thousand transistors per square, and the chip would have been too large by a factor of four.

I was happily stunned. But there was a second major problem with the Belle design. This problem may come as a surprise to a layperson. It certainly would have come as a surprise to a much younger me. When I was a little kid, higher quality radios were the ones with more vacuum tubes or more transistors. What could be more important to a silicon chip than the number of transistors it has? The answer is the number of wires, in particular, the number of *long wires*. The Belle move generator had too many long wires.

The Belle move generator produces six piece-priority signals, one per piece type, for each of the sixty-four squares of the chessboard. The piece-priority signals are used to order the moves by the *values* of the pieces, *before* the simple move ordering by piece *locations* based on the disable-stack. In general, we should firstly search moves that capture the most valuable victim with the least valuable attacker. This value-based move ordering can improve the efficiency of the chess machine dramatically.

The 384 (6x64) piece-priority signals get fed into a priority encoder, which is a voting circuit used to select the best move. The problem lies with the 384 piece-priority signals. They are 384 long wires.

For the 3-micron CMOS technology that was available, the 384 long wires alone would have covered half of the chip. I needed an alternative way to do the move voting. It took me less than one minute to find a working alternative. It was all a matter of luck. Back in those days, I subscribed to a lot of IEEE (Institute of Electrical and Electronic Engineers) journals. (IEEE gave students hefty discounts for journal subscriptions.) A few weeks before that fateful night, I had read an article in *IEEE Computer Magazine* about a new computer bus standard called Future Bus. The Future Bus used a "distributed arbiter" circuit to vote among circuit boards residing on the bus. The "distributed arbiter" required few wires and might be a good fit for my problem with the long wires in the Belle move generator. The magazine was lying right next to me. A quick check of the article verified that a slightly modified distributed arbiter would do the job. Instead of 384 long wires, the number of long wires would be reduced to forty-eight, a reduction by a factor of eight.

So, it might very well be possible to fit a modified Belle move generator onto a single chip using only a 40-pin package. As a matter of fact, there were reasons to believe that such a move generator could be more than ten times faster than the 64-chip move generator used in Hitech as well. The real chip in the end was closer to a factor of twenty times faster. It was over a thousand times (64×20) more cost effective.

Things were suddenly very interesting. Up to this point, I had always assumed that the Computer Chess Problem was out of reach. My belief seemed to have been confirmed by the 64-chip Hitech move generator design. If it took sixty-four VLSI chips to complete a relatively slow move generator, then the problem was indeed beyond reach. But now it appeared that you could build a move generator with only *one* chip. The Computer Chess Problem deserved a second look.

In the Belle chess machine, besides the move generator, the *evaluation function* was the bulk of the rest of the machine. Could the evaluation function be fitted onto a single chip as well? A good evaluation function will be far more complicated than the move generator. If it was barely possible to fit the move generator onto a single chip, what was the chance of doing the same for a good evaluation function? It doesn't look good, does it? There was one option: namely, we could trade space for time. Chess evaluation functions have spatially repetitive components, and it is possible to use a smaller circuit multiple times to do the same computation, albeit with a time penalty. An interesting fact is that we do not have to pay the time penalty all the time. The evaluation function can be partitioned into two components: material (basically the values of the pieces left on the board) and positional (anything else). The material evaluation can be computed very fast. The positional evaluation is the part that is time consuming. Usually, the positional evaluation also has relatively small values, frequently smaller than the value of a pawn. If the material balance is too far off, say one side is down a queen, the positional evaluation function can be ignored and does not need to be computed. Statistics measured later on real chess machines indicated that the full evaluation is only needed about 10–20% of the time. Multiplexing a smaller circuit in time to reduce the chip area appeared to be a viable option. A back-of-an-envelope calculation showed me that the 64-chip evaluation function did not make sense and at this point, I lost interest in helping Dr Berliner with his 64-chip evaluation function. The Hitech system was sufficiently slow that a time-multiplexed single chip evaluation function would still be more than fast enough.

The next day I sent an e-mail to Dr Berliner telling him that I was no longer interested in building the 64-chip evaluation function, and that it was possible to build single chip chess move generators and single chip evaluation functions. I also offered to do a simple version of the single chip evaluation function, if he was interested. Dr Berliner's first reaction was to try to get me to "design the whole chip the right way". That is, to design the chip as he specified, using the 64-chip design. I made it clear that I didn't want to do the 64-chip design. After a week of going back and forth, I sent Dr Berliner a one-page preliminary spec of a simple time multiplexed circuit that calculated a subset of the evaluation function. Dr Berliner was not entirely satisfied with what I was proposing. I decided to stand my ground and say that I did not want to be involved if my proposal was not acceptable. Perhaps I was a little too blunt. I was not planning to do anything more with computer chess at this point, and I had a serious thesis proposal to work on.

Shortly after, I had a meeting with Professor Kung and told him about what had happened. Professor Kung strongly suggested that I write up the ideas for the single chip designs and give a presentation to a few faculty members. Professor Kung did not say it, but from his tone, I got the feeling that I might have major problems at the faculty Black Friday meeting (the faculty meeting held at the end of each semester to decide the fate of each and every graduate student in the department). In my blunt response to Dr Berliner I had effectively claimed that Hitech was passé, without presenting the reasoning. My standing in the eyes of the faculty was already shaky from my earlier escapade over the Arpanet. If I wrote the paper and did the presentation, then the faculty would know that I did not make the claim frivolously. For the next few weeks, I dropped my work on my thesis proposal and wrote up a technical report. I also gave a presentation to faculty members the day before I was to get on the plane to Taiwan.

I spent most of May 1985 in Taiwan. Part of the time was

spent collecting books about Chinese fonts, calligraphy and so on for the printer controller idea. The rest of the time was mostly just vacationing. I was debating with myself whether I wanted to go into the computer chess arena. I did not go to Carnegie Mellon to work on computer games; working on computer chess would be quite a deviation from my original interest. Moreover, the commitment could easily take five to ten years. Writing the technical report and doing the presentation, however, made me realize that I had the basic blueprint to build the Mother of all Chess Machines, a machine that could defeat the World Champion. In other words, I had a chance to pursue one of the oldest holy grails in computer science, and possibly make history. On the negative side, the printer controller looked quite promising as well, and it was not an idea that could wait. Personal laser printers were still in their infancy and there was a limited time window to make a custom printer controller chip widely adopted before the industry standard set in. There was some chance that the printer controller idea could make me financially independent. There was practically no chance that solving the Computer Chess Problem would ever provide any financial reward commensurate with the time and efforts required. If I went after the Computer Chess Problem, I would be going for the glory of knowing that I solved the problem. I probably would not be financially destitute, but there would be major personal sacrifices. The opportunity cost would be extremely high. I could be spending many of the most productive years of my life on a project that had a very slim payoff.

The decision was a difficult one. In the end, after serious soul searching, I decided to go for the glory. You don't get a chance to make history every day.

At Least Two Years

Sometimes, nothing is more important than being at the right place at the right time.

If I had not been at Carnegie Mellon, I would not have had Mike Browne and Andreas Nowatzyk as my office mates. If Mike and Andreas had no interest in chess or computer chess, my interest in computer chess probably would have completely dissipated by the time Dr Berliner asked me to help. If I had not had both the Belle paper and the IEEE magazine in my apartment on that fateful night, I probably would not have figured out how to fit a chess machine onto a single chip. If Dr Berliner had accepted my suggestion, I probably would have just done what I could and gone on with my original research project. If I had been at some other Computer Science Department, and, if Professor Kung had not been my faculty advisor, I might not have had the freedom as a graduate student to start a project on my own. The fact that it was 1985 when I began the project was also important. Five years earlier, the technology would not have been sufficiently advanced for fabricating a single chip chess move generator. Five years later you would be able to put the Belle move generator, as it was, onto a single chip, and somebody else would have beaten me to it. It was more or less an accident that I ended up on the path that I took.

When I first became Professor Kung's advisee, many years before the troublemaker label, he told me that graduate students were the ones with the real power in the Department, as they were the ones with a true grasp of the research projects. Professor Kung was probably encouraging me to be more assertive, as many Asian students had the problem of not speaking up.

After my return from Taiwan, I told Professor Kung about my decision to go after the Computer Chess Problem. Professor Kung was surprised but receptive. He hinted that I might have only limited time to work on the chip. He did not mention the reason, but it did not take a genius to realize that I could not afford to take too long. The Department already had a computer chess project. Starting a new one without fast progress would be an academic suicide.

Before I could work full time on the chess chip, something else happened. A few days after my return, Professor Kung informed me that the GE people were having problems simulating the chip that we designed with them and they needed help.

By this time Teiji had already returned to Japan, and Alan Sussman and I were the only people who might be able to help. Both of us wanted to spend time on our own research, and we did not sign up to do the simulation to begin with. Eventually, we both got involved. I took over the bulk of the work in the end, as I realized that it was not a waste of time, at least not in my case. The chip we designed with GE had quite a bit of transistor level circuitry, so we had to do a significant amount of "switch level" simulation, where the transistors were simulated as if they were on-off switches. The new move generator had not been designed yet, but I knew that it would be mostly dynamic [10] transistor level circuitry, and the experience from the GE chip would be quite useful.

The GE work was not finished until late August 1985. Just before its completion, I took over the maintenance of the VLSI CAD (Computer Aided Design) tools, as the previous maintainer had just become a father. It was in my own interest to take over the work, as I was to become the only user of the tools for a while. I was ready to begin my new project.

The Hitech 64-chip chess move generator designed by Carl Ebeling took over three years to complete. I did not have that much time to spend on my move generator chip. I planned to complete my goal of beating the World Champion in five to ten years, and I could not afford to spend three years on just the move generator. I decided to go full steam ahead and complete the chip in six months. Why the six-month target? Well, Joe Condon and Ken Thompson finished the Belle chess machine in six months, and if they could build a complete chess machine in that time, I should be able to complete a VLSI chess move generator. At the time, all the chip projects of any significance at Carnegie Mellon, and possibly every other university, took over a year to complete. If I pulled it off, it would be a speed record of sorts.

The first phase of the project, the circuit design, was straightforward, and largely drew from my experience with the GE joint project. It was hard work, but there was no major surprise along the way. The complete circuit design of the move generator, down to the transistor level, was finished in one month. The full chip was also simulated in its entirety down to the transistor switch level in the same period.

Next came the hard part. The physical layout—the drawing of all the geometry, including the transistors and the wires—was the next step. Nowadays, most designers would be using automated tools to do the layout. The tools available in 1985 could not do it, so to a great extent I had to do the layout manually. But there was another problem. I wanted to fit the chip into a 40-pin package and the die size for such chips was severely limited. The largest die, size for chips in production quantities today are around 2 cm (0.79

---

10 "Dynamic" has special meanings for chip designers. The states or memories of a dynamic circuit are stored as charges on capacitors, which have to be refreshed constantly.

in) on a side. The maximum die that could fit into the MOSIS[11] 40-pin package was about 0.7 cm (0.28 in) on one edge, or roughly twelve percent of the area of today's big chips. My task was to fit the design into the limited die area and to do it with the tools at hand. There was also the small problem that I had essentially no experience with the physical layout step of the chip design.

In the circuit design phase, I reduced the core logic to about 550 transistors on average for each of the sixty-four squares of the chessboard. Owing to edge effects and the fact that a pawn moves in a different way on different ranks, the circuits for the squares were not identical, but they did share a lot of common logic. As a first step, I picked one of the squares and did a trial layout of the square. This took about a month. At the completion of the trial layout, there was good news and bad news. The good news was, that based on the area used by the trial layout, the chip might fit with a lot of work. The bad news was that the trial layout I had for one square had the wrong shape. It was too tall. To get the maximum chip area, essentially, the chip would have to be a square. The maximum dimensions allowed were 6812 by 6912 microns, or 0.6812 cm by 0.6912 cm. Since a chessboard is 8x8, the circuit for each logical square would have to be physically laid out as a square as well.

The next two months were spent correcting the shape of the layout and creating variations for all the different squares. The number of different squares quadrupled when, in order to reduce the chip area, it became necessary to tile the squares to an exact fit in both X and Y dimensions. By tiling the squares to an exact fit, I could share wires and contacts (connections between wires on an IC) between adjacent squares and squeeze out a few microns for every pair of adjacent squares. The easiest way to do the tiling was to mirror the squares in both X and Y directions. This mirroring meant that, even for squares with identical circuits, there were four different versions of the layout: northeastern, northwestern,

---

11 MOSIS (MOS [Metal-Oxide-Semiconductor] Implementation Service) is a low-cost prototyping service for VLSI circuits. Initially, MOSIS served only government agencies and universities. Today, MOSIS also provides services to commercial firms. While I was at Carnegie Mellon, almost all the chips designed at US universities went through MOSIS. The chips were effectively free as government sources such as DARPA and NSF (National Science Foundation) bore the cost.

southeastern, and southwestern. The final layout of the chip core, which was logically an 8x8 chessboard, looked more like a 4x4 pattern as a result. The pattern was rather pretty and somewhat quilt-like. (When Deep Thought, the chess machine based on this chip, became widely known, a poster vendor asked me whether he could have the right to produce posters based on the die photo.) While the end result might have been aesthetically pleasing, the two months of hard work had been hellish for me personally. The work was tedious and consumed far more time than I had expected. I had to work longer and longer into the night to keep up with my schedule. Of course, my weekends had already become workdays earlier during the logic design phase.

It was December by this time, and there was another Black Friday coming up. Professor Kung asked me to give a presentation to the Hitech group. Dr Berliner started to show some interest before the presentation but, again, our interests did not really align. I was simply going to build a very fast machine, see what it could do, and decide what to do next. Dr Berliner had a completely different idea.

Dr Berliner was a leading authority in the computer chess field, and his words carried a lot of weight. He was publicly stating that brute force [12] searching, such as I was planning, would not go very far and it was time to go back to the old idea of selective searching [13], in particular, to the idea of the B-star (B*) search algorithm, an algorithm that Dr Berliner had come up with in the 1970s. Most of computer chess researchers appeared to agree with Dr Berliner that brute force searching was reaching its limit, but the suggestion that B* could rule the day was not universally accepted.

My intuition was that B* was a dead end. Anyway, I gave my presentation and Dr Berliner gave me references about B*. I did not

---

[12] Brute force searching in computer chess means logically examine every possible move, in contrast to selective searching where some of the moves might be pruned away.

[13] Selective searching means different things to different people. In general, selective searching has two flavors. One is to search "interesting" lines deeper (also known as selective deepening). The other is to search "uninteresting" lines shallower, or not at all, that is, to prune away the "uninteresting" lines (also known as selective pruning). It is possible to mix the two flavors in the same program. Some people consider selective deepening as modified brute force searching and not selective searching.

really have the time to go over his references until the chip was done.

Andreas Nowatzyk had frequent contact with several members of the Hitech group. A few days after my presentation, he told me that the Hitech group, or at least someone in the group, believed that it would take me "at least two years" to finish the chip design. I was quite amused. I had just given the Hitech group a presentation about a chip that was completely simulated, and almost completely laid out, and yet at least one person still believed that it would take me two more years to complete the design. I had completed the layout of all the squares, and I could see that I had a good chance to finish the chip in six months as I planned. The two-year prediction was probably based on how long it had taken Carl to finish the Hitech move generator, which was about three years. I was not necessarily a better chip designer than Carl, but I had better tools, I did not have to answer to a committee who changed the design spec from time to time, and I was determined to finish the chip in as short a time as possible. If it meant that I had to spend long hours on the project for sustained periods, I would not hesitate to do so. On top of all these reasons, I had Carl's indirect help. During his work on the Hitech move generator, he produced a tool that could be used to compare one netlist (the list of all the transistors and the connections between the transistors) with another. By comparing the netlist for the layout with the netlist for the logic design, a designer can verify that the layout matches the design. Carl's tool was quite important in the final verification phase of the design.

After two months of laying out all the squares of the chessboard, I had a new problem to deal with. Even with all the squares fitting tightly together, there was not much space left on the rim of the chip. In the remaining space, I had to squeeze in the edge wiring for the squares, the control logic for the chip, the interface logic to the world outside the chip, the wiring between the interface logic and the IO (input/output) pads, and, of course, the IO pads themselves. The main trouble was with the pads. The existing pads available from MOSIS simply would not fit. The pads connect the chip, usually through mechanically bonded gold wires, to the outside world. Given the mechanical nature of the wire bonding process, the wire landing area for an IO pad is fairly large in comparison to other chip features. The wire landing area, however, is only a small portion of an IO pad. The rest of the area is taken up with special protection circuits, which protect the chip from external electrostatic discharges, and the IO driver circuit, which boosts the internal signal to adequate strength for driving external circuits. The MOSIS IO pads were long rectangles, with the wire landing area near one of the short edges of the rectangle. The problem with these pads was that the long edges of the pads were perpendicular to the chip edges. They were fine if you needed to place, say, more than a hundred IO connections around the chip, but not so good if you didn't need a lot of IO connections. With the MOSIS pads, the IO ring around the chip would be a very thick ring. If I decided to go with the MOSIS pads, the move generator chip would have been about 1000 microns too wide, and too tall, or roughly thirty percent too large in terms of die area.

I had designed my move generator to use no more than 40 pins, so I did have an alternative, namely, getting a new set of pads. Viewed from the chip edge, the MOSIS pads were tall and skinny. My new pads would have to be short and fat. Since there was no expert with design experience for IO pads available, I just went ahead and designed my own. The layout of the pads and the remainder of the chip circuits took about a month. Five months from the start, I had a first cut of the complete chip layout. It barely fitted into the maximum die area allowed. I had no more than five microns to spare in either X or Y direction—not even enough to squeeze in one more wire. Talk about cutting it close.

At this point I was feeling good and getting bold. It would be another year before I presented my thesis proposal to the Department at large, but I was quite certain what my thesis would be. I also had a good idea about my choice of the outside thesis committee member. At Carnegie Mellon, the thesis committee normally had three members from the university itself and one outside member. Professor Kung would automatically be the head of the thesis committee and normally he would play a leading role in finding the outside member. Without telling Professor Kung, I sent an e-mail directly to Ken Thompson, asking whether he would mind being on my thesis committee. I did not tell Ken the minor detail that I did not have a thesis committee yet. Normally, you don't just ask a Turing Award winner to be on your committee; I was relying on the shock value of the request to get Ken interested. He was suitably shocked, and asked for more information on my work. I sent him the technical report that I had written before my trip to Taiwan and, after reading it, he agreed. I don't know why I did not ask Dr Berliner, who was very well known in the computer chess field, to be on my committee as well. It might have been that I simply wanted to emphasize that the thesis was really about hardware design and computation theory instead of computer chess *per se*. With hindsight, however, I might also have had some subconscious concern about a potential conflict of interest.

I had one month left of my original six-month schedule. The chip still had to be verified. First, I needed to re-simulate to verify the chip's functionality. This was straightforward, but there was one thing that I had to do before the re-simulation. During the layout process, I made changes to the circuit to allow more efficient layout, but I had not yet updated the circuit schematics to reflect the changes. The updates were made and the circuit was re-simulated. The next step, and this was where Carl's tool came in, was to verify that the re-simulated netlist and the physical netlist were identical, transistor for transistor and wire for wire. There was a slight problem associated with this last step—Carl's tool had its own idea on how the netlists should look. I wrote a translator to create netlists of the right form, and then compared the two new netlists. Usually, most designers would compare the netlists in a *bottom-up* fashion, that is, starting by comparing the netlists for the smallest sub-circuits, then the netlists for higher levels of circuits, and eventually the netlists for the top level. Just in case I got lucky, I compared the top level of the netlists first.

Not surprisingly, the comparison failed. There were too many mismatches. In particular, the power and the ground were shorted (directly connected) in the physical netlist. I would have one HOT chip that could be used to boil an egg if I submitted the chip the way it was. On the top level of the circuits, there were tens of thousands of connections to the power and the ground pins. Naturally, it was not possible to tell from the top level of the netlists where the power and the ground were shorted. The obvious strategy was to divide and conquer, namely, to compare the two netlists in the *bottom-up* fashion. Once the real netlist comparison started, I found numerous other errors. Luckily, all the errors could be corrected without increasing the already tight die size. By February 1986, six months after I started, the chip was designed, laid out, verified and ready for fabrication.

Now, the big question. Would the chip work the first time? Or would the person in the Hitech group be correct in predicting that it would take me at least two years to get my move generator working?

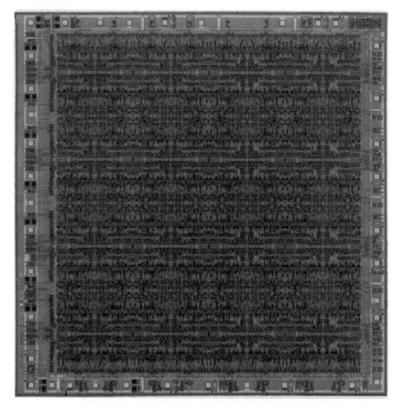

A Silicon Chessboard.
Aluminum on silicon canvas, drawn in 1985–1986, Feng-hsiung Hsu.
Also acts a single chip chess move generator and was the core of
the top chess machines from 1987 to 1995

Tom Sawyer's Trick

The semiconductor industry went through a major transition in the mid-1980s. In the early 1980s, NMOS (N-type MOS [Metal-Oxide-Semiconductor]) was the low cost, high volume technology. By the mid-1980s, CMOS (Complementary MOS) was slowly replacing NMOS as the dominant low cost technology. The CMOS technology uses both the P-type MOS transistor, where the main charge carrier has a positive charge, and the N-type MOS transistor, where the main charge carrier has a negative charge. CMOS circuitry has lower power consumption, but the process is also more complicated than NMOS.

MOSIS, the silicon broker providing chip foundry service to

US universities, started to offer a CMOS fabrication service in about 1985. In the beginning, few university researchers used the CMOS service. One reason was the lack of experience with CMOS design, and a second was that the CMOS process provided by MOSIS was not mature yet—rumor had it that someone got working CMOS chips from MOSIS, but no one saw them. To be fair to MOSIS, most of the designs submitted to MOSIS, either NMOS or CMOS, were probably flawed to begin with.

I submitted the CMOS chess chip in March 1986. Normally, it took about six to eight weeks before the packaged chips came back, and I had some time to work on something else. I took a closer look at the references related to B*, but I was not impressed. The reading confirmed my first intuition [14]. Contrary to the claims, the numbers appeared, at least to me, to show B* to be inferior to the simple-minded approach of just searching every move to the same depth—the so-called *brute force* approach.

Of course, some sort of cooperation with Dr Berliner might still be possible. After all, I would need a good chess player on the team, and Dr Berliner was the best player around, being a former World Correspondence Chess Champion.

Up to this point, I was making the assumption that I would find some way to parallelize the search. There were two steps in my plan to create a chess machine a thousand times faster than Belle. The first was to create a chess machine that was either a single chip or a small number of chips. The second was to find a way to use a massive number of chess machines in parallel to effectively speed up the search process. Given that the single-chip chess move generator had already been designed, I was part way through the first step. The second step was, however, an entirely different matter. At the time, no one knew how to effectively parallelize the search, despite many years of active research. I simply *believed* that a solution would be found. It did not matter to me whether I would be the first person to find a solution; as long as one was found before the final encounter with the World Champion, I would be fine. Of course, it would be so much sweeter if I could find the solution myself.

The problem turned out to be simpler than I thought. By April 1986, I had a decent solution that appeared to work well in pre-

---

[14] A B* version of Hitech appeared in early 1990s. Its public tournament results were no better than those of the brute force version of Hitech.

liminary simulations and could be proven theoretically to have some fairly good properties. At about this time, I heard that the fabrication run for my submitted chip had run into some problems and it would take quite a while before the chips arrived. Shocked by the news, I submitted the chip again in early May. Two days after my submission, MOSIS sent me a message saying that the chip I submitted in the first run was too large to fit into the 40-pin packages that I specified. I informed them immediately that the chip was at exactly the right maximum size. A few hours later, I got an apology—a software glitch had added a few microns to my chip in their calculation, and the chip got bumped into a larger die. The chips would be packaged in 64-pin packages, which were about three times bigger than the 40-pin packages. I did not know for sure that the second run would go correctly and, given the successive glitches, I submitted the chip twice more in late May and late June.

I received the first thirteen chips on 28 June 1986. To my surprise, they were from the second run and were packaged in 40-pin packages. The foundry used on this run had a bad reputation, and I was a little bit apprehensive. I measured the resistance between power and ground, and several of the chips were shorted. My heart sank a little. The CAE workstation that I used to design the chip had an attached hardware hookup that could be used to test the chips functionally. I hooked up the chips that were not shorted. No go. None of the chips showed any glimmer of life—they were not passing even the simplest test. I opened some of the chip packages and placed the chips under a microscope; defects were plain to see. I sent a report to MOSIS, telling them about the defects. Their first response was a request for one of the bad chips. Then I got another response questioning whether I had worked on any large project or had any experience testing chips. I was more than a bit annoyed, to say the least. Apparently, no other people were reporting zero yields on the very day they received the chips. It was very likely that I was the only one complaining at the time.

The next batch of chips arrived two weeks later on July 14. These were from the long-awaited first run, and were packaged in 64-pin packages. The test setup was for 40-pin packages. Andreas soldered together a 40-pin socket with a 64-pin socket to act as an adaptor, and I was able to test the new chips using the adaptor on the old setup. The chips behaved much better this time. Most of the chips passed some tests, and two of the chips passed all the tests. Bingo. The chip worked the "first time". The percentage of good chips (also known as the *yield*) was a little bit low, and looking at the non-working chips under a microscope showed that the metal wires were wider than they should be.

I sent out another report to MOSIS, mentioning that these chips were the same design as in the zero-yield run. This time I got a reply indicating that the chip vendor *dry* etched (etching without using wet chemicals) the metal layer, but MOSIS had prepared the mask for *wet* etch. This explained the initial delay for this run. A few days later, the third run arrived, with chips in 40-pin packages. This run had better yield and about half of the chips worked. The fourth run arrived a month later, was fabricated by the same vendor as the second run, and again had a zero yield. MOSIS this time took the report seriously, put the vendor on the watch list, and even suggested using the chess chip as a test chip for qualifying the vendor.

When I got the first two "working" chips, I verified that the chips worked *as designed*. But the design itself was not verified to work *within* a real chess program yet.

At Carnegie Mellon, the CS Department had a support organization known as the Engineering Lab to take care of the departmental network and machines, and to provide engineering support for the researchers. Several of the staff engineers there were good friends of mine. One of them, Lawrence Butcher, lent me a computer bus interface card and gave me a small empty wire-wrap board. (A wire-wrap board is a prototype board where circuit connections are made by wrapping wires around posts on the backside of the board.) I wire-wrapped a simple nine-chip chess chip interface on the wire-wrap board. Lawrence helped me make a cable connecting the two boards. Now, the problem was finding a machine to put the bus interface card in. One possibility was to put it in one of the machines in the Engineering Lab, but the Lab was on a different floor from my office. Then I hit upon a great idea.

In Mark Twain's classic novel *The Adventures of Tom Sawyer*, Tom was ordered to paint the fence. He pretended that it was fun painting the fence, and got the other kids to think that it was such fun that they were willing to *pay* Tom to do his work for him. Being a lazy person myself, this story made quite an impression on my young mind when I first read it as a small boy.

Mike Browne, my office mate, wrote a chess program while I was working on the chip. I tried to interest him in porting his program to run with the chess chip, not that I wanted to have a competitive chess program, but I did want to make sure that the chess chip worked. If I could get the chip to run inside a working chess program, preferably with someone else doing the work, I would be sure. My direct approach with Mike did not work. Remembering Tom Sawyer, I went for a sneakier approach.

Thomas Anantharaman and I were in the same incoming class of CS graduate students. He was in the speech group, but he was also in the VLSI group that I was in, so we had a lot of contact. Thomas had quite an unusual upbringing. His father, a retired professor of Metallurgical Engineering, was also an expert Yoga practitioner. His German mother was a student of Indian Philosophy. Thomas graduated from the Institute of Technology at Benares Hindu University in India. I don't know how, but he seems to be capable of thinking in different ways than I do; sometimes, he reaches conclusions that I would never dream about in a thousand years. Thomas' office was on the same floor as mine and it was only a few doors away.

Like Mike, Thomas had also written a chess program for his own amusement, and he had an office workstation that was compatible with my interface to the chess chip. Had I known how my next action would impact on Thomas' thesis research, I would have refrained from doing it (although, when all was said and done, he did all right in the end). Anyway, I persuaded Thomas to let me put the interface card into his workstation. I then wrote a more detailed testing program to test the chips. Whenever a new batch of chips came in, I could test them all within five minutes, at about ten seconds per chip. I placed the source of the testing program in a public place that Thomas could access, and then I got back to my simulation on how to parallelize the search, pretending to ignore Thomas for the moment.

A few days later, Thomas informed me that he had adapted his chess program to use the chess chip, just as I had secretly planned. Thomas was able to get his program, with the chess chip, to search about 30,000 positions/sec. The fastest PC-based chess programs today can search at least 10 times faster, but in 1986 only special purpose chess machines, and chess programs running on supercomputers, were faster. The first game that Thomas' new program played was against Murray Campbell, a fellow graduate student and chess expert, as well as a student of Dr Berliner's. Murray had done some work on Hitech, although not as part of his main research. He certainly had good ideas about how to play chess against computers. Yet, Murray lost the game. I was quite certain that the chip was correct after my own detailed testing, but seeing it used in a working chess program dispelled any residual doubt.

At the time that Thomas got involved, I had not really planned on forming our own computer chess team. I had assumed that I would find some common ground and work together with the Hitech group. Getting Thomas to port his chess program was just a short cut to avoid doing a piece of work that I should be doing myself. My plan at the time was to create a three-chip chess machine. Besides the already completed move generator chip, the two new chips would evaluate chess positions (the evaluation chip) and control the search (the search controller). I never did complete the chip set because of technical difficulties. One of them was that the evaluation chip would need to have RAMs (Random Access Memory) on it. Designing RAMs without detailed process control, as in the case of MOSIS service, was no trivial task. The other major technical difficulty was that I really did not know that much about chess at the time. When Thomas and I decided to enter into computer chess competitions later on, the plan for the chip set became permanently shelved.

CHAPTER 4

The Chess Machine That Wasn't

Seven Weeks

Thomas Anantharaman's exploit in creating a very fast chess program did not go unnoticed in the Department. The fastest chess programs in 1986 were Belle, Hitech and Cray Blitz. Belle and Hitech were special purpose chess machines roughly the size of an office refrigerator. Cray Blitz was a chess program running on a multi-million-dollar Cray supercomputer. The top programs at the time were searching in the range of 100,000 chess positions per second. Thomas was getting 30,000 chess positions per second with a vanilla office workstation plus a chess chip interface card about the size of a paperback novel, although with a *brain damaged* chess evaluation.

The frequent TG (Thank God [It's Friday]) parties were some of the unofficial fringe benefits of being a graduate student in the Department. They were not always held on Friday, and could be held for all sorts of reasons. The Department sponsored some of them, but the graduate students and faculty members sponsored at least half[1].

It was at one of these TGs that Gordon Goetsch, a graduate student working with Dr Berliner on Hitech, jokingly suggested that Thomas and I enter the program into the annual ACM (Association for Computing Machinery) Computer Chess Championship upcoming in Dallas. Gordon was of the opinion

---

[1] Later on when our chess machines, ChipTest and Deep Thought, scored major tournament victories, we sponsored four TGs ourselves to celebrate the wins.

that the programs in the tournament, despite claims to the contrary, had very little chess knowledge, and a fast and dumb program, such as Thomas', would be able to do serious damage. It would not win—there were faster programs that were not as dumb—but it would be fun to watch what would happen. Neither Thomas nor I took Gordon's suggestion seriously at the time.

After the TG, Andreas Nowatzyk and I ended up in the Engineering Lab with some of the staff engineers. I did not intend to do what Gordon suggested, but I had a lingering question about the chess chip. With Thomas' program running at 30,000 chess positions/sec, I knew that the chess chip worked, but I had no idea at what speed it could run without overheating. If I stuck with my original plan of building a chess chip set, it would be at least another year before I knew the answer. That would be a risky proposition. I probably should build something that could exercise the chess chip at a higher speed. If I built such a speed tester, then modifying it into a "poor man's chess machine" and entering the ACM competition would be quite interesting. Of course, there were a few obstacles.

First, there were only seven weeks left before the ACM competition. Second, I only had a student budget, namely, nothing. Last but not least, I needed help if I wanted to participate in the ACM Tournament, with a competitive program, in seven weeks time.

Andreas provided the first piece of help when I mentioned the idea of the speed tester to him and the staff engineers. His eyes lit up and he suggested a source for getting a prototype board that could be used to make the tester—the departmental scrap heap for Perq workstations. The first computer workstation to hit the market, the Perq, was both before its time and beyond its time. The workstation market eventually took off, but the Perq, stuck with an older multi-chip CPU (central processor unit) design, was taken over by nimbler competitors that used cheaper single-chip microprocessor CPUs. Three Rivers Computers, the manufacturer of Perq, went out of business in 1986, and the Department retired most of the Perqs. The scrap heap was full of Perq prototype boards, and it would be a simple matter to outfit one of them with wire-wrap sockets as a substitution for a full-sized, wire-wrap board. Lawrence Butcher, the engineer who lent me the bus interface card, volunteered to wire wrap the board when the design was complete. There was one more problem—getting the electronic parts for the tester. Professor Kung had a lot of spare parts in his cabinet for a DARPA project. I decided to borrow some parts from the cabinet—if they ever became needed, they could always be reclaimed from the tester board. That night, I took an inventory list of the spare parts in Kung's cabinet, and Andreas located a Perq prototype board in decent shape. The tester would be designed using only the parts in Professor Kung's cabinet, although he did not know about the borrowed parts until after the chip tester was completed.

The next morning, I had a chat with Thomas. I briefed him on the chip tester, what the new software interface would look like, and what kind of new hardware functions would be provided. The most important new function was the ability to do searches directly in the tester hardware, which would then allow us to search faster and exercise the chess chip at higher speed. The searches performed in hardware would necessarily be simple minded, given the design time constraint. The hardware searches would not know about either castling moves or underpromotion moves (promoting a pawn to a rook, a bishop or a knight, instead of a queen as in a normal pawn promotion). That is, the hardware would not even know all the legal chess moves. Moreover, the hardware would not know that repeating a position could lead to a rule draw in chess. Also, since it was going to be just a chip tester, the hardware would evaluate a chess position based only on a piece-placement table (a table tabulating the value of every piece on each square of the chessboard). It could be used as a chess machine, but a very crude one. To compensate for the hardware limitation, the first few plies examined along any line during the search would be done in software, thus knowing about all the legal moves and the repetition draws. The last few plies would be done in hardware. The overall speed would be close to the hardware speed, since there are far more new positions, say, 10 plies away from the root[2] position than new positions, say, six plies away. It was also possible to add more complicated chess evaluation in the software part of the search tree.

The changes that we needed to make to Thomas' program

---

[2] The positions traversed by a chess program during a search can be viewed as a search tree, with the position on the physical chessboard acting as the root position. The moves searched become the tree branches, and the positions searched become the branching points.

were relatively simple, and he agreed to make them. Thomas was a good programmer but neither of us was a chess player. We needed at least one decent chess player to write the evaluation software and to prepare the opening book (the moves that the computer would play at the beginning of the game).

I tried to get Mike Browne interested again. He was one of the best programmers that I knew, and he had played chess competitively in high school but he was preoccupied with other things. There were a few other graduate students who were good chess players in the Department. One of them, Peter Jansen, expressed some interest, but he was busy with course work.

Murray Campbell, the first victim of Thomas' hardware-assisted program, was perhaps the strongest chess player among the graduate students, and he had worked on computer chess before. Murray was a chess prodigy, twice representing the Province of Alberta in the Canadian Junior Championship. He had quit playing serious chess when, in his last chess tournament while he was still in the prize hunt, he agreed to an early draw so that he could play tennis. In his words, "That was when I knew that I didn't want to play competitive chess any more." He would have been a great addition to the team, but there was one complication. He was in the Hitech group, and it would not be proper for me to go after him.

Two weeks after the conversation in the Engineering Lab, I got a surprise e-mail from Murray asking whether the piece-placement table on the tester board was adjustable after each move. If it was, he had some ideas on how to get the program into reasonable positions after the first few moves, assuming that we were interested. The table was indeed adjustable and, after finding out that Hitech was probably not going to play in the tournament, we took him up on his offer. I submitted the entry, without a finished design and without a working program, to the ACM tournament committee at about this point. We called the new program ChipTest, in part because of the chip tester nature of the hardware, and in part because we wanted to stress that it was not a real chess machine.

Four weeks into the seven-week period, the hardware design began taking shape. I felt comfortable enough to go out in the open and posted an electronic message seeking additional help. Since Murray had not promised to work on the evaluation function, I talked with a few other chess players but with no luck. However, I did get one positive response to my message from Guy

Jacobson. Guy was not just a garden-variety graduate student. He was one of the authors of Rog-O-Matic, an automatic program that played rogue, a popular computer game among graduate students at the time. By all accounts, he was one of the premier programmers in the Department.

Thomas, Murray, Guy, and I had a meeting. Thomas would do the bulk of the programming. Murray would take up the tasks of preparing the opening book and writing software for the piece-placement table, which was effectively the main evaluation function. Murray expanded his involvement when it became certain that Hitech would not play in the upcoming competition. Guy would work on a software evaluation for pawn structure so that the program would know how strong or weak the pawns were in the software part of the search tree.

The hardware was ready for wire wrapping by the end of the fifth week, and Lawrence Butcher completed overnight the job which would have taken me a few days. The hardware had about ninety chips which would have cost about $500 if we had had to acquire the parts ourselves.

Because of the time constraint, I designed the tester with a minimalist attitude. Unfortunately, I went too far—the tester contained absolutely no circuitry for testing *the tester itself*. The tester was, however, microprogrammable; that is, it could be programmed with a microprogram, which controls all the hardware circuits directly. In theory, the tester could be tested to some extent, assuming that I had the testing microprograms. But in order to verify the correctness of the testing microprograms, I needed to have working hardware. It was the classic chicken and egg problem.

Andreas came to my rescue by creating a high quality microassembler (a program that converts the microprograms into appropriate bit patterns for controlling the hardware) that made the coding of the microprograms much easier. It still took about one week and several microprograms to complete the testing of the hardware. There was one more microprogram to write—the one that controlled the hardware search function. Time was getting short.

Meanwhile, Guy did not get around to work on the program which meant we would not have a software evaluation for pawn structure. Oh, well, Guy's help was a gift to begin with.

It wasn't time to panic yet, but we needed to have a contingency plan. We could still play without the hardware search, but we would suffer a heavy speed penalty. The search microprogram was much bigger than all the test microprograms combined, and it was also far more difficult to debug. I did not sleep the night before I was to leave for Dallas, site of the ACM tournament, but continued working until I had to get on the plane. Andreas drove me to the airport, and I was silent the entire way. Thomas would pick up the work on the microprogram while the competition was going on. We did not have a working microprogram for the entire tournament.

The previous year I had asked Ken Thompson to be on my thesis committee, but I only met him for the first time in Dallas. He was there as a tournament official, but after Cray Blitz pulled out, citing unavailability of machine time, Belle was drafted to play and Ken became one of the competitors. The top seed that year was Bebe, and we were paired against the Bebe team in the first round. The authors of Bebe were Tony and Linda Scherzer, a couple from the Chicago area. My first conversation with Tony did not go too well. I tried to explain why ChipTest would not be at full speed by telling Tony that we had started to build it seven weeks before the tournament, and that we needed another week or two before we could get to the top speed. Tony said, "Yeah, they all said that they were off by a week." To him, I must have sounded like a braggart (and there were plenty of them around in the computer chess world). Bebe, which was another special purpose chess machine, proved to be the stronger player and ChipTest went down without much of a fight. Tony turned out to be a nice guy when I got to know him better. He was quite open about what he was doing and I had many mutually beneficial conversations with him.

In the next round we played Monty Newborn's Ostrich. Monty organized the ACM tournaments from their beginnings in 1970, and this was Ostrich's last tournament. Ostrich was a contender in earlier days, but it was no longer considered a strong program. ChipTest got a winning position fairly easily against Ostrich, and then disaster struck. There were still a few bugs in both ChipTest's software and hardware, and Thomas put in a "cure". Unfortunately, the "cure", being very simple minded, turned out to be worse than the disease. Whenever the program detected that it was having problems, it would just play the first move generated by the hardware move generator, which was effectively a randomly chosen move. In this game, ChipTest played a move out of the blue as the result of the "cure". The move sacrificed a rook for a pawn, and with the rook, the game. Thomas worked overnight and replaced the "cure" with a safer alternative, that is, to record what was previously the best move and whenever the program ran amok, play the recorded best move.

ChipTest won the next game against Rex without much difficulty, and recorded its first win. The next round, it played Merlin from Germany, a well-respected program. ChipTest won the game by outsearching Merlin, but not without some incidents. It played an illegal castling move, but it also stated that the castling move was illegal and that the program was in an inconsistent state. The tournament director and our opponent agreed to let us restart the program. It played a legal move after the restart, and ChipTest went on to win the game.

In the last round, ChipTest played against Recom. Recom was a predecessor of Rebel, one of the best commercial chess programs today, and it was a strong program even back in 1986. ChipTest was playing well early on, but the problems from the Ostrich game resurfaced. With the new "cure", it played moves that did not get killed outright, but the position was getting really bad.

Then a miracle happened. ChipTest suddenly claimed that the game was drawn, and it played a move that sacrificed another rook for a pawn. But unlike the sacrifice in the Ostrich game, this was a good sacrifice. I got so excited that I was jumping up and down. Recom, after a while, realized that the game was indeed drawn, and we called the truce. Every time that I met Recom's operator since, he always brought up this scene of my jumping up and down at the end of this game.

For some unknown reason, the wrong game score was posted for the Recom game in the official bulletin. Dr Berliner found the posted final position a dead loss for ChipTest and was surprised enough to e-mail me asking whether Recom had crashed. No one else seemed to have caught the mistake. The real game score is given in Appendix B, courtesy of Ken Thompson.

ChipTest's debut was not quite a coming-out party, but an even score (two wins, two losses and one draw) on the first try was not exactly a bad result.

Singular Extensions

Despite being the top seed at the 1986 ACM tournament, Bebe did not win the Championship. Given the use of the "Swiss" tournament format, this was not really a surprise. In a Swiss tournament, players with similar scores who have not yet played against each other are paired together for the next round. A Swiss tournament is better than a knockout tournament in that there is some chance to recover from an early loss, but the odds are still not good for the top player to win. The probability of the strongest program winning the ACM or a similar tournament is actually quite slim.

In 1986, Bebe lost to Belle, the eventual winner. In the battle for second place, Bebe was defeated by Lachex (Los Alamos CHess EXperiment), a program running on a Cray supercomputer at the Los Alamos national lab. Tony Scherzer was quite disappointed about the loss. He told everyone who would listen what had happened in the game, and it was an intriguing story.

Bebe and Lachex somehow went into a sequence of forced moves where both sides had only one single good choice along the way. Neither program had any idea about who would come up ahead in the end. Both sides just kept on playing the "only" moves until, suddenly, both programs realized that Bebe was a dead loss. Bebe was one of the top programs, and Lachex was no slouch either. How could both programs be so clueless? And what could be done about the problem?

The ACM tournament was not just a competition; it was also the annual gathering of computer chess researchers. Between rounds, impromptu discussions took place whenever a small group of people got together. One of the discussions that I had with Tony Scherzer and a few others was about the idea of selective search. Tony made a blanket statement that the old idea of "selective pruning" (discarding "unpromising" moves from consideration) was dead, replaced by the new idea of "selective deepening"[3] or "selective extensions", namely, searching *interesting* moves more deeply.

Could the idea of "selective deepening" be used to solve the problem that showed up in the Lachex-Bebe game? Well, it could if we had some way to detect that there was only one *good* move for the present position. I thought about it briefly, and reached the conclusion that there was no sure way to obtain the information without paying for it. In some very rare situations, the information is free, but we were talking about perhaps once in a million. I put

---

[3] Tony might have been the first person to use this phrase.

the question in the back of my mind until the next day when I got on the plane back to Pittsburgh.

The way people had been doing selective deepening or selective extensions was mostly based on chess knowledge. If one side is in check, examine the position deeper. If a pawn is about to reach the eighth rank and become a queen, search the position deeper. In the case of ChipTest, it was very difficult to put in the chess knowledge for more selective extensions. But, if we could get the microprogram working, we would have the fastest chess program on the planet, and searching would be comparatively cheap. At least that was how the idea of "singular extensions" began. It was not really necessary to have a fast program. In any case, I reasoned that we could afford to slow down the program a little bit by modifying the search or doing extra searches to gather information about whether a move is *singular*, or the *only* reasonable move. Once we verified that the move is *singular*, then we could search it more deeply. One way to gather the *singularity* information is to explicitly search all the alternative moves and to test whether they are significantly worse than the move in question. This could be done fairly efficiently along the "principal variation", or PV (the line where both sides play the best moves), as all the alternative moves along the PV have to be examined in a normal search anyway. This basic idea later became the "PV singular extensions". Anyway, I deemed the idea a theoretical curiosity at the time. I had more important things to attend to when I got back to Pittsburgh. It was about time to present my thesis proposal.

Even though Ken Thompson had been on my thesis committee for over a year, I had not yet presented my thesis proposal. After I finished the design of the chess move generator chip, Professor Kung suggested that Dr Berliner should be on my committee. It seemed a good idea at the time that if I wanted to eventually build the *ultimate* chess machine, I would need the cooperation of at least one good chess player at some future date. Dr Berliner was without doubt the best chess player at Carnegie Mellon as well as a World Correspondence Chess (chess played by mail) Champion. His world title did not mean that he was of the top echelon in regular chess, but he was still of International Master [4] strength, which would have placed him among the top fifty over-the-board players in USA. To be such a strong player is a considerable achievement in itself. He could play simultaneously against twenty players of my strength and win every single game. Ironically, having Dr Berliner on the committee probably doomed any possibility of cooperation [5]. Anyway, I took Professor Kung's suggestion, and Dr Berliner became the third member of my thesis committee. Alan Fisher, a professor in the VLSI group, was the fourth member.

When I got back from the ACM Tournament, Thomas had cleaned up and rewritten the search microprogram. It was working but not yet optimized, and there were still some hardware bugs that crashed the microprogram from time to time. I worked on both the hardware and the microprogram off and on while preparing for my thesis proposal. A month after the ACM tournament, I presented my proposal, which was to complete the design of a real chess machine and work out the details of how to use multiple chess machines to get to unprecedented search speed. The thesis, when it was finished, became the blueprint of the future Deep Blue chess machine.

Shortly after the proposal, I debugged the ChipTest hardware and optimized the microprogram. Thomas also had some free time to work on the software. Two months after the ACM Tournament, ChipTest played its first game against Hitech. The two teams were on cordial terms at the time and both were interested in getting a sparring partner [6]. ChipTest won the game, but Hitech was probably still the stronger program overall. ChipTest, however, was clearly already one of the top chess machines in the world, just two months after its lackluster debut. It was searching about 300,000 chess positions per second, approximately three times faster than any other chess program. Not bad for something that was designed as a chip tester.

After ChipTest became a stable chess machine, I had some dis-

---

4 From the top, the chess players can be ranked in the following order: World Champion, Grandmaster (GM), International Master (IM), senior master (SM), master, expert, class A, class B, class C and so on. The first three are international titles. FIDE Master (FM) is a relatively new international title. An FM is roughly comparable to a senior master in playing strength. A Super Grandmaster is a very strong Grandmaster, but the term is mainly one of praise and not an official title.

5 The arrangement created an unintentional public perception that the ChipTest team worked for Dr Berliner, which later became a source of friction.

6 Dr Berliner had unrestricted access to ChipTest which he used as a sparring partner for Hitech extensively. We kept logs of all ChipTest games, so the sparring games played by Dr Berliner were of use to us as well. We also ran games against Hitech to debug ChipTest. Murray, who also worked on Hitech, conducted the debugging sessions for the ChipTest team.

cussions with Murray Campbell about the idea of PV singular extensions. Not being a real chess player myself, I used Murray as a sounding board to find out whether the idea made sense. Murray was of the opinion that it deserved serious testing. Thomas implemented the idea during a weekend, and we pitted the version with PV singular extensions against a version without it in a twenty-game match. The result was a big surprise. The new version beat the old version by 15 to 5. A win-loss ratio of three to one corresponds to a difference of 200 rating points, or a full chess class. It is about the difference between the World Champion and a typical Grandmaster. It is huge. We were all very excited, although our excitement was tempered by the knowledge that the match result was between two closely related programs, and the strength difference was probably greatly exaggerated. The twenty games were played from ten different starting positions with alternate colors. For the pair of games from the same starting position, usually the two programs would play exactly the same moves until a critical position where the new version managed to avoid an immediate disaster and ended up drawing or winning the game. Taking an analogy from 'Star Trek', the two versions of the program could be viewed as two identical Enterprise-class starships, one with all the long-range sensors disabled and one with all but the front long-range sensors disabled. As both starships head towards a massive black hole, the starship with the working front long-range sensor will be the one that detects the black hole, and escapes its deadly clutch in time.

No self-respecting starship captain would allow his ship to be without the full complement of long-range sensors for long. What if there was an interesting planet starboard in the distance? Without the starboard long-range sensor, the planet would be missed completely. We found ourselves in a similar situation. PV singular extensions allowed the program to discover the potential disaster with the current best plan, but the extensions did not help the program find interesting alternatives to the current plan. In chess jargon, PV singular extensions does not help the program discover combinations, that is, non-obvious sequences of moves that lead to significant advantages. We needed a new idea. Could we extend the idea of PV singular extensions to attack the problem?

If an alternative chess move is not as good as our current best move, then our opponent must have refutations to every possible continuation that we could play. To verify that a move was not the best move for us, we needed to find one working refutation move for our opponent against our move. What if our opponent had *only* one working refutation move after our move? Then it seemed to make sense to search deeper after our opponent's *singular* refutation move. Intuitively, if a player has only one good move, it is possible that the move is the only one left that *delays* the inevitable disaster for the player. This is the main reasoning behind what we called *fail-high singular extensions*. (Computer chess researchers refer to refutation moves as fail-high moves.)

The introduction of fail-high singular extensions produced a quantum leap in ChipTest's ability to detect combinations. But the newest version did not play measurably better than the older version in head-to-head competition against each other. The extra computation cost of the fail-high singular extensions wiped out the gain. We decided to keep the new extensions, figuring that they might have a positive effect against human players. At the very least, the extensions would make it impossible for the human players to guess whether the program would see a particularly deep combination.

A couple of years later, Thomas decided to abandon his original thesis topic and do a detailed study of singular extensions and a few other search extensions that we used. There was some debate among the team whether some of Thomas' conclusions in his thesis should be taken at face value. Thomas' results were obtained using an unproven indirect measurement technique with Deep Thought, our next chess machine. His results were suggestive, but they provided more questions than answers. According to Thomas, singular extensions had little effect on program performance, at least as implemented in Deep Thought. It was not until 1991, when Deep Thought II became operational with an entirely new implementation of singular extensions, that we verified that the effects of singular extensions were quite substantial. But this was after we introduced several additional new ideas, which were not present in Deep Thought, on how to control the singular extensions and their derivatives. In particular, the Deep Thought II implementation also extended the search on moves that were not really singular. For instance, when the move was one of the only two good moves, Deep Thought II would still extend the search, although not as much as when the move was singular.

Beating "World Champions"

ChipTest was playing on roughly equal footing with Hitech after the introduction of singular extensions. It was tactically stronger than Hitech, but it had close to zero chess knowledge. We could have added some simple software evaluation to improve ChipTest's strength, but I had something else in mind.

When I started the project, I planned to design an evaluation chip to go with the move generator chip. I had some rough idea on how the design would look, but I had no idea on what kind of chess evaluation function to put in. With the Hitech team around, I hoped that I could draw on the local expertise and experience. The problem was that Hitech was designed with a different philosophy, and was not compatible with my idea of fitting an entire evaluation function onto a single chip. By the time that ChipTest was up and running, I concluded that I needed to gain some design experience with chess evaluation function first hand before I could seriously entertain the idea of an evaluation chip.

By then, the first field-programmable gate arrays (FPGAs) had just become commercially available. These FPGAs allowed logic circuits of moderate complexity to be implemented with off-the-shelf components. They seemed to be ideally suited for the task of an experimental hardware evaluation function in a real chess machine. Professor Kung had some discretionary funds and agreed to foot the bill. This new machine would be mainly a learning experience on how to design chess evaluation hardware. But, based on the performance of ChipTest, the new machine could be expected to be a stronger chess player than any existing chess machine. I was also hoping to kick some butts at the 1987 ACM tournament! Given the crude nature of FPGA design software at the time, and the fact that I had never designed with FPGAs, the chance of entering the new machine in the 1987 tournament, however, was not good.

One month before the 1987 ACM tournament, it became clear that there was absolutely no chance of getting the new machine ready in time. We drew up a contingency plan. First, we added to ChipTest the software evaluation of pawn structure that we had planned back in 1986. Second, we made sure that both the hardware and the software were in good shape by doing serious play testing, both against ChipTest itself and against Hitech[7]. Third, we "acquired" the fastest workstation that we could lay our hands on. We did not own the workstation—it was borrowed through our connections with the Engineering Lab staff. Officially, the workstation was being tested before its installation in its real owner's lab. The faster workstation reduced the software overhead and ChipTest was able to search about 400,000 chess positions per second, a thirty percent increase in speed.

After the addition of the software pawn structure evaluation, ChipTest became about 100 rating points stronger in games against machines. Since Murray was officially in the Hitech group, one big question was whether Hitech would be playing in the ACM Championship. It did not play in the 1986 tournament because its hardware was being modified. Dr Berliner decided to skip the competition again in 1987, citing the desire to concentrate on competitions against human players, so there was no problem with Murray continuing to work on ChipTest.

Despite the absence of Hitech, the 1987 ACM tournament in Dallas had a strong field. The top finishers in the 1986 World Computer Chess Championship were all present with the exception of Hitech. ChipTest was seeded third, behind Cray Blitz, the winner of the 1986 World Computer Chess Championship on tiebreak, and Belle, the winner of the 1986 ACM Championship. Bebe and Phoenix were seeded fourth and fifth respectively but tied for first at the World Computer Chess Championship.

ChipTest beat Cyrus 68K in round one easily. Round two brought a more difficult opponent, Lachex, which had finished in second place in the 1986 ACM tournament. ChipTest won a pawn early in the game, but it was a difficult endgame to win, going on until 3:00 am, Central Time, and was the last to finish. Pittsburgh is in Eastern Time so, biologically, it was 4:00 am for me and way past my bedtime. I was very tired but happy to have won the game.

In the next round, we moved to the top board to play against Cray Blitz. We had Black.

ChipTest played an opening called the center counter defense, in chess parlance. The defense did not have a good reputation. The main criticism of the center counter defense is the fact that the Black queen moves out into the open at a very early stage and can be subject to attacks. I grimaced when I saw the opening. One of the introductory chess books that I had read gave this particular

---

7   We did not really do much play testing against Hitech ourselves. Dr Berliner was using ChipTest as a sparring partner against Hitech. We just checked out the game logs to make sure that nothing strange happened.

opening as an example of how *not* to play in the opening phase of the game. Murray did not have a lot of time to prepare the opening, and decided to use the defense since it was relatively easy to prepare. Ken Thompson came by and asked, "How can you play this garbage *again*?" In the Lachex game, ChipTest had also played the center counter defense. Having seen the Lachex game, the Cray Blitz team prepared a better offensive line for White.

Pretty soon after the opening phase, the board position looked a little bit dicey for ChipTest, and at this point it suddenly predicted that Cray Blitz would win a pawn. ChipTest went into what we called panic mode, trying to find a way out by going through all the moves. After about thirty minutes of calculation, it went for a sharp surprise continuation that would still lose the pawn but with some compensation. Mike Valvo, the tournament director, was quite shocked that any program would spend thirty minutes on a single move, and praised ChipTest for spending time wisely at a critical juncture. In reality, the reason why ChipTest spent thirty minutes on a single move was because singular extensions tend to cause the search tree to explode in size when used in conjunction with the Panic Mode. We had learned about this in our test games and therefore we gave ChipTest a very large time allocation whenever it was in panic mode.

Given the surprise move from ChipTest, Cray Blitz inexplicably decided not to win the pawn. Had ChipTest played the normal continuation that Cray Blitz was predicting, Cray Blitz would have gone ahead and grabbed the pawn immediately. Cray Blitz had been calculating its response to the normal continuation during the entire 30 minutes of ChipTest's calculation. I breathed a sigh of relief. Cray Blitz's opening edge had dissipated. The game seemed to be about even for a few moves. But then, out of nowhere, ChipTest declared that it was winning. It had calculated a very long forcing line as a result of singular extensions and, was reporting that at the end of the line, it would win major material. Cray Blitz simply had no idea that its position was about to collapse like a house of cards. It took Cray Blitz three or four more moves before it realized that the game was lost. The game lasted only twenty-seven moves and was probably the shortest and worst loss of Cray Blitz's career up to that day. It was probably also the first public game where singular extensions played a major role.

In the last round, we had White against Phoenix, a program

that ran on a network of workstations. We were thoroughly out-prepared in the opening. Phoenix had many more moves in its opening book than ChipTest. Since ChipTest had White, being out-prepared in the opening was not fatal. We did lose the advantage of the first move, and the game reached an endgame with equal possibilities for both sides. The author of Phoenix, Jonathan Schaeffer, was a master level chess player; after Dr Berliner, Jonathan might very well have been the strongest chess player among the active computer chess researchers. Former World Champion, Mikhail Botvinnik, was supposed to be working on a chess program, but he probably could not be considered an active computer chess researcher, as no one outside of his group had ever seen his program play a single move. Being a weak player myself, I listened intently to what Jonathan had to say about the position, and constantly checked his opinion against ChipTest's assessment of the position. Jonathan was later quoted as saying that I, being a weak player, was one of those guys whose emotions went up and down with their own program's evaluation of the position. This was certainly true in this game. Jonathan thought his program was in a better position, but with ChipTest thinking the position dead even, I was unconcerned. Jonathan was still in a cheerful mood when ChipTest's evaluation started to creep upward in its favor. Then it dawned upon Jonathan that Phoenix might be in trouble. Phoenix's position was no longer tenable. ChipTest had already seen ways to win material. A few moves later Jonathan resigned for Phoenix, and ChipTest won the Championship with a clean sweep.

ChipTest was probably at this point *the* best chess machine in the world. It had won the ACM title ahead of three of the top four finishers in the 1986 World Computer Chess Championship. Hitech was the only one among the top four at the World Championship that was missing, and ChipTest had held its own against Hitech before the ACM tournament. How strong was ChipTest? I have reasons to believe that it might have been the first senior master machine. ChipTest was never fully rated in human tournaments, so this is just a guess.

ChipTest received a $2000 prize for the win, which was more than the estimated $500 cost of building it. To celebrate the win, we used part of the prize money to hold a TG party for the whole Department in ChipTest's honor. It seemed very appropriate, given how ChipTest was born in the first place.

An Invitation from California

During one of the conversations at the 1987 ACM Championship, Jonathan Schaeffer, the author of Phoenix, said that there were two people whom he really looked up to in the computer chess field.

The first person was Ken Thompson. Jonathan respected Ken not just for his achievement and contribution to computer chess, but also for his unselfish acts. He mentioned a few of Ken's deeds, one of which I observed myself. Each year at the ACM Championship, Ken would collect the game scores after each round, enter them into the computer, and then post them to the rest of the world. Not something you would expect from a busy and important person who had won the Turing Award, the equivalent of the Nobel Prize for a computer scientist.

The second person that Jonathan looked up to came as a big surprise to me. It was Dr Hans Berliner. Looking back, I was surprised partly because of my professional differences with Dr Berliner, and partly because I considered him not the easiest person to work with, but I guess I can understand why Jonathan thought highly of him. When Jonathan looked at Dr Berliner, he must have seen quite a bit of himself, or at least something of what he would like to be. They were both very good chess players doing research in computer chess. Jonathan was still an up-and-comer, while Dr Berliner was well established. Dr Berliner had worked on computer chess since 1970 when he entered his first program in the ACM competition. Having garnered the title of World Correspondence Chess Champion earlier, Dr Berliner may have hoped that he could be the person who would finally solve the Computer Chess Problem, creating a chess machine that could beat the World Chess Champion in a match. He went back to graduate school at a fairly advanced age, earned a PhD degree, and became a research faculty member at Carnegie Mellon University, where the Computer Science Department had a history of pioneering work in computer chess. He gathered together a group of graduate students with varying skills and led them in the creation of Hitech. There are very few people who could match Dr Berliner's drive.

A few weeks after my conversation with Jonathan, the friendly competition between the ChipTest team and Dr Berliner suddenly turned into an open rivalry.

Before I tell you the story, I need to put you in the right frame of mind. First, the story is important. Things like this do happen. I don't enjoy telling it, but the events in the story marked an irreversible transition in the relationship between the ChipTest team and Dr Berliner. Second, the story may make you look at Dr Berliner unfavorably. Before you do that, please think twice about what you would have done in his place. Imagine that you have a lifetime goal, a higher calling. You have worked for decades to reach the goal, making many personal sacrifices. You are now a widely recognized authority in your chosen field. You have achieved great successes in the last few years and your goal seems to be in sight. Now imagine a bunch of students coming out of nowhere. They are not from your field and they have different ideas. You have little persuasive power over them since they are not your students. Their approach is the exact opposite of what you are advocating. To make matters worse, they seem to be making rapid progress, which makes it even harder to persuade them to follow your vision. What would you do? What can you do? It is a very tough situation.

Andreas Nowatzyk, my office mate, was spending time at NASA's Jet Propulsion Lab (JPL) in Pasadena, California. He met Stuart Cracraft, a computer chess enthusiast, who happened to be working at JPL at the time. Stuart asked Andreas a lot of questions about ChipTest. A big chess tournament, the American Open, was about to take place in Los Angeles. Stuart apparently had good contacts with the tournament organizers and suggested that we enter ChipTest into the tournament. Stuart mentioned that he had friends who would gladly help with setting up communications and operating the machine remotely. Andreas thought that it was a good opportunity to see how well ChipTest would do against human players.

Thomas was all for entering the tournament. Murray did not want to take sides, as both he and I knew that Hitech was going to the same tournament. I was against participating, but not because Hitech was playing. I found that I was spending too much time watching ChipTest play and not getting much work done. I was not quite as disciplined as I would have liked. If ChipTest started playing in tournaments, the new machine that I was working on might never see the light of the day. Anyway, I sent an e-mail to Dr Berliner asking for his opinion.

The next morning, Dr Berliner sent back a message vehemently against ChipTest going, giving three reasons. The first was that ChipTest was totally untested against human players. The second was that Carnegie Mellon's reputation could be hurt. His third was that it was foolish to let an outsider, not affiliated with the university, operate ChipTest.

From my point of view, ChipTest being untested against human players would have been the perfect reason to take it out for a spin. We were in a research university after all. Furthermore, I had never heard of a university's reputation ever being ruined by student projects doing poorly in chess tournaments. Dr Berliner's third objection brought up a valid concern, but ChipTest was a student project with a zero budget, and I did not see any strong reason against getting outside help to operate the machine. Otherwise, we would have to shell out a serious amount of our own money to fly to Los Angeles [8].

I disagreed with Dr Berliner's reasoning, but since I did not really want to enter ChipTest into the tournament I just forwarded Dr Berliner's message to Andreas.

Andreas replied in the afternoon that the potential operator did have an affiliation with CMU. He was Jim Gillogly, one of the early pioneers in computer chess and a PhD from the Department at roughly the same time as Berliner. A couple of hours later, Jim sent me an e-mail formally agreeing to be the operator, if needed. I passed this information on to Dr Berliner.

Dr Berliner was probably taken off guard. This time he came up with a different reason. The ChipTest team had not published the paper on singular extensions yet, but Dr Berliner knew about them. The Hitech group was just in the process of getting singular extensions to work on their machine. Since Hitech did not have Singular Extensions, Dr Berliner worried that it could finish behind ChipTest, and the Hitech group would look bad. Well, it was not completely unreasonable. We had come up with the idea of singular extensions ourselves without any help from Dr Berliner, so in that sense his request was unreasonable. On the other hand, we owed Dr Berliner something. When Murray agreed to help Thomas and me with the evaluation function for ChipTest, he did not start from scratch. Unbeknown to me at the time, Murray used the

---

[8] The Department did pay for the trips to the ACM Championship, but competing in the ACM Championship was an academic activity.

"Cray Blitz Simulator" code [9] written by Dr Berliner as the starting template to create ChipTest's evaluation function. The Cray Blitz Simulator was a simple (compared to Hitech's) evaluation function used by Berliner to run on Hitech to simulate the expected behavior of Cray Blitz. The amount of code from Dr Berliner was less than a half of one percent of ChipTest's total code, but it was his nonetheless. I first learned about the nature of the code in question only a few weeks before the 1987 ACM Championship. Gordon Goetsch, who was in the Hitech group, was joking about the possibility of Cray Blitz being outplayed by the Cray Blitz Simulator.

If Dr Berliner had stated this objection right at the beginning, we probably would have just honored his request. By this time, I was a little bit mad at him. I had a discussion with Thomas and we came up with a compromise. We would go to the tournament only if Hitech has the singular extensions working. In reality, we were not making any travelling plans as we could not imagine they could have them working in time. I informed both Berliner and Andreas of the decision.

Andreas surmised that another possible reason for Dr Berliner's objection, may have been because Hitech was within sight of a major prize and Berliner did not want to be beaten at the post—a perfectly understandable stance given that the two teams were potential rivals. Back in the late 1970s, Professor Edward Fredkin set up a $100,000 prize for the first computer to defeat the World Chess Champion in a match. Carnegie Mellon University was entrusted with managing the Fredkin Prize, and Dr Berliner was the chairman of the Fredkin Prize Committee. To encourage steady progress in the field, two additional but smaller prizes, the Fredkin Intermediate Prizes, were set up. The Belle team had claimed the first Fredkin Intermediate Prize for master level performance. Perhaps Dr Berliner had set his eyes on the second Fredkin Intermediate Prize for Grandmaster level performance ever since Hitech had been built. Not fully aware of the rules for the

---

[9] How did ChipTest end up using this code from Dr Berliner? None of us knows for sure any more. Thomas Anantharaman believes that he might have retrieved the code after Gordon Goetsch suggested it to him. Gordon, in turn, might have been simply trying to help us make it to the 1986 ACM Champion in the short seven weeks that we had. Gordon, however, could not confirm nor deny what Thomas said.

award, Andreas pointed out that, with singular extensions, Hitech might just be good enough to achieve a 2400 rating and become the first computer senior master. However, the rules for the second Intermediate Prize specified a twenty-five-game performance of over 2500. I did not believe Hitech would be good enough, even with the singular extensions. Neither did I believe that ChipTest could do it. If Dr Berliner wanted Hitech to be the first official senior master then good luck to him. I had bigger fish to fry. Anyway, we had agreed that we would not go, although with a proviso.

For Dr Berliner, Hitech happened to be his last chess machine—it took years to complete and stayed in service for over a decade afterwards. ChipTest took seven weeks to put together, and was only one year old at the time. But ChipTest was effectively fully depreciated, having earned more in prize money than it had cost, and I had a new machine in the pipeline. ChipTest missing a tournament was not as important to me as getting the new machine finished.

Shortly afterwards, Professor Kung called for a meeting to discuss things and both Dr Berliner and I attended. Murray and Thomas were not present. The first part of the meeting was to talk about the invitation from California. Dr Berliner made his statement first, expressing his dissatisfaction that ChipTest was using the "Cray Blitz Simulator" code which was a surprise to me. I had never seen the code until after the 1986 ACM Championship but once I knew its origin I thought that Murray used it with Dr Berliner's blessing. For most of the year before, I had assumed that Murray wrote the code himself. Had Dr Berliner told us about his displeasure, we would have gutted the code and rewritten things from scratch. As it was previously noted, it was less than a half of one percent of the total code anyway. I explained that I knew nothing about it, and Murray was the one who knew anything about the code. (I did not know it at the time, but Thomas might have been the one who retrieved the code.) Dr Berliner accepted my explanation. I then reiterated that we did not want to play in the tournament, so the problem with the invitation was finally over.

The second part of the meeting was about my future. The Department had been mulling over the possibility of retaining me after my graduation. Naturally, they would prefer that Dr Berliner and I work together. I did enjoy life a great deal in the Department, but I had one major concern. What about the credit? Dr Berliner answered "The credit will take care of itself". I was not sure exactly what he meant by this, but I had seen what happened with Hitech. Most people referred to it as Dr Berliner's machine and Carl Ebeling was largely unknown to the outside world. This perception may well have been due to inaccurate reporting in the press, but the assumption stuck and I would not want anything similar to happen on any project I worked on. Well, it was an interesting offer, but I had to decline, since I had no confidence that the credit would indeed take care of itself. After graduation I would have to look for a job elsewhere to continue the work. The job prospects for a computer science PhD were not good at the time. Oh, well, what will be will be. The thing to do would be to make the new machine as successful as we could, in particular, to go after the Fredkin Intermediate Prize. We also needed to make it obvious to anyone that the new machine was completely separate from the work of the Hitech team.

I became a lot more sensitive to the credit issue after this episode. I didn't want to be mistreated, and I didn't want to see people mistreated. I swore after the meeting that our team would not have an official leader. The team was functionally partitioned, and it would be unfair to any one to declare a particular person as the leader.

Looking back, I wonder whether I was just lucky. All my project experience up to that point had been some sort of partnership—my undergradate project in Taiwan and the GE project had both been with partners. The attitude of my faculty bosses had been hands off and just letting us do whatever we pleased. So the decision to have no official leader was kind of natural. The chess project turned out to be a project that required complete dedication from every member of the team. This dedication was possible only because we were equal partners.

Several books and articles stated that the Hitech team and the ChipTest/Deep Thought team were bitter enemies. The relationship was more civil than that. For the Deep Thought team, it was easy—we ended up on the winning side. Also, things only really turned bad after the invitation from California. It is safe to say that neither team would invite the other to their private parties afterwards. After we left Carnegie Mellon, time and distance helped to heal the wounds; I think both sides mellowed. When Deep

Thought II became active, we no longer considered Hitech as a competitor. We still did not like the idea of losing to Hitech. Hell, we did not like to lose to anybody, Garry Kasparov included!

♟ CHAPTER 5

The Race for First Machine Grandmaster

Some 2200s

During the 1970s and 1980s, the British science fiction writer
Douglas Adams wrote a highly popular science fiction trilogy that
the BBC turned into both a radio show and a television series.
While I was serving in the Taiwanese Army, a local radio station
was carrying the BBC radio show based on the first book, *The
Hitchhiker's Guide to the Galaxy*. However, I did not get to read the
books themselves until I lived in the United States.

In the universe of the Hitchhiker's Guide, an alien race built
a computer called Deep Thought, to solve the question of "Life, the
Universe, and Everything". After eons of computation, it came up
with the answer "42". But no entity, including Deep Thought,
knew the original question any more. Deep Thought, however,
being the most powerful computer ever built, knew how to build
an even more powerful computer which would answer the question, of what was the question, to the answer "42".

Well, a machine that could defeat the World Champion
would surely be worthy of the name Deep Thought.

I did not believe that the machine we were building in early
1988, which was also our first real chess machine, would be sufficient to defeat the World Champion. It was probably at least 100
times too slow. Factoring in the speed discrepancy, the first version
of the new program was called Deep Thought 0.01. It later became
Deep Thought 0.02 after we got a dual-processor version working.
Eventually, when we decided to join IBM and build a new machine
with a new name, the name became simply Deep Thought.

Andreas came back to Carnegie Mellon from Pasadena after
the New Year. We talked off and on about the possibility of creat-

ing a program that could tune the chess evaluation function automatically. Andreas had an exciting new idea. The new idea, however, required that the evaluation function be written in a different way. Murray liked Andreas' idea and agreed to write a completely new evaluation function in the way Andreas specified. The new evaluation function was written in part to handle the new evaluation primitives supported by the Deep Thought hardware, which were about to be completed. The original reason for the new evaluation function, and the automatic tuning software, however, was to start from a clean slate. We needed to avoid any of the problems with the "Cray Blitz Simulator" code as we had had with ChipTest, so that we would be able to compete freely. The automatic tuning of the evaluation function was often mentioned as the most novel aspect of Deep Thought, but it came purely out of necessity. Andreas helped quite a bit in bringing up ChipTest earlier, and with this increased involvement I finally got him to agree to be seen as one of the authors of Deep Thought.

Once Andreas became seriously involved, I set my sight on Mike Browne, my other office mate. (Okay, being my friend has its drawbacks.) One of the biggest problems for ChipTest was its opening book, or rather, its lack of opening book. Mike agreed to write a program that automatically examined all the opening lines to look for opening traps (bad opening moves), and theoretical novelties (new opening moves that are interesting), and became the fifth member of the Deep Thought team.

During most of the 1980s, the Fredkin Foundation sponsored a series of annual computer chess events. The final event of the series took place in 1988, the year after ChipTest's win at the ACM championship. The money used to sponsor the events came from the interest accrued from the prize fund for the $100,000 Fredkin Prize. The Fredkin events, unlike the computer competition in the ACM championship, pitted the top chess programs against human chess players. Traditionally, the reigning ACM Computer Chess Champion was invited along with possibly some of the stronger programs at the time. The 1988 final edition was the Fredkin Masters Open, from May 28 to 30 on the Carnegie Mellon campus. It would be a six-round tournament, with two rounds per day. ChipTest, as the reigning ACM Champion, was invited, along with Deep Thought 0.01. Hitech, as the 1985 ACM Champion, was also invited. Hitech would be using Singular Extensions for the first time in tournament play.

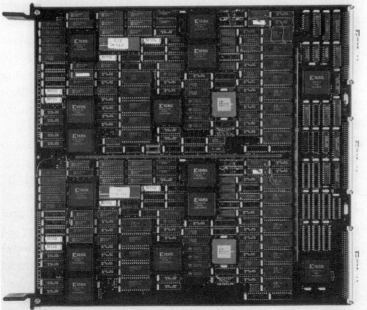

The two versions of Deep Thought 1.

The wire-wrapped (top) and the printed circuit (bottom) versions of the Deep Thought 1 board. The two wire loops on the right side of the wire-wrapped board are used to delay two critical signals by a few nanoseconds. (Electrical signals travel slightly less than one foot over the wires every nanosecond.)

When the work began on the Deep Thought hardware, I was hoping to get it ready for the 1987 ACM Championship but Deep Thought never made it. I was not going to miss the Fredkin Masters Open; however, I ended up cutting it very close. The most important new feature in Deep Thought, compared to ChipTest, was its hardware evaluation function which recognized many dynamic positional features, including chess concepts such as pawn structure, passed pawns, rooks on open files, and so on. The new hardware evaluation was implemented with field programmable gate arrays that took longer to program than I expected. The wire-wrapped Deep Thought board also had some nasty electrical problems that took a while to track down. Furthermore, the Deep Thought board, besides having the new hardware evaluation function, had two chess processors, and both needed to be fully tested. With the additional complexity, the cost for the Deep Thought board was close to $5000, or ten times the cost of ChipTest. Just procuring the parts for Deep Thought took longer than the time to design and build ChipTest. By March 1988, the Deep Thought board was partially working, but the debugging of the board, along with the creation of the new software, seemed to take forever. Two days before the Fredkin Masters Open, the Deep Thought board was still being rewired, and Thomas continued to add finishing touches to the new software until the event started.

The Pittsburgh Chess Club ran the tournament. About thirty players participated, approximately twenty at the master level or above. One of the out-of-town masters was Alexander Ivanov, a recent Soviet émigré. Alexander was rated 2597 on the US rating scale, which was close to Grandmaster strength, even though he did not have a title at the time. (He became a Grandmaster about a year later.) The top Pittsburgh master was Vivek Rao, a teenager rated at 2491 who also happened to be the top player in Pennsylvania. Vivek's rating put him at close to International Master (IM) strength. The masters from Pittsburgh were thought to be a particularly tough crowd for computers. Many of them had participated in earlier editions of the Fredkin events or played Hitech before. It would be a very good test for the computers.

I paid the tournament entry fees and US Chess Federation (USCF) membership dues for both ChipTest and Deep Thought, using ChipTest's prize money from the ACM Championship. After paying, I checked the wall chart for the participants. Neither ChipTest nor Deep Thought was rated at the time, and I was surprised to see ratings placed next to the their names. I asked the tournament director, and he said that the ratings for both machines were Dr Berliner's estimates. The programs were both listed as 2200, essentially very weak masters. Hitech was rated 2376 at the time. I winced but did not say anything as I could understand the reasoning for these ratings. The low estimate ratings in the strong field meant that for both ChipTest and Deep Thought our first round opponents would be strong masters.

Thomas was the operator for ChipTest and I operated Deep Thought. Deep Thought's first opponent Ross Sprague, rated 2339 on the wall chart, was a lawyer from out of town who played conservatively. The game was still undecided when it was time to adjourn till the next morning. Meanwhile, ChipTest scored its first win against a human opponent, a strong master.

I came back early the next day to finish the game with Ross. We both knew that the game was heading to a draw but that Ross could try to avoid the draw by playing a risky move. But first, he played on for a while to see whether Deep Thought would self-destruct. Finally, he figured that a 2339-rated human player should beat a 2200 machine and decided to take the risk. Deep Thought's evaluation immediately jumped up, and a few moves later, Ross threw in the towel. Deep Thought probably would have drawn the game, if not for the 2200 rating estimate. In the second round games, both Deep Thought and ChipTest drew against strong masters.

Deep Thought's third round opponent was Kimball Nedved. Kimball's son, Rudy, worked in our department, and Kimball himself was quite familiar with chess computers. He had both beaten and lost to Hitech before. Kimball was sufficiently comfortable that he would make comments from time to time during the game. He had drawn ChipTest in the previous round and was complimentary of ChipTest's play. Deep Thought was not quite stable yet, and all of a sudden, it played an instant move due to an internal inconsistency. I raised my eyebrows when I played the move. Kimball had no idea why I did this, and said questioningly, "Why? That is a good move." Well, it just happened to be. There were no more incidents in the game, and Kimball resigned without ever realizing that Deep Thought could run into the same problem again. Meanwhile, ChipTest won its third round in a hair-raising game. The fourth round saw Deep Thought winning another game and ChipTest drawing its game. We would be meeting the top players on the third day.

In the fifth round, Deep Thought was paired against Alexander Ivanov, and ChipTest against Vivek Rao. Deep Thought was still using the same opening book that ChipTest used in the 1987 ACM Championship, and that, of course, meant we were seeing the center counter defense, also known as the Scandinavian defense. I was surprised to see Alexander, the soon-to-be Grandmaster, spending a lot of time in the opening. He did say before the game that he had never studied the Scandinavian defense seriously. Maybe the center counter defense was not garbage after all. Alexander played carefully and powerfully. Then he went into deep thought over a position that looked quite dangerous for Deep Thought. It appeared to me that Alexander could unleash a very strong attack on Deep Thought's king. To my surprise, Alexander played a move that seemed to release all the tension in the position. What was he doing? It looked like an even ending to me. On a closer look at the board, I began to get a sinking feeling. It wasn't an even ending. Alexander had seen deeper than Deep Thought, and Deep Thought lost its first ever game. While Deep Thought was having its problems, interesting things were unfolding on ChipTest's board. Before Vivek's game with ChipTest, he was openly expressing his contempt of chess-playing computers, having had numerous pleasant memories at the expense of Hitech from earlier encounters. ChipTest forced Vivek to resign in twenty-two moves with an unexpected sacrifice. Hours after the game was over, Vivek was still showing other people ChipTest's surprise combination.

In the last round, ChipTest's undefeated record against human chess players came to a screeching halt, losing to a strong master. Despite Vivek's loss to ChipTest, he continued to express his contempt of chess computers, and got a chance to prove his point in the last round. He was paired against Deep Thought. Now chastened by ChipTest's tactical ability, Vivek went for a quieter game against Deep Thought. An "isolated queen pawn" position was reached. Deep Thought had more control in the center of the board, but also a potential weakness in its isolated queen pawn. Deep Thought's queen pawn did not have any friendly pawns on the adjacent files. If Vivek could drive the game into an ending with most of the pieces traded off, he would very likely win, as Deep Thought's queen pawn would become a major endgame weakness. Vivek managed to trade off two pieces, and seemed to have obtained a favorable position. Then Deep

Thought started playing dumb looking moves. A smile formed on Vivek's face. Did he sense a kill? Deep Thought remained unconcerned. Vivek continued his quiet maneuver with innocent looking moves. Then Deep Thought pushed its pawn on f file, threatening to open up the position. Its score jumped. Vivek froze up, took another look, and left the room for fresh air. It was a good move. He came back and sat at the table, this time with his hands over his ears. Someone opened the door and made a slight noise. Vivek hushed the guy. After thinking for twenty-five minutes, Vivek made his move. A series of piece exchanges ensued. After all the smoke cleared ten moves later, Vivek was down a pawn. A few moves later, when he was about to lose more material, he resigned. So the top player in Pennsylvania lost twice in the same day to the newest USCF players in Pennsylvania.

Ross, our first round opponent, dropped by after the Vivek game. He commented, "Some 2200s." He then added that if he had known what he was dealing with, he would have just taken the draw.

Alexander Ivanov won the event, scoring 5 points out of 6. Deep Thought tied for the second place with two masters, scoring 4.5 out of 6. ChipTest tied for fifth place, scoring 4 out of 6. Hitech had a bad tournament, scoring 3.5 out of 6. Deep Thought's performance rating was 2599 for the tournament, while ChipTest's was at 2521. Hitech performed at 2312.

If ChipTest and Deep Thought could be considered as a single machine, then its twelve-game performance would be around 2560. The rules for the Fredkin Intermediate Prize called for a twenty-five-game performance of over 2500. We had a very good shot, assuming that Hitech would not do it first. Before the Fredkin Masters Open, I did not believe that either Hitech or ChipTest could have done it. But it now looked like ChipTest could do it, and who could say for sure that Hitech could not do it too? We had a new sense of urgency. Deep Thought had the best shot of the three machines, but it would be a race. We had the lead and the stronger machines. But don't forget what happened to the hare in the race against the tortoise.

Thank you! Thank you!
One of the drawbacks of constantly bringing new machines to chess competitions, is the need to deal with the numerous exciting

bugs waiting to happen. ChipTest had a memorable first outing at the 1986 ACM Championship. The debut of Deep Thought 0.01 in the Fredkin Masters Open certainly had its tense moments, but there was nothing obvious, at least from our opponents' viewpoints. Deep Thought 0.02 played its first tournament at the 1988 US Open held in Boston from August 7 to 19. It was an experience reminiscent of ChipTest's first tournament.

Deep Thought's wire-wrapped card had two chess processors on it. At the Fredkin Masters Open, only one of the processors was in use; there was no time to get a dual-processor version working. The single-processor version that played at the Fredkin Masters Open was adapted from ChipTest, using the old search code but with the brand new evaluation function. For reasons now lost in antiquity, we did not bother to play in tournaments in the two months leading up to the US Open. Perhaps, we wanted to get the dual-processor version as soon as possible. The other possibility was that we wanted to get a decent opening book.

The ChipTest opening book was grossly inadequate for playing against human players. Murray Campbell received his PhD degree before the Fredkin Masters Open, and was offered the faculty position of Research Associate at the CS Department. The position was equivalent to Assistant Professor but in a research track. Berliner was his semi-official boss [1]. After the Fredkin Masters Open, Murray was told that he was not to spend any time on either Deep Thought or ChipTest—after all, he was employed to work on other projects. Murray followed the directive to the letter in office hours, but continued to work on the two programs in his leisure time. With Murray's time becoming a scarce resource, we moved the new opening book to the top of the to-do list. Since Murray would not have enough time to work on it, we sought help from outside the university. International Master, Larry Kaufman, offered to provide us with the opening book that he had prepared for the Rex chess program, and we took him up on his offer. Ironically, Rex had been ChipTest's first victim at the 1986 ACM Championship.

While we were bringing up the new version, Hitech played in the 1988 Pennsylvania State Championship from July 23–24, won the title, finally getting its rating over 2400, and became the first

---

[1] Dr Berliner was a Senior Research Scientist, which was equivalent to a full professor but in a research track.

official computer senior master, three years after its birth[2]. Both ChipTest and Deep Thought were higher rated than Hitech, but had not yet played twenty rated games, the minimum needed to be official senior masters. While there was no prize associated with the senior master title, there were some misgivings among the Deep Thought team members, that we should have sent out the single-processor version of Deep Thought to tournaments. Anyhow, Hitech the tortoise was catching up, and we could not wait any longer.

The US Open, the showcase event for the US Chess Federation, was a twelve-round tournament held in Boston. Thomas Anantharaman had a friend with whom he could stay in Boston, so he volunteered to drive to Boston, and be the operator. Thomas' expenses would be paid from our earlier winnings in the ACM Championship and the Fredkin Masters Open. As computers were not allowed to get the prize money in regular chess tournaments, we would not be getting any more winnings, and had to watch how much we spent. We would be playing with the dual-processor version for the first time.

The first three games at the US Open were played with the dual-processor code, and the results were disastrous. The first game was drawn as a result of a bug at the interface between the hardware and the software code, although we were not certain of the cause at the time. Deep Thought 0.02 managed to win the second game when the opponent resigned early, but had he known what was to happen in the third round, he probably would have played on. In the third round, we got an expert-level opponent who simply refused to resign when his position was clearly lost. Deep Thought 0.02 was up by a rook, but the opponent played on. Then strange things started to happen. Deep Thought 0.02 started playing nonsensical moves. The opponent made a move threatening to checkmate it on the next move, and Deep Thought 0.02 did not bother to defend against the threat. The opponent just made the mating move, and then exclaimed "Thank you! Thank you!" as he ran off.

It turned out that Thomas' new dual-processor code was accessing the hardware in a different way from the single-processor code. This had the side effect of causing the hardware

---

2 In the first edition of his book *Kasparov vs. Deep Blue*, Monty Newborn erroneously stated that Hitech became a senior master in 1987.

microprogram to reverse the sign of the value for checkmates under certain conditions. Instead of avoiding being checkmated, Deep Thought was enjoying being checkmated!

With Thomas in Boston, it was difficult to debug the dual-processor code, and we reverted to the more reliable single-processor program after round three. In the next five games, Deep Thought 0.01 allowed one draw, winning the other four.

Round nine brought the first major opponent, International Master Igor Ivanov. (Years later, I picked up a book on the early career of World Champion Garry Kasparov, and was surprised to read about a tournament where Igor and Garry tied for first place. But I am getting ahead of myself.) I had seen Igor in action much earlier, even before ChipTest's existence. It was a tournament game between him and Hitech, played on the University of Pittsburgh campus, a ten-minute walk from my office. In that game, Igor effortlessly arranged his pieces for an attack and slaughtered Hitech. Gordon Goetsch of the Hitech group pointed to this game as an example of how far computers had yet to go. After ChipTest was built, I tested out positions from the Igor vs. Hitech game and was quite impressed with his play. ChipTest probably saw Hitech's demise a few moves earlier than Hitech did, but also had no idea what he was doing. Igor was of Grandmaster strength, but he did not have a Grandmaster title. He had defected from the USSR during a tournament held in the West, and this might have made it difficult for him to obtain the title. He was the Canadian co-champion, and at 2641 on the US scale was one of the top players at the Open.

How would Deep Thought do against Igor Ivanov? In Pittsburgh we were obviously nervous. In Boston, Thomas was probably ignorant of his history but his rating alone would be sufficient to impress. Igor had Black. Later, Thomas mentioned that Igor was reading a magazine during the early part of the game; he had no respect whatsoever for Deep Thought. The results from the Fredkin Masters Open were still largely unknown in the chess world.

The game against Igor turned into one of the strangest affairs that I have ever seen. Deep Thought liked to push its pawns. In chess terms, it liked to increase *space*. Good chess players are taught at an early stage that pushing pawns too far could create weaknesses. The "hypermodern" chess school of thought is to deliberately provoke the opponent to push their pawns, hoping that the pawns become over-extended and difficult to maintain. If that was Igor's intent, he succeeded brilliantly, at least for the provoking part. By move nineteen, all of Deep Thought's pawns had advanced at least one square; in fact, with the exception of the two pawns on the edges, all of them had advanced by at least two squares. With Deep Thought pushing pawns with abandon, I was quite concerned, but it really liked its position. What was going on? According to Thomas, by this time, Igor had put down his magazine for several moves; he had seen something that he did not like. Deep Thought's next move pushed all of his pieces back to the first two ranks, and he could hardly move. Its pawns were not over-extended—they were dominating the position. Two moves later, Igor's position deteriorated and became critical. On move twenty-nine, he resigned just as he was about to suffer heavy material loss.

The 1987 US Open Champion, Grandmaster Lev Alburt, rated slightly higher at 2652 than Igor, was paired against Deep Thought in the tenth round. Igor's loss to Deep Thought had been a big upset, and Lev was adequately warned about what he would be facing. Lev played cautiously and entered the endgame with a promising position. On move nineteen, Deep Thought's position became critical, and it pushed a pawn in front of its king by two squares. Lev was surprised by the move which was probably the only move that held the position for Deep Thought. While Deep Thought's position looked ugly, it was not losing. The wily Lev, however, found a way to make progress. The game then became a rook ending where both sides had only one rook and five pawns each. Lev still held the edge, but rook endings are notoriously difficult to win. Perhaps we could get a draw. Deep Thought indeed had a repetition draw in hand by move fifty-two, if only it had played the drawing move. For reasons unknown, Deep Thought found the move, but then decided to look at an alternative drawing move. The new move, however, lost outright. Deep Thought found that the new drawing move did not work, but the software controlling the time allocation was not smart enough to allow it to switch back to the real drawing move. All of us watched in agony while Deep Thought spent twenty minutes trying to find the drawing move that it already knew about. It did not rediscover the move, and we resigned for the computer on move sixty-one.

Deep Thought won the next game against a master player, and then drew the final round game against a senior master. Its provisional rating dropped from 2599 to 2495, mostly as a result of its buggy performance in the first three rounds. If we take out the three games in question, and only count the games played by Deep Thought 0.01, then the performance for its fifteen games (six from the Fredkin Masters Open, and nine from the final rounds of the US Open) would be around 2592. Had Deep Thought 0.01 drawn the game against Lev, its fifteen-game performance would be around 2634.

The US Open was a sobering experience. First, we had bugs to fix. Second, the Fredkin Intermediate Prize was obviously within reach, but the question was whether Hitech would beat us to it.

Hitech was not doing much tournament-wise, so we had some time to regroup. We spent the next two months ironing out the bugs in Deep Thought 0.02. During the process, we found another major bug. Deep Thought was not generating *en passant* [3] moves for the part of the search controlled by the microprogram. It had been puzzling us for a while that Deep Thought 0.01 was not playing better than ChipTest in head-to-head competition, despite having far more chess knowledge than ChipTest. The *en passant* bug might be the main culprit.

Deep Thought 0.02 played in two more tournaments in October 1988, the American Open from October 8 to 10 in Los Angeles, California, and the US Class Championship from October 28 to 30 in Somerset, New Jersey. Stuart Cracraft and Jim Gillogly graciously served as the operators for us in the American Open. Andreas traveled to New Jersey where Deep Thought defeated two more International Masters. After the US Class Championship, Deep Thought had played twenty-nine rated games. The overall performance for the twenty-nine games, including the three games marred by the mating bug, was 2509. The best twenty-five-game performance, again including the three bad games, was 2519. In

---

[3] For people who do not play chess, here is an explanation of the *en passant* rule. In chess, all pawns start on the second rank of the board. Before Renaissance, pawns could only move one square forward at a time. To speed up the game, during the Renaissance, the rules were changed to allow the pawn to move two squares forward on its first move from the second rank. This, however, allowed the pawn to escape being captured by opponent's pawn(s) on the adjacent files that normally could capture the pawn on the third rank. The *en passant* (in passing) rule was added. *Immediately* after a two-square pawn move, the opponent can, with an adjacent pawn, capture the pawn *just* moved as if it were a pawn on the third rank.

other words, we could have claimed the Fredkin Intermediate Prize right after the US Class Championship. However, we had no idea that Deep Thought had already achieved the milestone; we only knew that it was close, based on the wall-chart ratings, which were a few months out of date. Not knowing that we had already won the race turned out to be a good thing. The following month Deep Thought was about to shock the chess world.

Given that ChipTest was slightly ahead of Deep Thought 0.01 up to the US Open in head-to-head competitions, it was entirely possible that it could have claimed the Fredkin Intermediate Prize in 1987, if only we had let it play in human tournaments. But then, the development of Deep Thought would have suffered.

Ahead of a World Champion

In January 1988, at a press conference in Paris, World Chess Champion Garry Kasparov was asked whether a computer could defeat a Grandmaster in tournament play before the year 2000. He replied, "No way, and if any Grandmaster has difficulties playing computers, I would be happy to provide my advice." Garry had no idea what was about to happen in the very same year. Nor did he have any inkling as to what kind of difficulties he himself would be facing nine years later in 1997, three years before the year 2000.

At the time Garry made the prediction, it seemed to be a safe one. Computers had indeed beaten Grandmasters in blitz (five-minute) games more than a decade earlier, with Grandmaster Michael Stean and Grandmaster Robert Huebner as the victims. But under tournament conditions, computers had never drawn even a single game against a Grandmaster. While ChipTest was already in its full strength, it was unknown outside the computer chess community. As a matter of fact, not even the team really knew how strong ChipTest was, since the program did not have a rating until the Fredkin Masters Open. Cray Blitz was the World Computer Chess Champion, but International Master David Levy humiliated it in a 1984 match, winning all four games. The highest rated chess computer, Hitech, for years only hovered between 2350 and 2400 on the US scale. Grandmasters were typically rated above 2550 on the same scale. Surely, Garry's prediction had the ring of truth to it.

In 1988, the Hall of Fame Chess Festival tournament was held in Canton, Ohio, from November 4 to 6. Deep Thought played with Mike Browne as the operator. Deep Thought had a good tournament, winning the first four rounds, including one over another International Master. In the fifth round, Deep Thought played Igor Ivanov for the second time in its short career. Igor had White and this time did not do any magazine reading! The game ended in a fighting draw. Deep Thought had its first tournament win, as it tied for first with Igor.

The next weekend, Deep Thought played in its first ACM Championship in Orlando, Florida. Deep Thought won the title on tiebreak over Fidelity Challenger, which it drew in the first round. In this tournament Deep Thought played Hitech in public for the first time and won. (Deep Thought played Hitech three more times in computer chess events, lost one of them and won the other two. The winning ratio of 3 to 1 between the two programs is consistent with the roughly 200 rating points separating the programs.) Deep Thought was the clear winner or the co-winner of all the Computer Chess Championships that it played in. But luck played a big part in the results. Given the Swiss tournament format of these Championships, Deep Thought, despite being the heavy favorite, had only about fifty-percent chance of winning each individual event.

Between November 24 and 27, the Software Toolworks Championship was held in Long Beach, California. With a total prize fund of $130,000, it was one of the top three US chess tournaments in 1988. Besides several strong US Grandmasters and International Masters, there were three invited legends: the former World Champion Mikhail Tal, the former World Championship Candidate "Great Dane" Bent Larsen, and the former World Championship Candidate Samuel Reshevsky. Both Mikhail and Bent were still active and ranked high on the world-rating list, sixteenth and forty-second in the world, respectively.

Again Stuart Cracraft, and Jim Gillogly offered their invaluable help to be the remote operators. Jim, who happened to know one of the founders of Software Toolworks (known as Mindscape these days), smoothed the problems with the phone line with the help of Toolworks' personnel. Professor Raj Reddy, then a senior professor in the Computer Science Department at Carnegie Mellon[4], offered to foot Deep Thought's bill for the tournament.

---

[4]   Raj later became the Dean of the School of Computer Science at Carnegie Mellon University.

(It would be many years before I knew that Raj was also instrumental in setting up the Fredkin Prize in the first place.) By the time of the tournament, we knew that Deep Thought might have already won the Fredkin Intermediate Prize but there was some ambiguity on how the "performance" should be calculated. Deep Thought would have fallen short if the mathematically incorrect formula were to be used. We would have needed two more good games in that case.

While Deep Thought had played in tournaments for half a year, the chess world was mostly unaware of its existence. The tournament director did a double take when he heard Deep Thought's rating and phoned the US Chess Federation to make sure that it was correct. An old acquaintance of mine, Sanjoy Mahajan, was playing in the tournament and chanced on IM Patrick Wolff, who later became a Grandmaster and US Champion. Patrick asked what Deep Thought's rating was at the beginning of the tournament. Sanjoy said it was 2510, to which Patrick said, "No way is it that strong." Patrick was to change his tune considerably as the tournament progressed.

Deep Thought won the first two games without much trouble. As far as the Fredkin Intermediate Prize was concerned, we were home and dry. Stuart was the operator in the second game. The normal etiquette at the chess table is that one does not announce that one is about to checkmate the opponent. The old masters from the last century were known to announce checkmates, but it is considered bad form today. At the end of the game, Deep Thought calculated that it could checkmate its opponent in 19 moves, that is, 19 moves by Deep Thought plus 18 replies by the opponent, for a total of 37 plies. Stuart was so excited that he told the opponent. The opponent resigned promptly. The position was quite lost even without the immediate mating possibility.

The next day, we got word from California that our third round opponent was none other than the "Great Dane", Bent Larsen himself. Bent was one of the most successful Grandmasters in the postwar era. He has been a World Championship Candidate, not just once, but in four different World Championship cycles. In "the USSR vs. the Rest of the World" team match held in 1970, he played the first board for the Rest of the World, ahead of Bobby Fischer. At his peak, he had been as high as number 2 in the world. After the thrill of winning the Fredkin Intermediate Prize, it was time for a reality check. Bent would have White. I was hoping for the best and bracing myself for the worst. I was also a little bit envious of Stuart and Jim. One does not get to see, let alone face, a legend every day.

Bent was not known as a conformist, and he played unusual chess even when facing a computer. A few years before this game, I had read a biography that mentioned his predilection for pushing the rook pawns, the two pawns on the outside edges of the chessboard. Deep Thought had showed a similar tendency in its first tournament, but I am quite sure that it had entirely different reasoning from Bent's. True to Bent's form, in this game, he allowed Deep Thought to have an advanced center pawn, and he did push both of his rook pawns before either of his center pawns. It is difficult to judge the position even after all these years. A human commentator asserted that Bent had an edge after the opening phase of the game. Deep Thought was quite happy about its position. It had an advanced pawn that cramped Bent's position. In return, he had considerable pressure on the advanced pawn. Against a human player, it might indeed be a decent position for Bent, as human players might have problems handling the pressure on the pawn. A computer would just calmly calculate all the variations, making sure that the pawn is not lost or at least not without exacting comparable compensation. As the game progressed, Deep Thought's evaluation climbed up in its favor. I was beginning to think the unthinkable. Could Deep Thought indeed have the better position?

Recent analysis, with a more powerful chess computer (Deep Blue Jr), showed that Deep Thought could have played a combination and possibly won the game outright on move seventeen[5]. Deep Thought did not play the combination, but the position was probably still favorable. The human analysts were universally of the opinion that Bent had the better position throughout the early part of the game. My observation over the years is that only really good analysts can stay objective when analyzing human vs. computer games.

Slowly, Bent improved the scope of his pieces. The position was very dangerous for both players, probably more so for him. Then on move twenty-six, Bent made a slight error. He moved his king and it happened to block the retreating square for his bishop.

---

[5] See Appendix B for the game score and the potential combination.

Deep Thought threatened to trap the bishop with its next move. Bent could have just moved his king again to create an escape square for the bishop, although with a loss of time. When interviewed by IM David Levy a few weeks later, Bent mentioned the king move as "one very bad move". In reality, the bad move was the next one. Not willing to concede the mistake over the board, he lashed out at Deep Thought's king by pushing one of his pawns forward. The position was close to losing for him, and after his next move, Deep Thought calculated a forced win. Fifteen moves later, Bent resigned and became the first Grandmaster to lose to a computer under regular time control in a tournament. In Pittsburgh, we looked at each other in disbelief. We were on an emotional high. But we would come down to earth within a few hours.

In the fourth round, Deep Thought played against six-time US Champion Grandmaster Walter Browne. Walter had played against computers in public before. In 1978, he lost a game against the Northwestern chess program, Chess 4.6, but he was also playing against forty-three other opponents at the same time! This time, however, he was playing against Deep Thought with undivided attention. There is an old saying in chess, "Sometimes you give them lessons, and sometimes they give you lessons." In this game Walter gave Deep Thought a good lesson. Deep Thought at the time did not understand the value of a bishop controlling an "open diagonal" or the value of a "permanent pin" [6], and Walter exploited the weaknesses beautifully and won the game fairly easily. Deep Thought put up quite a struggle, but it was not enough.

Deep Thought drew with an IM for the second time ever [7] in the fifth round game against Vince McCambridge, and then won the next game against a strong master. In the seventh round, it was paired against new IM Alex Fishbein. A couple of years ago, at the ACM Championship, IM Danny Kopec brought in an article he wrote about the ending rook and bishop vs. rook. According to chess endgame books, this is a typically drawn ending. Danny Kopec's article, however, mentioned that even Grandmasters fre-

---

6 An open diagonal is a diagonal that is no longer impeded by pawns of either side. A permanent pin is an unbreakable pin, typically formed when a piece is pinned against its own king by an opponent's bishop.

7 Up to this point, Deep Thought had won all its games against IMs, with the exception of one draw against Igor Ivanov.

quently made game-losing mistakes in this ending. Since ChipTest had no problem finding the mating sequence from Danny's sample winning positions, we made a conscious decision to allow ChipTest, and later, Deep Thought, to play into the ending. Prior to the game against Alex Fishbein, Deep Thought had won twice from the stronger side of this ending against players of expert level and this decision seemed to be sound. I greatly regretted the decision when Deep Thought allowed Alex to convert from a clearly lost position into the weak side of rook and bishop vs. rook ending. Theoretically, the position on the chessboard was a draw with perfect play.

Sanjoy Mahajan talked with senior master Adam Leif and IM Patrick Wolff, who both thought Alex should know how to play it. "He's just the kind of player who'd know it," said Patrick. For a while, Alex was maintaining the draw. Since the final round was coming up, the tournament directors adjourned the game to be played after the last round game. There was an interesting debate

The Deep Thought team.
From left to right: Murray Campbell, Feng-hsiung Hsu, Thomas Anantharaman, Mike Browne, and Andreas Nowatzyk. In the foreground are the Deep Thought board itself and the CDC plaque (plaque donated by the supercomputer company CDC for the ACM Championship). Taken after Deep Thought won the Fredkin Intermediate Prize for its Grandmaster level performance in 1988.

among the tournament directors about how Deep Thought should be paired in the last round. If the game had been paired as a win for Deep Thought, our last round opponent would have been British Grandmaster Anthony Miles. Instead, the game was paired as a draw, and we ended up playing IM Jeremy Silman who happened to be Stuart Cracraft's chess teacher, and Stuart was nervous facing his own teacher. Of course, Deep Thought did not know who Jeremy Silman was. Jeremy managed to steer the game into an even position, but then lost in fifty-seven moves in a difficult ending.

The adjourned game against Alex Fishbein was played after both players had finished their last rounds. Alex lost his to GM Anthony Miles, who was leading the tournament with 6.5 points out of 8. Deep Thought was the only player that could catch up with Anthony. Alex's sealed move turned out to be a losing one

With Ken Thompson and David Slate.
Standing from left: *Ken Thompson (Turing Award winner*
for UNIX and one of the authors of Belle)
and David Slate (one of the authors of Chess 4.X).
Taken at the 1989 WCCC (World Computer Chess Championship).

Claude Shannon presents the author with a horse's head.
Taken at the 1989 WCCC.

and Deep Thought quickly found the winning sequence. This time Stuart did not announce the mate, and the game was played out to move eighty before Alex conceded.

GM Anthony Miles and Deep Thought were the co-winners of the tournament, ahead of six other Grandmasters, including the former World Champion Mikhail Tal. This was the first time that any computer finished first in any tournament ahead of Grandmasters, let alone a former World Champion. Since Deep Thought was not eligible for prize money, Anthony Miles was awarded sole possession of first prize.

The race for the Fredkin Intermediate Prize was officially over. Deep Thought performed at 2776 on the US scale for the tournament, slightly behind the Hall of Fame result, which was 2790. In 1988, Deep Thought played forty-two rated games, and the performance over all forty-two[8], including the ones played with serious bugs in the US Open, was 2598. The best twenty-five-game performance over the period was 2655 or 155 points higher than

---

[8] It is a strange coincidence that 42 appeared repeatedly in this chapter, first as Deep Thought's answer to the question of "Life, the Universe, and Everything", then as the world ranking of Bent Larsen, and the number of rated games by Deep Thought in 1988.

the performance rating requirement for the Fredkin Intermediate Prize.

A few months after the Software Toolworks competition, Deep Thought became a World Champion in its own right in Edmonton, Canada, at the World Computer Chess Championship tournament that was held every three years. Computer chess competitions, however, were becoming less interesting to us. Our full attention turned to the ultimate quest of beating the human World Chess Champion.

As a final note, in 1989 the organizers of the Software Toolworks Championship arranged for Deep Thought to play GM Anthony Miles, in an exhibition game as the unofficial tiebreaker for the 1988 Championship. Deep Thought won the game.

CHAPTER 6

"Knock, Knock. Who's There?"

The Man Who Likes to BE Your Friend

Frederic Friedel is a German freelance journalist, that is when he is not too busy working for the two computer chess-related companies that he co-founded. One of his companies publishes a computer chess magazine *Computer Schach und Spiele*, which reviews and recommends chess computers and chess software, while the other company, ChessBase, produces chess software. There is a potentially serious conflict of interest. But Frederic is not someone who would be stopped by a mere conflict of interest, and he is quite open about it.

Andreas Nowatzyk knew Frederic from his time at the University of Hamburg. He had met him a couple of times through some friends who were active in computer chess. Andreas described Frederic as someone who drove fast cars, wore designer suits, and hung out with famous people. The "hung out with famous people" part is still correct, but the Frederic I know today is a family man with a loving wife and two bright kids.

Frederic had organized some fairly large computer chess events on German soil. One of them was the 1979 TV match between IM David Levy and Chess 4.8. Either Frederic was very persuasive or David was very brave. A gigantic industrial robot made the moves for chess 4.8 over the chessboard. The robot could easily have made David a very famous but damaged IM, if there had been a power flicker or two.

Frederic was a friendly sort of guy who could be very helpful, especially when the help was mutual. Since both of Frederic's companies are in computer chess, he socializes with many of the top chess players, usually offering them free chess software and databases of chess games. He became a close friend of Garry Kasparov very early, possibly even before Garry was crowned the World Chess Champion. Garry was said to be instrumental in the formation of ChessBase itself. Apparently, the ChessBase software, which is a database program for chess games, was created to satisfy Garry's needs and many of the features of the program were based on Garry's specifications.

In late July 1988, Andreas received at our office a phone call from Frederic. Afterwards, he sent an e-mail to the rest of the team summarizing the conversation. Frederic was inviting us to play in an exhibition event in Germany. I was quite surprised. Although ChipTest had won the 1987 ACM Championship, Hitech was the better known machine. In fact, *Europe Echecs*, a French chess magazine had a report after the Championship that said Hitech was beating ChipTest by the ratio of 2 to 1. The *Europe Echecs* report probably misquoted or cited a wrong source, as the tally from ChipTest's log showed something completely different. Anyway, to the outside world, Hitech was the uncrowned king. The results from the Fredkin Masters Open for Deep Thought and ChipTest dispelled the myth, but it was unclear as to whether they were well known outside of Carnegie Mellon. How did Frederic find out about us?

It turned out that Frederic had befriended Ken Thompson back in Belle's heyday. Ken was spending a sabbatical year from Bell Labs in Sydney, Australia. Since Ken was on my thesis committee, I kept him updated about what was happening with ChipTest and Deep Thought, and he apparently told Frederic about us. Sometimes, it pays to know the right people.

The German invitation was part of a birthday celebration in the fall for Conrad Zuse, Germany's most prominent computer pioneer. Conrad had made a prediction fifty years earlier that a computer would defeat the chess champion within fifty years. A big event was planned to match the best computer against Garry Kasparov. Frederic was organizing it, and wanted Deep Thought to be the computer. It was definitely too early to face Garry but it was too good a chance to pass up. Anyway, it would be an exciting thing to do.

Since we were busy chasing after the Fredkin Intermediate Prize, we did not really keep track of what was happening with the invitation. Andreas maintained contact with Frederic and kept the rest of the team informed. Frederic also offered to provide Deep

Thought with game databases, and the offer was gladly accepted. By mid-September 1988, there were a few new developments. A TV scheduling conflict meant that the match was delayed until January. Another complication was that IBM Germany was the sponsor and was pressing hard to run Deep Thought on an IBM host computer. Deep Thought could not run on an IBM host at the time so the funding for the match was in doubt. A week later, we were informed that the match was off. Thus ended the first attempt to arrange a match between Garry and Deep Thought.

Frederic kept in touch with the team over the years. Since he was also close to Garry, we got to hear some of the Champion's opinions about chess computers. The following excerpts came from a letter he sent me in 1989:

> Beginning 1988: "Computers will never beat Grandmasters."
> Mid 1988: "Computers will never beat strong Grandmasters."
> End of 1988: "Okay, yes, Bent is a strong Grandmaster. But a
> computer will never be able to beat Karpov or me."

Murray Campbell had an interesting observation in regard to this last statement. Murray had been in the computer chess field far longer than I had. Over the years, he had observed that when computers were much weaker, chess masters would say that computers would never beat chess experts. Of course, experts are one level below masters in playing strength. As time progressed, the same pattern repeated with players of greater strength. Anatoly Karpov happened to be the second strongest player of the world behind Garry Kasparov when Garry made his prediction.

The IBM Connection

IBM Germany called off the German match with Garry in September 1988. Meanwhile, IBM Research in the US had been talking with us for some time about the possibility of continuing our research at IBM. As far as I know, IBM Germany had no idea that we might be moving to IBM after graduation.

The first hint of IBM interest came from Kai-Fu Lee, a Carnegie Mellon graduate student working in the speech recognition area. Kai-Fu talked to some IBM speech recognition people about what the Deep Thought team had done, and got the feedback that IBM might be interested in supporting our research. One of the IBM people that Kai-Fu talked to was Peter Brown.

Peter and I had been in the same 1982 incoming class at Carnegie Mellon. We knew each other, but were not really close. I bumped into Peter in the Computer Science lounge a few weeks before the Fredkin Masters Open, and mentioned what I was doing. Peter was asking a lot of questions, but I had no idea that he was thinking about getting IBM to hire us.

Years later, Peter described how he got the upper management in IBM interested in continuing the project inside IBM. It was around the time of the Superbowl season. Peter happened to be in the men's room with Abe Peled, the IBM Research Vice President of Computer Science. They started talking about how expensive the Superbowl TV commercial spots were. Peter suggested that he knew a way to gain much greater publicity at far lower cost. He knew this group of graduate students working on computer chess at Carnegie Mellon, and he believed that this team would create the first chess machine to beat the World Champion. Given the historical significance of the quest, and the latent public interest, IBM could stand to gain huge advertising value from the endeavor. Oh, yes, members of the team were world-class people that IBM would be interested in hiring anyway. Abe got interested and asked Peter to look into it.

John Cocke, the now retired IBM fellow and Turing Award winner who pioneered the idea of RISC (Reduced Instruction Set Computer) among other things, was also instrumental in getting the team hired. John is a good friend of Professor Edward Fredkin, who donated the money to set up the Fredkin Prize for computer chess. John was quite excited about the possibility of the top computer chess team coming to IBM, and his excitement was contagious. By early November 1988, a couple of IBM managers were interested and we were asked to send in applications. This was before we made the splash at the Software Toolworks Championship.

Thomas, Murray and I visited IBM Research separately and gave our sales pitch. The idea was to integrate an entire chess machine onto a single silicon chip, and then use a massive number of the chips to build the "ultimate" chess machine—a chess machine that could beat the World Champion. I would be the one doing the chip work, while Thomas and Murray would develop the software first on an intermediate machine, and then port it to the final machine. By early March 1989, both Thomas and I were offered regular positions at IBM Research to work on the chess machine. There were some complications with Murray, and it took another month or so before he was offered a post-doc position. His position later became a regular one.

A few weeks before the notice from IBM, I received an e-mail from the manager of the Computer Science Laboratory at Xerox PARC (Palo Alto Research Center), asking me to consider PARC. Xerox PARC was a legendary place for computer science research. Some of the most exciting computer science research in the 1970s and 1980s came from there. For instance, the main idea behind the Apple Macintosh can be traced to the PARC lab. Some of the most innovative early VLSI design software also came from PARC. In addition, the lab atmosphere was much closer to what I was used to at Carnegie Mellon. PARC was also right in Silicon Valley. I had been there a few times, and really enjoyed the different atmosphere, not to mention the weather! The fact that Silicon Valley was much closer to Taiwan was a bonus. I quickly sent in my vita to PARC and received a positive initial response.

When the IBM offer came in, I was still considering PARC as an alternative. Both Thomas and Murray accepted the IBM offer immediately, while I was still waiting to find out whether PARC provided a better option. I was in a fairly awkward position. If I were to decline the IBM offer, Thomas and Murray would need to find a new project at IBM, and I did not want to put them in a difficult situation, especially after what we had gone through together. But I had also promised the PARC people to give them a fair look. Furthermore, I liked the idea of going to California. "Go west, young man." I always thought I would end up in Silicon Valley. A lot of my college classmates were there, and several of my good friends at Carnegie Mellon were also heading that way. I decided to delay the decision until I found out what PARC had to offer.

Xerox PARC was a very interesting place, especially to someone who worked in the VLSI area. However, I did have some reservations. Would Xerox, which was not really in the computer business, be willing to support the effort long term? I also did not know what decision I would make if Xerox offered to support the project, but hired only one of us.

Part of me welcomed the idea of working alone again, at least for a while. The team had been working in an assembly line fashion, with me completing the hardware first, and the others finishing the software afterwards. Theoretically, the hardware and the software can be developed simultaneously, but that is only possible when the hardware is well defined, which was certainly not the case with the new chess chip. Also, the new chip could easily take a few years to design, while the software could be completed in say, 6 months to a year. IBM's hiring of the team had the advantage of keeping the team intact, as well as providing IBM immediate external visibility. But as far as the project schedule was concerned, there was relatively little to be gained; in fact, the need to provide external visibility could easily delay the project, as we would then have to build an intermediate machine to ensure that we remain on top of the computer chess world. Working alone, I would have been able to go directly to the new chess chip, which was what I really wanted to work on.

Anyway, I did not tell the people at PARC that I would consider the option of working alone. Perhaps, subconsciously, I did not want to face that difficult choice should it arise. I did mention what IBM was willing to offer. In the end, PARC decided that they could not match IBM's offer to hire a full team, and I informed IBM Research of my acceptance.

The Poor Lieutenant Colonel at DARPA

After the arguments over the invitation from California in 1987, I avoided dealing with Dr Berliner as much as possible. He was still on my thesis committee of course, but it made no sense to rock the boat given the less than ideal relationship we had. Allen Newell, who was one of the founders of the Department and also one of the pioneers of computer chess, replaced Dr Berliner on my thesis committee in April 1989. In retrospect I wondered if the reason for Dr Berliner leaving the committee were more to do with an investigative reporter than with the man himself.

Deep Thought's defeat of GM Bent Larsen, and tying for first in the 1988 Software Toolworks Championship, were big news in the chess world. At the same time of the Toolworks Championship, the twenty-eighth Chess Olympiad was being held in Thessaloniki, where nearly all of the world's top chess players competed for their national teams. When the news of Deep Thought's win in Long Beach was wired to Thessaloniki, it became the talk of the day. Probably most of the top chess players had never heard of Deep Thought until then.

It took a while before the general press picked up on the news. On December 22, a month after the tournament, the front page of the *International Herald Tribune* carried the headline "A Computer First: 'Deep Thought' Stuns the Chess World". None of us on the team had any idea that we had made the front page of an international newspaper. As far as we knew, we did not make the front page of any national newspaper in the US, and certainly we were not expecting to see the news showing up in an international newspaper. This headline caught the attention of a reporter in London who decided to start an "investigation".

We learned about the reporter's interest in the project from Dr Berliner, who called us to say that a reporter was interested in playing a demo game with Deep Thought. Dr Berliner added that the reporter was from a well-respected magazine. Since we were starting to look for jobs and could use the publicity, we readily agreed to set up the demo. At the agreed time, the reporter called and introduced himself as Dominic Lawson from the British magazine *The Spectator*. I found out later that he was the Deputy Editor of the magazine (he is now Editor of *The Sunday Telegraph* newspaper in Britain). Dominic lost the game and we thought that was the end of the story. He made no attempt to interview any member of the Deep Thought team and seemed only to be interested in playing the game.

Then on 27 February 1989, someone showed me the column of Charles Krauthammer, syndicated from the *Washington Post*, in the *Pittsburgh Post-Gazette*. It was a very well written article about Deep Thought's success in Long Beach and its implications, and quoted *The Spectator* as the source for some of the material.

One of the libraries at Carnegie Mellon had a subscription to *The Spectator* and I found the article quoted by Charles Krauthammer. It was not just an article, but the cover story of that issue. On the cover, an airplane, with the fuselage in the shape of the chess piece bishop and four engines in the shape of chess pawns, was flying over a checkered field. An American flag was prominently displayed. The cover headline read "Playing to Win" and the smaller headline read "Dominic Lawson reveals the Pentagon's war moves". I frowned, "Andreas is not going to like this." Andreas had a sympathetic view for Germany's Green Party, which was into environmental causes and pacifism. Supporting any sort of war effort would be completely counter to his beliefs. For that matter, none of the other members of the team was thrilled about the connections that were made.

In one sense, Dominic's article was hilarious. *The Spectator* appeared to be a magazine that took itself seriously, but the article seemed to me to be pretty groundless. The subtitle inside the magazine read "Dominic Lawson investigates the Deep Thought project, and discovers that the Pentagon is harnessing chess to the arms race". Okay, I did not know—and I still do not know—whether the Pentagon was harnessing chess to the arms race. But I do know that Deep Thought was not started because someone in the Pentagon wanted it done.

Once I started reading the article, factual errors kept on popping up, and that was just for the parts that I knew for sure were wrong. One section of the article read, "The Deep Thought project, and other computer chess developments at Carnegie-Mellon, have been paid for *in their entirety* by DARPA, the Pentagon's Defense Advanced Research Projects Agency". So, the money we paid out of our student pockets belonged to DARPA as well!

Then I read what was the most amusing part of the article. "I asked Lieutenant Colonel Robert Simpson, DARPA's head of funding for expert systems research—which includes the Deep Thought project—to give me one clear military application of Deep Thought." First, Deep Thought was not an "expert system", which means something quite specific in the research field of Artificial Intelligence. Several members of the team would probably consider it an insult to call Deep Thought an expert system. In fact, at least two members of the team had used the word bullshit to describe "expert systems", or for that matter, Artificial Intelligence. Second, the Deep Thought research was supported in part by the VLSI project, and none of the money came from the DARPA funding for expert systems research. Lieutenant Colonel Robert Simpson had to my knowledge never received a single scrap of paper describing the Deep Thought project.

Just imagine the situation that this Lieutenant Colonel was placed in. A reporter calls you up and asks you about a project that you know nothing about. You have to say something. Well, Lieutenant Colonel Robert Simpson had a quick mind.

" 'Navigation in a battlefield situation,' he replied promptly. 'A machine like this, programmed with knowledge of the terrain a pilot is flying through, can digitize all the various route choices, explore them, and choose the optimum route. That is exactly what Deep Thought is doing.'" Interesting, I hadn't thought that Mr. Kasparov would make a nice cruise missile.

Then I came to something quite annoying. "The head of the Deep Thought project and of the Carnegie-Mellon computer science department, Professor Hans Berliner, warned me that in about three years his team would have produced a son of Deep Thought, which would be stronger at chess than the world champion, Garry Kasparov. 'It's a pity, really,' he sighed. 'Just as chess players were beginning to make a decent living.'" Dr Berliner was neither the head of the Deep Thought project nor the head of the department, and he was a competitor. What had gone on in Dominic's interview with Dr Berliner, who had had absolutely nothing to do with Deep Thought?

When I calmed down, I realized that the reality might be that Dominic had a good story in mind, and may not have had the time to check all the details. Dr Berliner had after all erroneously been named as leader of the project in other media coverage of Deep Thought.

Anyway, after the rest of the team had seen the article, we decided to send a letter to *The Spectator*. I also sent an e-mail to Dr Berliner asking him to please make sure that other reporters would not make the same mistake. We were still looking for jobs, and the wrong attribution could affect our chances. One thing led to another, and a month later, Professor Allen Newell replaced Dr Berliner on my thesis committee.

A few weeks after we mailed the letter to *The Spectator*, a massively modified letter appeared in their letters section.

> Sir: The article, 'The Pentagon Plays Chess' (28 January), contains several gross misconceptions and factual errors.

(This is different from what we actually wrote, but the essence is the same.)

> The Deep Thought project is not entirely funded by DARPA, the Department of Defense, or the Pentagon directly. The support includes industrial funding, National Science Foundation funds, and, to some degree, Department of Defense money.

This is drastically different from what we wrote, which was "The Deep Thought project is not funded by DARPA/DOD, or the Pentagon directly, and certainly not in its entirety. The Deep Thought effort was a recreational exercise where several graduate students applied what they learned about VLSI circuit and hardware design. The first result was ChipTest, which we built entirely out of scraps from other projects in spare time. After ChipTest's success in the 1987 ACM Computer Chess Championship, one of our advisors, Prof. H. T. Kung, helped us with a modest $5000 out of his discretionary fund, which was used to construct the current Deep Thought. This money is not directly related to any official project, but is part of normal operational expenses of typical universities. As such, it includes industrial funding, tuition, NSF (National Science Foundation) funds, donations, and to some degree, DOD money. In addition, some of the various expenses for Deep Thought came right out of our own pockets."

The published letter continued.

> We very much doubt that Lieutenant Colonel Robert Simpson was aware of the nature of Deep Thought which is completely unrelated to expert systems research. Deep Thought is a special purpose engine for playing chess and chess only. The principal algorithms used by Deep Thought had been known for decades, and the structure of Deep Thought has no utility for battlefield navigation whatsoever. To quote Ken Thompson of Bell Labs, "the only military application for Belle [a chess machine like Deep Thought] is to drop it from an airplane and kill someone."

This paragraph was given in its entirety.

The following did not show up in *The Spectator*. "Dr Hans Berliner is a senior research faculty member of the CMU Computer Science Department, and heads the research project on the Hitech chess machine. He is not head of the Computer Science Department, who is Professor Nico Habermann, nor is he involved with the Deep Thought effort in any way.

Mr. Lawson, in his 'investigation' of the Deep Thought project, managed the unusual feat of interviewing not a single member of the Deep Thought team."

The letter must have been too long.

From Chess to Wall Street

Once I decided to go after the World Chess Champion, I read Grandmaster Robert Byrne's columns in the *New York Times* whenever I could lay my hands on them. When ChipTest became operational, I would check out Robert's analysis with ChipTest.

Sometimes ChipTest would come up with ideas that he missed, but frequently he would have some deep analysis that ChipTest had a hard time replicating.

When ChipTest won the 1987 ACM Championship, Robert wrote an article about it but we did not really have contact with him until after the 1988 ACM Championship where Deep Thought defeated Hitech. Mike Valvo, the tournament director, was providing Robert with background information about Deep Thought. Since many people did not realize that Dr Berliner was unrelated to Deep Thought, we asked Mike Valvo to help clarify the situation. It was our first indirect contact with Robert.

While Deep Thought was never an Artificial Intelligence project, the AI community treated Deep Thought as one of their own, and we were invited to play an exhibition match with none other than GM Robert Byrne at the 1989 International Joint Conference on Artificial Intelligence. Neither player was on site. Deep Thought played from Pittsburgh, while Robert played from his home in New York State. The moves were relayed over the USA Today Sports Center, an on-line service similar to AOL or MSN today. Deep Thought won the game, but a few days later Robert returned the favor in a second game arranged by the Sports Center. Robert and Deep Thought played two more games with one win each.

After these four games, the *New York Times* took an interest in the project, and Robert was asked to write an article for the Science Times section of the paper. He visited Carnegie Mellon for the article, and it was the first time we met him face to face. He looked like a distinguished old gentleman—the most frequent description used when people got to know him was "a sweet gentleman". We all liked him immediately. After we joined IBM, we found out that Robert was living close by. An avid tennis player as was Murray (before Murray's daughter was born), they would frequently play on weekends. Once in a while, Robert would drop in and play some games with our latest machine. Except for the Grandmasters who worked on the project, Robert probably knew more about our machines than any other Grandmaster.

Robert's article in the *Science Times* was the cover story, spanning two pages. In it, Andreas' work on the automatic tuning of the evaluation function was described. A CEO of a Wall Street stock and commodity trading firm saw the article and gave Andreas a call, offering him a high paying job. Out of curiosity, Andreas went to New York and met the Wall Street people. Wanting to impress, the CEO took him to the stock exchange, but Andreas was wearing jeans, and jeans were not allowed on the floor. The CEO had to talk the security guard into looking the other way. The following floor trip was supposed to be for a peek only, but somehow it became a more detailed tour. The security cameras caught Andreas wearing jeans on the exchange floor, the security people descended, and an argument ensued. I don't know about Andreas, but if I were in his place, I would have had a hearty laugh once I was cleared from the floor. Wall Street was a different world.

While the Wall Street proposal was interesting, Andreas turned it down. The Wall Street firm continued to sweeten the offer, but Andreas remained uninterested.

In February 1990, Andreas accepted a job at Sun Microsystems in California, with the starting date in June 1990. He still had some writing to do for his thesis. By this time both Murray and I had already left for IBM. The Wall Street firm came back with an offer for Andreas to do some consulting work while he was finishing up the thesis. Thinking of the consulting work as a paid vacation from writing his thesis, Andreas went to New York for four months, with occasional trips back to Pittsburgh. At the time, the software used in the Wall Street firm was in pretty bad shape. It worked, but at the speed of a snail. For the piece of software that Andreas was working on, the total storage for the data was something like 10 megabytes. The software always went back to the disk for the data, even though the disk access speed was more than a thousand times slower than the main memory access speed. Andreas rewrote the software to read in all the data into main memory, and voilà, it now ran more than a thousand times faster. The Wall Street people were impressed. Andreas did some other amazing things in their eyes. To them, Andreas was like someone who could walk on water. Today, many real computer scientists work on Wall Street and the problem that Andreas found is unlikely to reappear.

After Andreas went to work at Sun Microsystems, the Wall Street firm refused to give up on him and offered him a proposal that they thought he could not refuse. The proposal went something like this: the firm would create a company in Silicon Valley with a hefty annual budget. Andreas would head the company and have full say on what the company would do, but half of his time had to be spent on continuing what he was doing for the firm. Andreas would be free to hire people who would also be given profit sharing deals and so on. Andreas asked Thomas Anantharaman and Mike Browne, as well as John Zsarnay, a staff engineer at the Engineering Lab, whether they were interested. They were. John went to California and started setting up the infrastructure. But then Andreas had second thoughts and backed out of the deal. The firm renegotiated the deals with Thomas and Mike, and John was moved back to the East Coast. John soon left and joined Rambus, a startup at the time in Silicon Valley. I was quite unaware of all this until much later, but the whole episode eventually would have an unexpected influence on the project at IBM.

None of us on the Deep Thought team ever imagined that our work would have some link with Wall Street. The automatic tuning part of the project was an interesting topic in its own right. But the main reason for doing it came from the incident with the California invitation. Who would have thought that the invitation from California for a chess tournament would lead to some of us working for a Wall Street firm? Sometimes, life is full of the strangest twists and turns.

Intermezzo

♟ CHAPTER 7

First Date with History

A Phone Call from New York

After Deep Thought became famous in the chess world, phone calls started to come in from all sort of places. Usually, they were put through to our offices. One night, however, I got a call at home from some guy I had never heard of, who was asking lots of questions. He was supposedly calling from somewhere in Minnesota, was not associated with any news organization, but was calling purely out of personal interest. Apparently, he found my phone number in the white page. He seemed harmless, but I did get nervous talking to him. For several months until I left Carnegie Mellon for IBM, he would call every few weeks trying to find out what was new with Deep Thought.

I was therefore a little bit nervous when I got another unexpected phone call at home. Although the voice did seem somewhat familiar, I was sure that it was not someone I knew. "Not another one," I thought. The caller introduced himself as Shelby Lyman.

Before "the match of the century [1]" between Bobby Fischer and Boris Spassky in 1972, chess was not telecast in the USA. Shelby Lyman and his friends persuaded PBS (Public Broadcasting Systems) to do a TV show on the match, with Shelby being the main commentator. For a while, with the Fischer-Spassky match grabbing the attention of people on the streets, Shelby was an instant celebrity. The public's interest in chess waned after Bobby Fischer refused to defend his title under FIDE's conditions against his Russian challenger Anatoly Karpov. Shelby, however, main-

---

[1] Hey, hyperbole is free.

105

tained a good relationship with PBS and was able to get PBS to broadcast more TV shows covering the World Chess Championships.

I started viewing some episodes of Shelby's show after deciding that I wanted to beat the World Champion. To tell the truth, Shelby's show was a little bit slow and too artificial for my taste. The show might have worked in 1972 when the interest in the Fischer vs. Spassky match was high, but with the MTV and video game generation, the show simply did not resonate.

Shelby asked whether we would be interested in playing an exhibition match with Garry Kasparov, the World Chess Champion. Of course, the answer was yes. We were not really ready to play the world champion, but we did not want to miss the chance. I did have some doubt whether Shelby could make the match happen. The earlier exhibition match proposal from Germany was scrapped in the end, despite the close relationship between the potential organizer and Garry.

At the time that Shelby called, I was designing a printed circuit board version of Deep Thought. Professor Raj Reddy at Carnegie Mellon had taken an interest in the Deep Thought project, and offered to provide us with about $10,000 to make additional boards for a version of Deep Thought with more than two chess processors. The component cost had come down sufficiently that we could build four printed circuit boards with two chess processors on each board. In theory, for the proposed match we could have a new machine running that was up to five times as fast as Deep Thought (four new boards plus one existing board).

Not knowing much about the mechanical design of printed circuit boards, I made a serious error. The Deep Thought boards were the size of a large pizza. For circuit boards of this size, the heat expansion from the soldering process can cause severe warping of the circuit boards. While I did place a board stiffener on the new printed circuit board to prevent warping during normal handling, it was not strong enough to prevent warping resulting from the soldering process. All four boards were quite visibly warped. Probably because of the warping, one of the four new boards never worked. It might have been possible to fix the bad board with a lot of work, but I had a thesis to defend and lots of packing to do before I left for IBM. Therefore, the maximum number of boards that we could really have for the match was four.

After my initial positive response, Shelby came back with

more details for the proposed match. NYNEX, the Telephone Company for the New York area, would sponsor it. I mentioned to Shelby that some of us would be moving to IBM, but NYNEX apparently had no problem with the IBM connection. The match would be a short one, lasting only one day. Two games would be played, and the games would be played with 90 minutes to each player for the entire game. Each game would last at most three hours. Garry Kasparov's one-day appearance fee, not including expenses, for the match would be $10,000, which was supposedly heavily discounted. He viewed the match more as an experiment than as a real match and he was willing to give a discount. Anyway, $10,000 for one day of work is still a tidy sum. (In 1997, I was asked by IBM Asia Pacific to give a lecture and presentation tour for near-ly a month, stopping in seven countries. The total expenses, including the plane fare and hotel accommodation, came to slight-ly more than $10,000. Nowadays I believe that Garry's fee for a one-day appearance is something like $30,000, enough for me to take a three-month business trip around the world.)

Murray joined IBM in September 1989 after finishing his stint as a research associate at Carnegie Mellon. I joined IBM a month later, after my thesis defense [2]. Thomas was still quite a way from completing his thesis and stayed behind at Carnegie Mellon. Prior to our leaving the university, IBM and Carnegie Mellon reached an agreement that we could take the three working Deep Thought printed circuit boards with us to IBM. Since Thomas was staying behind, I brought only one board with me. The other two new boards and the original Deep Thought board remained at Carnegie Mellon so that Thomas could complete the parallel code using all three boards. The three boards would be placed inside three work-stations, with one board in each. The workstations would then communicate over the departmental local area network at Carnegie Mellon and negotiate how the search would be run in parallel. This configuration was what we used at the Deep Thought vs. Kasparov match. It ran at two to three times the speed of the regular Deep Thought. It would not be competitive with Garry, but at least we could hope for a good showing.

---

2 Well, if you were expecting any fireworks at my thesis defense, I have to say it went smoothly. The defense was open to the public and Dr Berliner attended it as a member of the public. While Dr Berliner might have disagreed with the directions that I was taking, he did not give me any trouble.

But Not Karpov and Me

I first heard the name Garry Kasparov from Mike Browne, my office mate at Carnegie Mellon, probably in late 1983, in the middle of a World Chess Championship cycle. At the time I had no idea who the big names in chess were. Mike had to explain to me that Anatoly Karpov was the World Champion. Among the possible challengers was Victor Korchnoi, who had lost two championship matches to Anatoly under, according to some, highly unfavorable conditions. Victor had defected and his family in the USSR suffered some persecution as a result. There was a rumor that Victor's family would be tortured if he won either of the matches. Mike thought Victor would be the most likely challenger, but he did not believe that he could win against Anatoly. Mike then mentioned the name Garry Kasparov, describing him as a flamboyant attacker with lots of talent. Mike thought that Garry would be a more exciting world champion than Anatoly, who was generally considered a little bit boring. But, again, Mike did not think Garry, being too young and too inexperienced, would be able to beat Karpov either.

In 1984, Garry emerged from the Candidate matches[3] as the challenger to Anatoly. On 9 September 1984, the first World Championship match between them began. Whoever scored six wins first would be declared the winner of the match. Anatoly quickly scored four wins in the first nine games, while Garry was not able to win a single game. It looked bleak for Garry. Then he dug in, and drew game after game. Weeks grew into months, and the reporters started to leave. But the match went on, and Anatoly scored another win in game 27. Garry won the 32nd game and then the 47th and the 48th games.

On 15 February 1985, the FIDE (the international chess federation) president Florencio Campomanes announced "the termination of the match without a conclusive result". Garry complained that Campomanes was in league with Anatoly and was stopping the match to give Anatoly much needed rest. A new 24-game match, with the initial score of 0–0 and with draws counted as half a point each, would begin on 2 September 1985. In the case of a tie after 24 games, Anatoly would retain his title. I was busy

---

3 The system for selecting the challenger for the World Chess Champion changed from time to time. For most of the recent history up to the mid 1990s, the challenger was selected by a series of elimination matches also known as the Candidate matches.

working on the move generator chip and was not paying attention to the match. In this match Garry prevailed by the score of 13 points to 11 points, and became the World Champion.

By October 1989, Garry had successfully defended his title twice against Anatoly. He was officially about to become the first and, to the date of writing, the only chess player to have a FIDE rating of 2800 or above. None other than the legendary Bobby Fischer held the previous rating record of 2780.

A few days before the scheduled match between Deep Thought and Garry, we got a call from CBS. "CBS This Morning" wanted to do an interview with Garry and the Deep Thought team. Jerry Present, who handled the public relations of the chess project for the Communications department at IBM Research, made the detailed arrangements with CBS. Murray and I stayed overnight at a hotel in New York City so that we could get to the studio on time.

We woke early and arrived at the studio at about 5 o'clock in the morning, more than two hours before the show was to start. CBS wanted us to hook up Deep Thought remotely from the studio and play a few moves during the segment. After setting up an IBM PC and testing the phone connection to IBM Research, we were led to a waiting room to have some breakfast. Garry had not arrived yet. Several monitors in the room were showing the on-air shows from CBS, other networks and the local TV stations. One of the CBS people stuck around and gave us some insider comments. This went on for a while. Then we heard the sound of footsteps. A familiar face appeared at the door. It was Garry.

From the photos that I had seen, Garry appeared to be an intense person with a very high energy level. Seeing him in person confirmed the assessment. Photographs, however, could not really convey the intensity that came from his presence. Behind his dark eyes, there was a smoldering fire. Garry once referred to playing chess as "controlling chaos". Was there a fight going on between order and chaos behind those eyes?

We introduced ourselves and chatted a little bit. A CBS person led Garry away to his makeup session. We followed shortly. After the makeup sessions, our conversation naturally turned to chess. Garry was about to overtake Bobby Fischer as the highest rated chess player ever, and we talked about the validity of comparing ratings from two different time periods. Kasparov declined to comment directly about the relative chess playing strength between

himself and Bobby. We did not bother to talk about the likely outcome of the match between Garry and Deep Thought—there was
never any doubt that he would win it easily. But what did Garry
think his chance was against the machine that we were going to
build at IBM? He made an interesting observation.

When the team joined IBM, we were planning to build a chess
machine that could search at least 100 million positions per second, preferably a billion positions per second. Garry thought that
a machine searching 100 million positions per second would be an
interesting opponent, and probably would beat the majority of the
Grandmasters. But even for a one billion positions per second
machine, Garry stated, "It might be able to beat the rest of the
Grandmasters, but not Anatoly and me." He then explained that,
in his opinion, he and Anatoly Karpov were the only *real* professional chess players in the world, and that they were the only ones
able to do proper preparations for the big match. Anatoly was rated
2730, and the players right behind him were Timman, Gelfand and
Ivanchuk. They were rated at about 2680, slightly behind Anatoly,
but not by a full class (200 rating points). If one just looked at the
rating scale, there was no reason to believe that the new machine
would fall in the narrow range between Anatoly and the other top
GMs. So what did Garry really mean?

There are two plausible theories.

One was that Garry knew subconsciously the machine would
be a serious challenge but, refusing to bow to the inevitable, he
placed Anatoly between the machine and himself as a buffer. This
was Murray's theory when he first read about Garry's "Not Karpov
and me" statement in Friedel's letter. Throughout the history of
computer chess, chess players had made similar assertions but
Deep Thought smashed the supposed barriers all the way up to
"strong Grandmasters". It was interesting to note that, during the
1997 match between Deep Blue and Garry, several Grandmasters
claimed that Deep Blue was playing at around number X in the
world. The number X happened to be slightly below the ranking of
the specific Grandmaster making the claim. Some of the
Grandmasters making the claims probably would have had their
hands full with the old Deep Thought.

The other plausible theory was that Garry really believed good
preparation would make a huge difference in match performance.
Actually, we believed this as well. In fact, the design speed for the
"ultimate chess machine" was specified so that the machine would

play at about 200 points stronger than an *unprepared* Garry, or whoever the World Champion might be. We had good reasons to overshoot. A well-prepared IM David Levy was able to slaughter Cray Blitz, which was supposed to be comparable to David in chess strength, by 4 to 0. So it was true that good preparation could make a huge difference against a slowly changing computer opponent. But why "Karpov and me"?

There was no fundamental reason why the other Grandmasters could not make comparable preparation but Garry and Anatoly did have more resources at their disposal than other Grandmasters. Grandmaster Joel Benjamin, who worked with us during the two Deep Blue matches against Garry, observed that Garry and Anatoly had lots of "slaves". Numerous Grandmasters wanted to be in the Champion's camp so that they could eke out a decent living or, in some cases, learn what it would take to be a World Champion. It was very difficult for a Grandmaster in the USSR to make a good living unless he was right at the top, and the collapse of the USSR and the subsequent loss of state support made the situation even more acute. Both Garry and Anatoly, each being a multimillionaire, became magnets to the ex-USSR Grandmasters. Western Grandmasters, like Jan Timman from the Netherlands, would have a much tougher time getting the same quality help. Furthermore, Garry and Anatoly had both successfully defended their titles. Who is to say that they don't have some secret formulae for top level preparation?

The live TV segment went smoothly. Garry and Deep Thought played a few token moves. The rest of the interview, not surprisingly, was centered on Garry. Murray and I were, after all, just insignificant students fresh out of graduate school. My impression, from what he said, was that he saw himself as defending the human race against machines. When I looked at my fellow team members, I saw human faces. We were simply approaching the problem of playing chess from, shall we say, a non-traditional direction. Maybe Garry needed to pump himself up for the matches to come. Well, that was fine with me. We wanted him to play at his best—okay, though perhaps not for the coming Deep Thought match where we were overmatched to begin with.

Who Wants to Win?

There was no doubt that Garry wanted to win the small exhibition match against Deep Thought with a perfect 2–0 score. We, on the

other hand, were only concerned about not embarrassing ourselves. Losing by 0–2 would not be a big deal for us; to be honest,
two losses by Deep Thought might even be the most desirable outcome. We certainly did not want our new employer to have the
unrealistic expectation that we were ready to tackle the World
Champion for real. Shelby Lyman, however, was not sure what
outcome he wanted to see. A 2–0 win by Garry would be fine, but
any half-point draw by Deep Thought would create huge head-
lines.

On Saturday 21 October 1989, the day before our first over-
the-board encounter with Garry, we visited the match site and
checked out the facilities. The match was to take place at the New
York Academy of Art, which seemed a strange place for a computer chess match. When we walked into the playing room, we were
greeted by an unusual sight. There were paintings and sculptures
everywhere. In one corner was a giant hand, roughly the size of a
love seat, possibly made from gypsum. Was it supposed to be the
hand of fate? Or did it symbolize Deep Thought, the tool we had
created with our hands, in its struggle with Garry?

The playing room was quite cramped, especially after all the
chairs for the spectators were added, giving an intimate feeling.
Garry had a room behind the small raised stage to rest in and
there was also a small area behind the stage that he could stroll
around while he was thinking. A few reporters were floating
around even though no press conference was scheduled for that
day. We set up an IBM PC, hooked up the phone line, and tested
the connection to Pittsburgh. One of the reporters wanted an
interview. It turned out he was from *Sports Illustrated*. We were not
in Kansas any more.

After the interview with *Sports Illustrated*, we went upstairs to
find Shelby Lyman. The commentary room, where the spectators
could hear the live commentary, was on the second floor, but it
was empty. When we found him, Shelby was quite agitated. It
appeared that Garry had refused to talk to one of the reporters who
appeared to have done something to upset him. Shelby and a few
other people were trying to make Garry change his mind. I was
curious as to whether Garry's mother, Clara Kasparova, was around
but Shelby indicated that Clara had not come to New York. So, as
I suspected, Garry did not consider the match a major event.
Clara's husband had died when Garry was still a little boy and he
and his mother had a very close relationship. In his autobiography,

Garry said, "The most important thing is that I can talk to her [his mother] as I can to nobody else." If it had been a major event, Clara would have shown up to cheer her son on. Garry, however, still did a thorough preparation for the match, as we would soon find out.

When we arrived at the venue on Sunday, we saw something that you don't normally see for a chess match. The line of people waiting to buy tickets circled an entire city block. Around thirty to fifty reporters were milling around Garry. A few noticed us and started asking us questions. After a while, the reporters got seated and ready for the pre-match press conference. Murray and I had a brief discussion and agreed that if Deep Thought's assessment of the position dropped below –700, which was roughly 5.5 pawns down[4], then we would resign. After the discussion I looked up and saw Garry smiling broadly at us; he had overheard the conversation.

Besides the reporters, several of the usual suspects from computer chess events were also present. Monty Newborn, the perennial organizer of the ACM Computer Chess Championship, was in the front row. So was our former rival, Dr Hans Berliner, apparently not wanting to miss the historic spectacle even though he probably wished that Hitech was the computer competitor. Jonathan "Almost Winning" Schaeffer, author of the chess program Phoenix, was also present. (Deep Thought had played Phoenix three times, winning all three. But according to Jonathan, Phoenix was always "almost winning".) Mike Valvo, the tournament director for the ACM and the World Computer Chess Championship, also showed up.

Deep Thought got White in the first game, and I was the operator. Murray manned the commentary room, relaying the moves from a PC. The PC, in turn, was following the game log on the computer in Pittsburgh.

The game started well for Deep Thought. Then I noticed that something strange was happening. For several moves in a row, Deep Thought wanted to castle its king, but then switched to moves that did not make any sense. Eventually, Deep Thought decided to castle for real, but Garry already had an edge as the result of the strange moves.

---

4 A pawn was worth 128 points on the Deep Thought scale. On the Deep Blue scale, a pawn was worth 100 points.

Three weeks later, Deep Thought played Phoenix in the ACM Championship. The same behavior happened again, and Deep Thought was objectively lost against Phoenix. (So Jonathan was correct in his "almost winning" assertion this time.) Luckily for us, Phoenix was only "almost winning", and Deep Thought won the game after a long struggle in the endgame. Thomas found the problem after the wakeup call from Phoenix. In the rush to get the three-computer version working in time for the Garry Kasparov match, a subtle bug had been introduced. If the castling move was made immediately in the software portion [5] of the search, then no castling bonus was awarded to Deep Thought's evaluation of the position. But if the castling move was delayed, and played into the hardware part of search, then Deep Thought would get the bonus. So Deep Thought would go to extreme contortions to delay castling until it was in the hardware portion of the search. In the Phoenix game, Deep Thought never did get to castle as a result. Jonathan had a very pleasant time for most of the game at my expense. In his own words, I was "fidgeting, scowling, concerned" [6]. But after the position turned in Deep Thought's favor, I was "giddy, smiling and exuberant". Jonathan took the game quite hard and soon gave up on computer chess [7]. We stopped using the three-computer version of Deep Thought permanently after the Phoenix game.

Anyway, in the first game against Garry, Deep Thought's pieces were seriously misplaced after the ridiculous contortions. Garry slowly increased his positional advantage and, after 52 moves, when Deep Thought's evaluation dropped below −700, I resigned for Deep Thought. The game was lost way before that.

While the first game was going on, a filming crew for the PBS

---

[5] In ChipTest, Deep Thought, Deep Thought II and Deep Blue, the positions most distant from the game position on the chessboard are searched by the chess hardware. These machines use special purpose chess hardware running under the control of a general purpose computer. For a 12-ply search, the first eight plies might be searched by the software on the general purpose computer, and the last four plies might be searched by the chess hardware directly.

[6] I tried to keep a poker face when operating the computer against human players but in games against computers, there was no need to hide my true feelings.

[7] Jonathan moved his attention to computer checkers, and eventually, with a few colleagues, created a World Championship level checkers program named Chinook. Chinook's story is described in Jonathan's excellent book *One Jump Ahead: Challenging Human Supremacy in Checkers*.

TV show *"Nova"* was taking shots of Garry. After the first game, the Nova producer mentioned that Garry was staring at me "as if you were the enemy". I had been so intent on not making operator errors that I had not noticed—sometimes, ignorance is bliss.

Garry, Murray and I traded places for the second game. Murray got to face Garry, while I relayed the moves to the commentators. Garry had White.

Before the match, Garry had requested that we send him all of Deep Thought's public games. We gladly obliged. We weren't really taking the match seriously. If it had been a genuine match, we would have done more than just give Garry the public games. We would have gone into training, prepared new openings, and drastically changed the program or even the hardware, if need be. Human chess players do the same type of secret training when they go into World Championship matches. Usually, both camps shy away from serious public appearances for, say, six months before the big match. Obviously, neither camp would volunteer any surprises that they had prepared for their opponents. This was the case when Garry played for the World Championship in his matches against Anatoly Karpov, Nigel Short (Great Britain) and Vishwanathan Anand (India). In this match, however, Deep Thought was an open book to Garry, and we paid dearly for this openness, or rather, lack of secret training, in the second game.

Garry used a move sequence that busted Deep Thought's opening for the Black side. The position right after the opening was difficult for Deep Thought, to say the least. Dr Berliner liked the position for White so much that he prepared and extended Garry's line for use by Hitech against Deep Thought. Three weeks after the Garry Kasparov game, Hitech played the White side of the same opening against Deep Thought. Deep Thought was lost right after the opening, but Hitech was not strong enough to finish off Deep Thought. Hitech was "almost winning". But once it was out of its opening book, Hitech immediately went astray. Deep Thought turned the tide and won the game. We did not have such luck against Garry. The castling bug, which existed in both games against Garry, did not help either. Deep Thought realized that it was in trouble right out of the opening, and it was straight downhill from there. Deep Thought never thought it was ahead in the game even when it was up in material at one time. The on-site commentary, however, was asserting that Deep Thought believed it was ahead. One book that described the game even went as far as saying Deep Thought's evaluation was such and such ahead for it. Based on Deep Thought's highly negative evaluation of its positions during the entire game, I believe that Garry simply busted Deep Thought's opening. Murray resigned for Deep Thought on move 37, but the result of the game was never in doubt after the disastrous opening.

The thoroughness of Garry's opening preparation for the second game was an eye opener for us. Deep Thought never got to really play the game. It lost the game to Garry's home preparation[8]. The easy win in the second game, however, might later have clouded Garry's judgment of what he could expect in the two matches he played against Deep Blue.

Mr Karpov Will Have White

Garry Kasparov's victory in the match against Deep Thought gave him by far the largest media coverage ever in the United States. After the match, Andrew Page[9], Garry's personal manager, was extremely happy about how well Garry was received. Garry took a risk[10] by agreeing to the heavy discounted appearance fee, but it would be an understatement to say that the publicity he received was well worth the discount. In certain aspects, Garry was getting even more coverage from the Deep Thought match than his World Championship matches.

Garry's media bonanza did not go unnoticed by the other chess players, and Deep Thought would soon take on three other chess players in exhibition matches. The last match of the three was against German Grandmaster Helmut Pfleger. The match resulted in two draws. The other two matches had more exciting results.

The first of these matches took place in December 1989, about two months after the Garry Kasparov match. The arrangements for this match, against International Master David Levy, were actually started before the Garry Kasparov match. David was best known for his taunting of computer chess researchers. In 1968, he had placed a bet with several computer scientists that no computers would beat him in a match within the next 10 years. He collected

8 Most likely it would still lose the game even if Garry had not busted its opening.

9 Garry fired Andrew Page after the 1997 Deep Blue match over financial issues.

10 Okay, $10,000 for one day's work is a risk that most people would undertake without any consideration.

the wager when Chess 4.5, a chess program from the Northwestern University, lost to him in 1978. *Omni* magazine then set up a $4000 Omni Prize, and David added another $1000 to the pile for the first computer to defeat him in a match. The Cray Blitz team tried to claim the Omni Prize in 1984, but was soundly defeated by David with the perfect score of 4–0.

When David played Cray Blitz, he adopted what he called the "Do nothing, but do it well" strategy. He deliberately avoided giving Cray Blitz targets, while keeping the board position closed so that the chances of immediate tactics were remote. The strategy worked exceedingly well against Cray Blitz. For that matter, it worked quite well against a lot of commercial chess programs, even at the hand of a weak chess player such as myself. Against David, Cray Blitz would muddle along until he set up some unstoppable long-term tactics and then Cray Blitz would crash and burn. Deep Thought had no problems spotting the long-term tactics used against Cray Blitz but, given that David was able to dispatch Cray Blitz with great ease, we were quite concerned before the match took place. When Deep Thought played Garry, it was acceptable that we did not score any point. Against David, we definitely wanted to win. Between the Garry Kasparov match and the David Levy match, we added thirty new terms to Deep Thought's evaluation function in preparation.

The match against David took place after Deep Thought's near disaster against Phoenix, and we were back to the single computer with two chess processors. The match was played in London. Peter Jansen, who became involved with the Deep Thought project in early 1989 [11], was the operator. In theory, the match could have been played using the machine in IBM, but since only the machines in Pittsburgh were available to all the Deep Thought team members, we used a workstation at Carnegie Mellon for the match.

Much to our relief, Deep Thought was able to do to David what he had done to Cray Blitz. David was gracious after his 0–4 drubbing, and did not make excuses for losing. In his own words, "I was not feeling particularly unwell; I was not sitting too close to

[11] Peter's main contribution to the Deep Thought project was endgame databases for selected pawn endings. He did not get actively involved in the programming of Deep Thought. Peter was more a user of the chess machines, using ChipTest extensively in his PhD thesis research. It had been left behind at Carnegie Mellon when Murray, Thomas and I went to IBM.

the heater; there was no disturbing noise outside the playing room; the lighting was not poor; the computer operator, Peter Jansen, was not smoking."

Deep Thought's next match opponent was none other than the former World Chess Champion Anatoly Karpov. With Garry getting so much publicity as a result of the Deep Thought match, Anatoly probably wanted his share of the attention. Was this the reason why he agreed to the invitation from the Harvard Chess Club to play Deep Thought? I don't know. I do know that the invitation from Daniel Edelman, the president of the Harvard Chess Club, for Deep Thought to play Anatoly did not come until after the Garry Kasparov vs. Deep Thought match.

Before his match Garry had requested the game scores of all of Deep Thought's public games. Anatoly did not make the same request and I assumed that he must have had the game scores already. I could not have been more wrong.

International Master Mike Valvo had been doing some chess work with Grandmaster Ron Henley for over a year. Ron was one of Anatoly Karpov's seconds (chess advisors) and, being an investment trader, he was also Anatoly's financial advisor. Mike Valvo, of course, was the tournament director for the ACM Computer Chess Championships, and thus was quite familiar with Deep Thought.

The match against Anatoly was supposed to take place on Friday 2 February 1990 at Harvard University. At about 9 pm on the night before the match, Mike visited Ron to deliver a laptop computer containing ChessBase databases for Anatoly's upcoming match against the Dutch Grandmaster Jan Timman. Mike was surprised when Ron requested Deep Thought games for Anatoly to look at. It turned out that Anatoly had not prepared for the Deep Thought match at all, even though the match was very likely the most important event during his short trip to the United States.

The first time I met Garry, he made the statement that only he and Anatoly were the true "professional" chess players. Well, compared to Garry, Anatoly was a quite different type of professional player. Garry studied all of Deep Thought's public games and its weaknesses, including its opening. Anatoly did not do anything more than a superficial study before his match with Deep Thought.

When the match was arranged, the Deep Thought team was surprised that it was going to be a one-game match. Chess matches are usually played with an even number of games so that both players get to play the same number of Whites and Blacks. The tradition for one-game matches was to select the playing color by a coin flip or some other chance event. The Harvard Chess Club organizers and ourselves all expected that the color would be chosen at random before the game, especially since it would be a one-game match. In hindsight, it seems that the Anatoly Karpov camp probably had a different idea early on.

Below is an excerpt from an article written by IM Mike Valvo on the match:

> ... Unlike both Fischer and Kasparov, however, Karpov is content to play for a draw with Black and only press with White.
>
> It seemed to me that Karpov had made up his mind to play 1. e4 after seeing the machine's handling of the Alekhine Defense [12]. I thought it was only fair to tell him that the machine could also play the Caro-Kann [13], but I had no intention of saying anything more as I was privately rooting for Deep Thought. I was taken aback at that point because Henley now phoned Danny Edelman and proceeded to convince him that Karpov should be given the white pieces without a coin flip. Edelman was clearly resistant to the suggestion, but Henley was quite persuasive.

Murray and I were stunned when we heard the news. Having been a World Champion for many years, Anatoly was used to special treatment. Had he asked to play White at the time of the match invitation, I would have felt no qualms about it. It was possible that we might not have agreed to play the match then, but it was also perfectly possible that we might. Anatoly's last minute demand left a very bad taste. Had we known that we would be playing the Black side earlier, we could have prepared a much better opening for Deep Thought. At high level chess, good opening preparation is crucial. Knowing well in advance which color you

---

[12] For the chess uninitiated, the Alekhine Defense is generally considered a somewhat suspect opening for Black. Deep Thought had good results against weak players with the defense, but Anatoly Karpov had been known to mow down top grandmasters daring to play the Alekhine Defense against him.

[13] Caro Kann is a relatively sound defense for Black. Ironically, it was also Anatoly's favorite defense when he played Black at the time.

will play against a specific opponent can be the difference between winning and losing. We were very unhappy about the turn of events, but we agreed to the demand in the end, for two reasons. First, we did not want to make a scene. The Harvard student group had put in a lot of work to make the event happen and we felt obliged to help them make it a success. Second, we were no longer only representing ourselves. Had it been entirely up to us, we might have said, "Good bye, nice meeting you, Mr. Karpov." Everything happened too fast, we had to make a snap judgment, and being forced to play Black seemed to be the least of our worries.

Anatoly looked quite different from what I expected. Most descriptions portrayed him as someone who looked relatively delicate. When I saw him for the first time on 2 February 1990, he appeared quite healthy, although a little bit tired from his trip. Anatoly had remarried shortly before the match, and married life seemed to agree with him.

After an opening speech by Anatoly, the game was under way. As Mike Valvo surmised, Anatoly played 1. e4, the king pawn opening. Between the Garry Kasparov and the Anatoly Karpov matches, Deep Thought had gone through the David Levy match and one computer chess tournament, during which Ken Thompson had provided us with his opening book for the Caro Kann. Mike Valvo was aware of this arrangement, and hence his deliberation about whether to tell Anatoly about the Caro Kann during their earlier meeting. As it happened, in the two intervening events none of our opponents played 1. e4, so there was no public game where Deep Thought played 1. ... c6, the Caro Kann, against 1. e4. Anatoly did not show any visible emotion when I made the Caro Kann defense on the chessboard. Unlike Garry, Anatoly's facial expression was not as easy to read.

The game was played at a faster time control than in the match against Garry. The Anatoly Karpov game was played with one hour to each player, while the Garry Kasparov match was played with 90 minutes to each player. Surprisingly, by move 16 Deep Thought had a chance to make a sacrifice that would have placed Anatoly under tremendous pressure. Had the game been played with a regular time control, then Deep Thought would have made the sacrifice. The 3-workstation version of the program that played Garry potentially could find the sacrifice within the game time, assuming that we had got it working for the match. It is amazing how a minor difference could have changed the history dramatically.

Since Deep Thought could not find the sacrifice over the board, it played the second best move and Anatoly obtained a slight edge. On the 27th move, Deep Thought played a move that at first glance looked quite ugly and the audience laughed. After the game, Anatoly commented that that ugly move was the only good move. I could not tell one way or another. All I noticed during the game was that the ugly move played was one hundredth of a pawn better than a more natural looking move [14].

Unfortunately, Lady Luck did not stay with Deep Thought very long. The game entered into a rook ending, where each side had a king, a rook and a bunch of pawns. The rook ending was objectively drawn. The game remained drawn for many moves, and at one point Deep Thought had a chance for a draw by repetition, but it spurned the draw as it erroneously assessed the position to be in its favor. Anatoly, being the virtuoso endgame player, knew better and he found some resources in the position that Deep Thought did not understand. Deep Thought ended up losing the game after 65 moves. Anatoly was down to his last minute when the game ended, while Deep Thought still had about twenty minutes. The audience was a little bit surprised when I resigned for Deep Thought, given the limited time that Karpov had left. In my view, it was an exhibition game, Anatoly obviously knew what he was doing, and there was no sense wasting everybody's time to force him to play the game to the bitter end.

After the game, Mike Valvo said to the audience that the game could be viewed as a moral victory for Deep Thought. I viewed it not so much as a hollow moral victory, but rather a good chess lesson given by one of the top chess players in the world. We needed to do some solid work about Deep Thought's or its successor's endgame play. The design of Deep Thought II was influenced quite substantially by the Karpov game, and there were very few games that had similar effects on the design of Deep Thought or its successors. When all was said and done, Anatoly Karpov's chess ability had to be respected. If letting Karpov play White was the price for the lesson, it was not so bad a deal.

---

14 Chess programmers usually don't admit it in public, but this happens all the time. The "brilliant" moves are frequently only "better" than the losing moves by the slightest difference.

IBM

 CHAPTER 8

We Need a New Name

A Cultural Shock

The move from the familiar environment at Carnegie Mellon University to the IBM T. J. Watson Research Center in Westchester County, New York took me a while to get used to.

A couple of months before we joined IBM Research, we got a call from Randy Moulic, who was to be our manager. Randy was excited about the project and wanted to visit us in Pittsburgh before we joined IBM. The meeting was mostly social. I was expecting someone relatively formal and much older than we were, but Randy turned out to be quite cordial, and only about ten years older. In fact, my first mental response was "our new manager has a baby face". Randy was quite young at heart and had a sunny outlook on life. Whoever selected him to be our manager did a good job; he was probably closer to our way of thinking than most IBM managers. The meeting went well, and I thought that the transition to life in IBM would be relatively smooth. I underestimated the cultural shock that I was about to receive.

Life as a computer science graduate student at Carnegie Mellon was comfortable. The stipend from the Department was adequate, and the cost of living in Pittsburgh was relatively low. Everyone in the Department knew you to some extent, and you knew everyone in the Department at least by name. Anyone could have a great deal of autonomy and freedom if that was what they wanted. If I needed any help, I knew with whom to talk, or at least someone who might be able to point me to the right person. The Department effectively operated 24 hours a day. Even in the middle of the night, you could always find some fellow students or occasionally some faculty members about.

Compared to Pittsburgh, Westchester County had much higher living cost—the food at the supermarket was about 10–20 percent higher, and the rent for my new apartment was about three times more than in Pittsburgh. It was a good thing that my new salary was much higher than my old student stipend. The sticker shock took some time to get used to, but it was not as hard as the change in the work environment.

The Immigration Course at Carnegie Mellon did a good job of easing new graduate students into the new environment at the Department. IBM Research did not have a comparable process to help newcomers. The first few months of my life at IBM were spent dealing with the seemingly never-ending paperwork, and trying to cope with the IBM computing environment, which was quite different from the computing environment in typical universities[1]. Furthermore, I no longer knew what the other people around me were doing. Everyone seemed to be busy with his own project, and there was very little communication outside one's own group. Most of the people also appeared to work regular hours. The building was usually almost empty by 7 o'clock in the evening.

However, the most amusing new experience was all the discussion about the name of the program. When I chose the name Deep Thought, it seemed to be appropriate for the machine that would defeat the World Chess Champion. I had no idea that some people might have problems with it. The first hint of potential trouble came at the very first computer chess tournament that Deep Thought played in, before we even started the employment talk with IBM. It was at the 1988 ACM Computer Chess Championship. Tony Marsland, a professor from the University of Alberta, organized a panel session alongside the Championship and I was one of the panelists. For some reasons, when introducing me, Tony used the name "Deep Throat" at least three or four times although immediately correcting himself each time. "Deep Throat" was the code name of the informer for the Watergate investigative reporters from the *Washington Post*, and it was also the name of a movie that you would not take your mother to see.

After the Garry Kasparov vs. Deep Thought match, complaints of the Deep Thought name poured in from both inside and outside IBM. It appeared that there were a lot of people who could

---

1 The amount of paperwork is much lower in IBM Research these days. The computing environment is also closer to what you see in the outside world.

not help thinking about "Deep Throat" when they heard the name Deep Thought. It got much worse. Murray Campbell's wife Gina was working at a Catholic college. The President of the college was an elderly nun, and during a conversation with Gina, the Sister kept on using the name "Deep Throat". Houston, we have a problem.

At Carnegie Mellon, we chose whatever name we liked. We could not do that at IBM. Given that IBM was a big corporation, we had to be careful not to infringe on someone else's trademark. It also seemed a good idea to get more IBM researchers involved in the naming process, so the Communications Department announced a contest for the name of the future IBM chess machine. Of the submitted entries, the name "Blue Chips" was my favorite, but a computer company was already using that name. A few other names also had the same problem. In the end, the name "Deep Blue" [2] was chosen, submitted by Peter Brown, that same classmate who was partially responsible for our being hired by IBM. For winning the contest, Peter was treated to a nice dinner with us, and a chance to play Deep Thought. He declined the second part of his award [3].

The Short-term View

When we joined IBM In 1989, it was one of the most profitable companies in the world, with very good financial years until 1993 or so. As a graduate student, I was used to operating with the minimum amount of outlay. We had a nil budget for ChipTest, and a $5000 budget for Deep Thought [4]. You had better be frugal when you have a budget as tight as we did. To me, it was already a big surprise that IBM agreed to hire a full team immediately, considering that most of the critical work would be in hardware during the early phases of the project. So when our manager Randy Moulic

---

[2] Deep Blue is a play on IBM's nickname Big Blue, which probably came from the blue color of its trademark. IBM does not own the trademark for "Big Blue" and never uses the term to describe itself.

[3] A few years later, Peter Brown, with the help of a strong master, played a casual game against a very early version of Deep Blue Jr. and lost. Peter wanted to be the first person to "play it".

[4] The commercial chess programmers, however, always referred to both ChipTest and Deep Thought as "supercomputers", implying that they only lost to multi-million-dollar machines.

suggested that we hire a Chess Grandmaster as a consultant, my immediate gut reaction was "What for?". My feeling was that we would indeed need help from Grandmasters for the final push, but we were not really ready to work with them yet, since the new hardware was still no more than a glint in the eye.

What I did not realize was that we could no longer afford to take only a long-term view. Back at Carnegie Mellon, Deep Thought was not an official project and the faculty did not have high expectations about how well we would do. Before we joined IBM, we had our own self-imposed milestones to meet, but we did not have to maintain a constant presence in the computer chess world. In theory, we could go back to the drawing board for years on end without showing up at any computer chess event. We did not have this luxury at IBM. Our arrival there was a high-profile one. Within two months, we were on the front page of the *New York Times* and the *Wall Street Journal* as a result of the exhibition match with Garry Kasparov. Such a high profile came with a price. We suddenly had to compete regularly in public and win. Providing short-term performance became an important concern for us even if it might be in conflict with the long-term progress of the project. It was most likely this concern that drove Randy to suggest hiring a Grandmaster.

Grandmaster Maxim Dlugy was born in Russia, but he came to the United States when he was quite young and received most of his chess education in the US. To some extent, Maxim was a cross product of both the American and the Russian cultures. His name came up when we talked with some of our chess friends and we invited him to come up to IBM Research for a visit. He was articulate and personable, and after some internal discussions he was hired as a chess consultant. Murray, being the chess expert of the team, would be the main person working with him.

When Maxim came on board, we had no clear responsibilities for him. In the first few weeks, he would come in, play a few quick games against Deep Thought, losing most of them, and then make a few comments. Later on, he would bring in some test positions, some from his recent tournament games, and see what Deep Thought came up with. Occasionally, much to his chagrin, Deep Thought would find that he had missed chances to win the games outright. The comments from Maxim were potentially very useful, but we were not in a position to make use of them without the new hardware at least partially designed.

Deep Thought had an opening book that was not up to Grandmaster standard, even though it was playing at Grandmaster level. After getting useful but not immediately usable work from Maxim, we asked him to work on a better opening book. In this new way of working, Maxim would first bring in an opening book fragment that he prepared at home. Deep Thought would check out all the positions for errors in the opening book, Murray would screen for the obvious errors, and then Maxim would check the flagged errors and come up with alternatives.

The Dlugy opening book, however, was never fully checked. In 1991, when Bankers Trust was recruiting top chess players as potential equity or currency traders, Maxim left IBM and joined them [5]. We used his opening book in a Deep Thought vs. the German national team match [6], with mixed results. Part of this opening book came straight out of the *Encyclopedia of Chess Openings* (ECO). The ECO is largely a collection of works from Grandmasters and some of the them were said to have deliberately laid opening traps in the sections that they wrote. Among chess players, it is well known that the ECO cannot be fully trusted. In one of the games against the German players, Deep Thought walked right into an opening trap. ECO assessed the position as playable for Deep Thought, but actually it was a dead loss. Had the position been examined, we would have noticed that Deep Thought assessed it as a full pawn down without any positional compensation, which is usually a good indication that the position is lost.

The Dlugy experiment was largely unsuccessful. His opening book was relegated to a backup role when Deep Thought II became fully operational. By the time of Deep Blue, most of the Dlugy analysis was no longer active. However, we did learn something from the process—how not to work with a Grandmaster. To work with them properly, we needed to set clear goals and establish some means to measure our progress.

---

5 This happened at about the time when Deep Thought II first became partially operational. See also the story on Deep Thought II and the Greener Pasture. According to my sources, Bankers Trust hired two other chess players in addition to Maxim Dlugy.

6 The match was billed as a Deep Thought II match, but Deep Thought was the player.

Deep Thought II and the Greener Pasture

Deep Thought II, also known as Deep Blue Prototype, served several useful purposes during its career from 1991 to 1995. It was the strongest chess computer until Deep Blue supplanted it in 1996. The decision to build Deep Thought II, in retrospect, was probably a mistake. Because of Deep Thought II, Deep Blue was delayed by about two years, although part of this delay was due to unforeseen personnel changes. On the plus side, without Deep Thought II, Joe Hoane, who became critical to the success of Deep Blue, might not have joined the team.

The initial decision to build Deep Thought II seemed to be a good one. Deep Thought was still about 200 rating points stronger than the nearest computer chess competitors, and would win three out of every four games against the best opponents. But the Swiss tournament format of the major computer chess events meant that its chance of winning an event was only about fifty percent, even though it was always the heavy favorite. When we were just graduate students, winning computer chess events was gratifying but otherwise unimportant. In a corporate environment, there was tremendous political pressure to keep on winning, even though the statistics were stacked against us. Officially, the reason for building Deep Thought II was to use it as a prototype for exploring parallel search algorithms. But the main reason was really to open up a large gap between our computer competitors and us, so that the project could go on for an extended period while I struggled through the design of the new chess chip.

From my point of view, there was another reason to build Deep Thought II. I wanted to force Thomas Anantharaman to rewrite the program for the chess machine.

Thomas and I went back a long way. He was the first person besides me to work on the Deep Thought series of chess machines. We were quite close, but by the time we joined IBM we had been in a long running debate on how to program the machine. Prior to his ChipTest days, Thomas had written a software-only chess program. In order to speed up his program, he violated many of the precepts of good programming and, in particular, his program was riddled with many "goto" statements, computer commands to branch to another place in the program. It was a classic "spaghetti" code—a program with convoluted, intricate control flow that could not be easily followed by normal human beings.

It was no longer necessary for Thomas to write chess programs in the "spaghetti" coding style when the ChipTest hardware started working. But since he was doing it as a hobby, I could not really force him to make the change. Beggars cannot be choosers. The ChipTest software became sufficiently unwieldy even for Thomas, and when Deep Thought was being built, he initially agreed to rewrite the software in a manner that the rest of the team could understand. But partly because of my delay in delivering the Deep Thought hardware, and possibly partly because of Thomas' work load related to his thesis research, the Deep Thought software was modified from the ChipTest software, and retained all of its "spaghetti" code.

After Deep Thought won the Second Fredkin Intermediate Prize, Thomas decided to drop his original thesis topic and turn his work on Deep Thought into a thesis, but the "spaghetti" remained. By the time we joined IBM, Deep Thought had about 100,000 lines of code, mostly in the "spaghetti" coding style, and even Thomas had a hard time keeping track of how the software worked. Deep Thought II, with many more chess processors (up to twenty-four) than Deep Thought, would require brand new software, and Thomas would finally have a good reason to change the program.

Things did not work out as I hoped.

When we started the design for Deep Thought II, Randy hired a contract engineer to work on the hardware design with me. He did a creditable job initially, freeing me to spend most of my time on the new chess chip instead of overseeing the design of the new machine. Before completing his work, the contract engineer left for a job outside IBM. Suddenly, I had to take over the whole design. This diversion took several months away from the chip work.

There were more problems to come.

When we were both graduate students at Carnegie Mellon, Thomas was working in the Speech group. For many years, he was running two programs, named "ex" and "lpc", on the same machine on which I was doing my chip design work. I had always assumed that the programs were part of his speech research—in particular, the "lpc" program sounded like a "Linear Predictive Coding" program, which is a well-established method used in speech recognition, and it made perfect sense for him to work on it. I only found out when I was about to leave Carnegie Mellon that neither of his programs was related to his speech work. The program "ex" turned out to be a program for the stock exchange [7], and the program "lpc" was used to predict the movement of the stock market. Thomas had had an interest in the stock market for a long while.

When Andreas Nowatzyk was approached by the Wall Street firm with the plan of forming a startup in Silicon Valley, he asked Thomas to work for the startup on a part-time basis. Andreas eventually turned down the deal but Thomas was sufficiently interested that he continued his own negotiations with the firm. After some time, he reached a deal, believing that there was no conflict of interest with his IBM job. Unfortunately, IBM lawyers disagreed, because the deal involved the transfer of intellectual property. Thomas ended up leaving IBM for the greener pasture of Wall Street, with a new salary more than twice what he had earned.

I was tinkering with the idea of creating my own version of the chess program before Thomas left. I had some new ideas for improving the search selectivity of the program, that is, making the program search much more deeply along "interesting" lines than Deep Thought ever had done. I wanted to see the ideas implemented [8] but, given my hardware design work, I was not really serious about writing the chess program myself. I was just talking and hoping that Thomas would pick up the ideas and run with them as he had done frequently when we were back at Carnegie Mellon. With Thomas now gone, I was forced to write a new chess program for real, myself [9].

Arthur Joseph Hoane, a staff programmer at IBM Research whom we called Joe, had previously expressed his interest in the chess project. With Thomas gone, we had an extra head count [10] and we needed someone to help program Deep Thought II. Joe was a graduate of the University of Illinois at Urbana-Champaign, and we knew him to be a self-motivated, excellent programmer. Deep Blue was not an ordinary IBM project; it was a project transplant-

---

7   Don't ask me what the program did. Thomas never explained it in detail.

8   After the Software Toolworks Championship, IM Mike Valvo challenged Deep Thought to a two-game correspondence match that he won easily. The correspondence games strongly suggested that it might be a good idea to have the program search a great deal deeper along "interesting" lines.

9   Murray was a decent programmer, but at the time, only Thomas and I could possibly write the new program as we were the only two with intimate knowledge of the hardware, the parallel search, and the selective search.

10 A head count is a hiring position.

ed from outside IBM, and with team members who were self-motivated. Before the team joined IBM, we explicitly told the company that we would not join unless we were given the chance to build the "ultimate" chess machine. Unlike typical IBM projects, the manager of the Deep Blue project was filling a support role, and not the project leader. As a matter of fact, there was *no* project leader. It was critical that members of the team be able to do things on their own. After some discussion and lots of paperwork, Joe was welcomed into the group. However, he was not yet ready to step into Thomas' shoes, so there was no break for me. I still had to program the new parallel search code and the new selective search code for Deep Thought II.

At Carnegie Mellon, I wrote a simulator for the parallel search algorithms described in my thesis. With this simulator as the starting template for the new program, I had an easier time. However, it was a slow process. Writing software was never high on my list of interesting things to do.

Deep Thought II had up to twenty-four chess processors, and the new chess program was designed to use all of them. The first version of the program did not implement any of the selective extensions used in Deep Thought, nor did it implement the search ideas that I had. It took several months to complete. The new program was about 5–8 times faster than Deep Thought. In his thesis, Thomas claimed that the search extensions used in Deep Thought produced only a small improvement in performance, which would not have been enough to compensate for the 5–8 times advantage in speed that Deep Thought II enjoyed. Yet, Deep Thought was on even footing with the first version of Deep Thought II in head-to-head competition. Maxim Dlugy had already left for Bankers Trust by then, but he still had some IBM contract hours to fill and he played a game against Deep Thought II. After the game, he opined that Deep Thought II was strong, but its play seemed to lack pizazz when compared with Deep Thought. In Maxim Dlugy's eyes, Deep Thought II played solid chess, but it did not seem to be capable of playing moves that surprised Maxim as Deep Thought had. I could not say conclusively that Thomas was wrong in his thesis, but the lab tests seemed to indicate there were reasons to doubt. Maybe the improvement was bigger than Thomas had concluded.

The new selective search ideas took a few more months to implement. At first, Deep Thought was still holding its own with Deep Thought II. We had a few public events scheduled for Deep

Thought II but since Deep Thought seemed as good as (or better than) Deep Thought II and was also the more stable program, we opted to let Deep Thought play in the events. The organizers, however, had already publicly billed the events as featuring Deep Thought II. As recounted earlier, during one of these events, we discovered the need of further work on Maxim Dlugy's opening book. By then, his contract had expired. Murray eventually gave up on the book and wrote a program to automatically generate new opening books, using the top players' opening repertoires gleaned from the public game records. One of the opening books that he generated was based on Anatoly Karpov's opening repertoire. This was accomplished by extracting the most common moves from all of Anatoly's public games [11]. This opening book was subsequently used in Deep Thought II's public debut.

For a while, it appeared that all my software work was for naught. Deep Thought II was no better than Deep Thought, despite all the extra processing power. The hands-on experience, however, proved invaluable and I certainly got to appreciate what Thomas did more fully. I also had a better idea about how to design the hardware to ease the software work. But, more importantly, I got some new insights into how to control the search more effectively. It was with these new insights that the final touch was added. The result was dramatic. Deep Thought II was suddenly outclassing Deep Thought. Deep Thought was already a chess tactical monster and yet, in game after game, Deep Thought II found deep combinations that escaped Deep Thought by a few extra moves. We had a new, number one chess program.

Deep Thought II played its first public event at the 1991 ACM Computer Chess Championship, held in Albuquerque, New Mexico from November 17–20. Instead of using the Dlugy opening book, the "Karpov opening book" was used. Deep Thought II won all its games; however, in one of its Black games, we had a scare, as the Karpov book allowed our opponent the option of getting a repetition draw right at the opening—Anatoly was well known to be willing to draw as Black. To me, the most impressive game played by Deep Thought II in this event was against Cray Blitz. For over

---

[11] Why did Murray choose to use Anatoly's opening repertoire instead of Garry's? Well, Anatoly played with a relatively narrow and safe opening repertoire while Garry's was very wide, rapidly changing, and sometimes risky. It would have taken a great deal of effort to ensure that a "Kasparov opening book" was safe to use.

ten moves (ten moves each by White and Black, or twenty plies total), Cray Blitz had no inkling that it was getting killed, while Deep Thought II was predicting the entire game continuation and assessing the game as completely won. Cray Blitz was one of the fastest chess programs around, and to outsearch it by this wide margin exceeded my wildest expectation.

Joe Hoane took over the chess program after the Albuquerque event. At the time I handed it over, Deep Thought II had only about 5000 lines of code, or roughly one-twentieth the number of lines of code in Deep Thought. The Deep Thought II code handled ten times more chess processors, and it also had new and possibly far more powerful search extensions. I was proud of the work, but the software effort took about a year of my time which would otherwise have been spent on the chess chip design.

A Trip to Denmark

Over the years, after every big event that ChipTest, Deep Thought, or Deep Thought II played in, I would post in the USENET newsgroup *rec.games.chess* my personal account of the event [12]. The following report on our trip to Denmark was adapted from one of the posts. There were other important chess events in the career of Deep Thought II, including a match win over Grandmaster Judit Polgar, one of the top players in the world and possibly the best female player ever [13]. The chess event in Denmark, however, was important for many other reasons. Historically, it was the first time that a chess computer defeated a National Team in a match. From the Deep Blue team's perspective, it was also the first time that we played in a serious match of classical chess (chess played at tournament time control), and in that sense, it was a dry run for the Deep Blue matches that were to come. The event, especially the games against the wily Bent Larsen, provided many useful chess lessons for us. There is one more very important reason why I included this event in the book. Joe Hoane had taken over the pro-

---

12 After the first Deep Blue match, I wrote a personal account but decided against posting it when the Communications Department at IBM Research persuaded me that it was probably better to publish it as an article in a serious magazine. As preparations for the second match were under way, the article never saw the light of the day. For the second Deep Blue match, I did not bother to write any post-match report.

13 The match was played under action time control (30 minutes per player for the entire game) and should not be taken too seriously.

gramming of Deep Thought II for just over a year when the event took place. By this time, he had made significant additions and improvements to the program, and Deep Thought II had more or less become his program. But it was only in this event that I really got to see Joe's dedication to the project for the first time. Joe was sick during part of the event, but he hung in there throughout, worked long hours, and made numerous improvements to the program. Murray, Joe, and I really solidified as a team during this trip to Denmark.

I was able to get back to the chip design after the Albuquerque event, but found that the earlier design work was no longer useful. It was too long a break and I lost track of what I had been doing. Meanwhile, our manager, Randy Moulic, had something else on his mind. IBM was forming a joint venture with another company, and Randy was going to be involved. Chung-Jen (C J) Tan was assigned as our new manager in the spring of 1992 but since Murray, Joe and I were all in the project for our own reasons, and effectively autonomous, the change in the management chain had very little impact on our day-to-day routine. To me, the project *was* my life and certainly close to the same thing for Murray and Joe. We would see the project completed no matter who the manager was. As far as we were concerned, the manager was a support role and, even if we were to get the pointy-haired boss from the Dilbert comic strip, we would have gotten the job done [14]. C J played a fine support role as the team was largely unaware of what he or the bureaucracy was doing. The team was well insulated from outside disturbances.

While I was restarting my chip design work, Murray discovered the Internet Chess Server, and Deep Thought II played anonymously on the server for a while before it was discovered. Deep Thought II became fairly well debugged during this period, and it was good preparation for our next event.

In late 1992, IBM Denmark talked with us about arranging chess exhibition matches, possibly in connection with IBM Sweden. At some point, there was talk about playing Swedish

---

[14] Okay, I will admit that it would have been very hard if the pointy-haired boss had been our manager. In all likelihood, the pointy-haired boss would have proclaimed himself our fearless project leader and ordered us to provide him free donuts at all the meaningless meetings he forced upon us.

Grandmasters as well, but the final arrangement was to play only in Copenhagen, Denmark, and only against Danish players.

Two separate official matches were scheduled, a four-game match against GM Bent Larsen and a four-game match against the Danish national team, with the last game against Bent also counted as part of the team match. So, there were actually only seven official games. Five additional one-hour exhibition games were also scheduled during the weekdays. The Copenhagen Chess Union co-sponsored the matches together with IBM Denmark. For this event, we hand carried the printed circuit boards for the chess processors to Denmark and shipped the rest of Deep Thought II in a large crate.

The main event against the Danish players was to start on Wednesday 24 February 1993. We arrived early on Friday 19 February in order to take part in a public event the next day with Garry Kasparov. We had dinner with Kasparov and the organizers in the evening of our arrival. During dinner, we first learned how well prepared the Danes were. Jens Nielsen, the creator of a well known test set of chess positions for computers, had made a notebook for the Danish players, containing the Deep Thought games, relevant articles, pointers about computers' weaknesses, and so on. We were concerned, but Deep Thought II was in pieces, and there were prescheduled weekend events. There was not much we could do before Monday.

Garry dominated the dinner conversation, but every once in a while he withdrew into himself and just listened. Maybe it was his cold. But it could also have been the case that something else was on his mind. A few days later, during one of our match games, we received a fax that Garry Kasparov and Nigel Short, his British Challenger, had decided to leave FIDE, the international chess federation. They were forming a new chess organization, Professional Chess Association (PCA), and would play their World Championship match under the auspices of PCA. Nigel did not like the conditions FIDE was imposing on the World Championship match without his consent, and with Garry in a prolonged dispute with the then FIDE president Florencio Campomanes, Nigel found a willing partner.

Garry was impressive on Saturday during the public event, despite having a cold. We could not put together the full Deep Thought II for the show, but we managed to get a version with only two chess processors up and running. Garry went over one of his recent games against GM Predrag Nikolic. In this game, Garry gave up major material for an attack, that in his judgment, was clearly winning. Deep Thought II, with reduced processing power, assessed the position as unfavorable for Garry initially, and gave some alternative defenses for the other side. Garry then proceeded to bust the new defenses given by Deep Thought II in real time on the stage. Deep Thought II clearly did not have a clue about what was going on in the game position. I was not precisely feeling gloom and doom, but it was clear that I would have a lot of work to do when I got back to the United States. The problems involved were more or less mine alone—the new chess chip would have to "understand" the positions in this game [15].

We started setting up the full machine at the match site on Monday 22 February. The machine room was not adequately cooled (there was no air conditioning) and one of the chess processors overheated and stopped functioning after a few hours. The ventilation was improved by Tuesday and a test game was played without further mishap.

The machine was referred to as Nordic Deep Blue by the organizers. This was the first time that the Deep Blue name was used, albeit obliquely. As far as I am concerned, Deep Blue did not exist until it was completed in 1996 for its first match against Garry. The machine that actually played in Denmark was Deep Thought II, although with a reduced number of chess processors. In Deep Thought II's public debut it played with twenty-four chess processors but at this time we were using only fourteen processors. Besides the one processor lost from the overheating, others were lost in a freak accident in our lab. The air conditioner in our lab iced up and stopped working. The ice then melted, dripped on the chess processors and caused some of them to malfunction. The peak speed of Deep Thought II was down to about 4–5 million chess positions per second for the Copenhagen events.

Day 1 (Wednesday, 24 February)
This was a disastrous day. It was the first time that we fully realized the seriousness of our own lack of preparation and how well

---

[15] Today, Deep Blue Jr., which has only one-thirtieth the computation power of Deep Blue, has no problem playing the sacrifice itself in about a minute. So I did learn something useful from Garry that day. The chess chip needed to recognize that certain piece configurations, in conjunction with open lines against the enemy king, could be very powerful in a king hunt.

prepared was our opposition. Frantic work followed after the games.

The first game was against Bent Larsen. This was the first official game of the match against him, and not part of the match against the Danish team. Bent adopted a simple strategy that worked surprisingly well. Bishops, operating on diagonals, are more powerful when the chess position is wide open with many "open" diagonals uninhibited by pawns. If the chess position is blocked by pawns, the knights might become more powerful than the bishops, even though bishops are normally superior pieces. Bent traded off all the knights belonging to Deep Thought II and tried to keep the position blocked. Deep Thought II retained a pair of bishops, which is usually considered an advantage. The problem was that we had never programed Deep Thought II to understand that it should trade some pawns to increase the scope of the bishop pair. Bent's strategy would not have worked if we had forseen this as a potential problem beforehand. Our opening preparation also left something to be desired. Bent won the first match game, and we were in a deep hole.

We played two short exhibition games after the official game. Again both ended in disaster. Our opponents were well prepared, and there seemed to be something wrong with Deep Thought II.

Day 2 (Thursday, 25 February)

The night before, a few modifications were made to the program. Joe put in an all-nighter. Murray also worked late. I was mostly a spectator. With the exception of the debut of Deep Thought II in Albuquerque, when I wrote the bulk of the chess program, my main work would have been completed usually by the time of a chess event. Overnight, Joe found some problems in the search extension code of Deep Thought II. Prior to our visit to Denmark, Joe put some debugging code into the program for testing, and this code was active during the games on the first day. The debugging code caused the program to behave quite differently and seemingly much weaker. Joe located the problems and corrected them.

Three exhibition games were played during the day, and Deep Thought II behaved much better than it had the previous day. The schedule for our Copenhagen visit was exceedingly tight, and with the continuous exhibition games, we did not have much time to make serious preparation for the official matches. The Danish team was probably using the exhibition games to look for additional weaknesses in Deep Thought II.

The second match game, and first game of the team match, was played in the evening against IM Henrik Danielsen of the Danish national team. Henrik was surprised by several sharp moves from Deep Thought II. Joe's late night changes seemed to have made a big difference. After one particularly unpleasant move from Deep Thought II, Henrik spent over fifteen minutes thinking about his response. The machine correctly predicted his response and was able to use the time he spent on the position to come up with a killer move that pretty much ended the game. If Henrik had responded quickly, Deep Thought II would have missed the killer move.

So after two days, Deep Thought II was 0–1 in the Larsen match, and 1–0 in the match against the Danish team. We slept easier that night.

Day 3 (Friday, 26 February)

It was a quiet day. Both match games against Bent Larsen and the Danish team, ended in draws.

Deep Thought II had good chances to win the second match game against Bent, but could not pull it off. He was under pressure throughout the game, and the game progressed into an ending where both sides had a rook and a bishop and Deep Thought II had an extra pawn. The problem was that the bishops were not on squares of the same color. It is well known that endings where the two sides have a bishop on the opposite color squares are notoriously difficult to win for the stronger side, since each bishop can only attack half of the chess board. Deep Thought II knew about this; unfortunately, it did not know that having only one additional rook on both sides did not change the situation much.

The second game of the day was against the Danish team member IM Carsten Hoi. Carsten achieved a good opening position in part owing to an oversight in our opening preparation. Deep Thought II played strongly, given the weak position, and presented Carsten with tricky choices. In one position, Deep Thought II appeared to be offering him a free pawn. Carsten thought for a very long time before declining the pawn offer and the game ended in a draw. Almost everyone in the audience expected Carsten to take the pawn and win the game. He explained afterwards that he did not see anything obviously wrong with taking the pawn, but his intuition told him that it might be a trap. Postgame analysis with Deep Thought II suggested that Carsten's intuition was excellent. Had he taken the pawn, either his knight would have been trapped or Deep Thought II would have had a very strong attack.

Day 4 (Saturday, 27 February)

Bent Larsen had White again. Murray could not find a good anti-dote to Bent's tactics in the first game so the old standby, the Center Counter Defense, reared its head again. Of course, in Denmark, it is better known as the Scandinavian Defense, and Deep Thought II happened to play the "Danish variation". We did not play the defense to honor our host. We were desperate. Shortly after the start of the game, Deep Thought II was in big trouble. Probably the only chess-playing entity at the match site that did not "think" that Bent was winning was Deep Thought II. But even the machine assessed its position as highly unfavorable. Bent, however, did have one psychological problem. Going into the game, he was probably expecting another slow positional squeeze. The position over the board was very good for him, but he would have to execute the attack perfectly. If Bent were facing a human player, the human opponent probably would have cracked under the pressure. If he were facing another computer, there would have been a very good chance that the computer would have made some critical mistake and gone down in flames. Bent executed the attack well for a while, but Deep Thought II walked a fine line and defended resourcefully. Slowly, his advantage dissipated. When the endgame phase was reached, it was Deep Thought II that had the better position. There were some debates as to whether the final position was winnable, but since Deep Thought II had no idea about the proper way to proceed, we called a truce.

The team match game against the third Danish National Team member, GM Lars Bo Hansen, was perhaps the best game played by Deep Thought II in Denmark. One commentator went so far as to say that Deep Thought II played like a Super Grandmaster. Lars had had previous successes against the opening line played by Deep Thought II, but said after the game that he might have to rethink the whole line. The game against Lars was the first time that we saw Deep Thought II outplay a Grandmaster in a regular tournament game by superior *positional* play. The final *coup de grace* was a tactical combination, but the game was finished before that. After this game, Deep Thought II clinched the match against the Danish National Team, leading by the score of 2.5 to

0.5. We were still behind Bent by 2 to 1, and we had one last shot to tie the Larsen match.

Day 5 (Sunday, 28 February)

The anchor game for both the Larsen match and the Danish National Team match was played on this day. Bent got into trouble early, underestimating a critical move. Deep Thought II probably had a winning edge at move twenty-five, but then it decided to go into another ending with bishops of opposite color. This time, both sides had a queen as well. After the second game, we increased the penalty for having an additional rook for both sides, but did not do so for having a queen for both sides. Did we goof? Deep Thought II was not able to make any progress. After a short while, we started discussing in the machine room whether we should just offer Bent a draw. IM Bjarke Kristensen came into the machine room very excited and started to explain to us that the position was a win for Deep Thought II, if the queens were traded off! We were shocked to hear that. Murray was the chess expert of the team, and he did not know about the possibility. Bjarke told us that once the queens were traded off, the pure "bishop of opposite color" ending would be won. Deep Thought II could then create two widely separated "passed pawns" (pawns that can no longer be inhibited or blocked by opposing enemy pawns), which would win despite the bishops of opposite color. The problem we had, however, was that Deep Thought II was explicitly programmed not to trade off its queen in this situation. We played on a little while longer, and then offered Bent the draw. After the match, thoroughly disgusted with this experience, I went through books on chess endings and added knowledge about all the "easy" endgame rules, including detailed rules on the "bishop of opposite color" endings, to the new chess chip.

The final tally for the Larsen match was Larsen 2.5 and Deep Thought II 1.5. The result was much better against the Danish National Team: Deep Thought II 3 and Danish team 1. The results, looking back today, are no longer important, but the match experience and the chess lessons we obtained from the trip were invaluable.

♗ CHAPTER 9

Bringing Up the Baby

Picking the Chip Vendor

At Carnegie Mellon, I never thought about the problem of choosing a chip vendor for the project. There was only one choice, MOSIS, the MOS Implementation Service. MOSIS provided low cost chips to the academic world by sharing the cost among multiple projects. NSF (National Science Foundation) and DARPA provided the funding for university MOSIS projects, and usually students had their chips fabricated for free.

To use the MOSIS service, I had to do the custom layout of the chip myself. Every single transistor for the 36,000-transistor chess move generator designed in 1985 was drawn by hand on a computer. I also hand routed every single wire on the chip. In 1986, when Teiji Nishizawa, my Japanese friend, visited Carnegie Mellon on his way to a conference, he was surprised that I managed to pack as many transistors as I did on a 3-micron CMOS chip. The commercial automatic layout tools at the time apparently did not do a very good job. I just had no idea how poor it was.

IBM Research had an excellent set of internal IC (Integrated Circuit) design tools that were said to be better than the commercial tools. IBM Microelectronics Division also had the most advanced IC processes, and still does. The problem was that when we started at IBM, IBM Microelectronics was set up for volume IBM internal production only. It was not set up to provide a silicon foundry service. Today IBM Microelectronics provides one of the best, if not *the* best service—if you want to build the fastest microprocessors using a foundry, you call IBM Microelectronics. In 1989, however, all the IBM researchers I met suggested that I find an outside chip vendor instead.

Among the US-based commercial silicon foundries, LSI Logic and VLSI Technology were the two main candidates. With both commercial silicon foundries, I no longer had to do the layout myself. All that I needed to do was to design the circuit, and our chosen vendor would complete the physical layout using their own in-house automatic layout tools. My initial thought was "This is going to be easy." The circuit design for the move generator chip used in ChipTest and Deep Thought took only a month. Okay, I would have to add in the one-month time used to verify the chip as well. That was still only two months. I reasoned, "The new chip should take no more than a year or two."

After some investigation, I was leaning towards VLSI Technology. In the early 1990s LSI Logic was concentrating more on the "gate array" business. In a gate array chip, all the transistors are prefabricated and the chip is customized by creating the metal inter-connection layers at the last steps. The gate array approach reduces the time from sending out the design to receiving the chip, but at the cost of circuit density and design flexibility. The main alternative is the "standard-cell" approach, which gives higher circuit density (by fabricating the transistors only where they are needed) than achievable with the gate array approach. The layout of the standard cell chips, however, could be automated in more or less the same way as the gate array chips. Furthermore, for chips that require sub-stantial on-chip memory, standard cell chips offer much better density, and improved performance. VLSI Technology had a more mature standard cell technology, but the clinching argument was their promise to lay out the custom circuit for detecting repeated chess positions, based on the design given in my PhD dissertation— for a tidy sum of money, of course. I would provide VLSI Technology with detailed transistor level schematics for the custom circuit.

During the evaluation of the tools from VLSI Technology, I did a trial layout of one square of a simplified chess move genera-tor. The trial layout was for a 0.8-micron CMOS process, which should have been about fourteen times denser than the 3-micron CMOS process that I used for the old move generator done in 1985. The trial layout generated by the automatic tool was only about twice as dense as my hand layout done in the 3-micron process. I was about seven times better at packing the transistors than the automatic tool. That was the good news. The bad news was that the automatic tool that I had to use was about seven times worse at packing the transistors than I was.

The poor packing density of automatic layout was the main reason for my decision to do a custom layout of the logic for detecting repeated chess positions. I thought the decision a necessary one, but it was a bad one. I would not make the same decision today. The custom design of the repetition detection logic interrupted the normal design flow, added new complexity to the design and delayed the chip design significantly. I spent over half a year just getting the transistor level logic correct for the repetition detector. The repetition detector was also the indirect cause of a traffic accident in which I was involved.

In the late spring of 1993, a few months after our Denmark trip, I delivered the final design data for the custom repetition detector to VLSI Technology's office in New Jersey. On my way back, a careless driver ran his car through a stop sign from a side road, only about twenty meters in front of me. It was a life-altering experience, but I would not recommend anyone to try it. When the other car suddenly burst onto the road in front of me, I thought that I was going to die and it would be the end of the project[1]. I managed to swerve my rental car sufficiently to avoid hitting the other car straight on. Had he seen me, and stopped in time, an accident would have been avoided. As it was, he went on without any regard to the road condition and a glancing collision took place. I was alive, but with the face bruised and cut by my glasses that were shattered in the impact with the air bag. I also had lacerations on my face and left arm. The occupants in the other car were uninjured. At a nearby hospital it was found that the cornea of my left eye had a nasty cut, and I had to wear an eye patch for a week. I did not really get back to serious work for about a month because of the problem with my eye[2]. By the time I got back to work, as a result of the prolonged break and possibly the trauma from the accident, I had a hard time understanding the existing design of the evaluation hardware. After spending about a

---

[1] When Andreas Nowatzyk read an early draft of this book, he was surprised at what I was thinking right before the accident. To me, the project was my life during this period. Also, I was returning from a business trip related to the project, and the project was on my mind. At that point in time, the survival of the project relied entirely on whether the new chess chip worked. Since I was the sole designer of the chip, if I had not survived the accident, the project would cease to exist.

[2] For over a year after the accident, I continued to have problems with my eyesight from time to time.

week going over the earlier design, I gave up and decided to redo the evaluation hardware from scratch. I had already spent about half a year on the evaluation hardware which was all wasted.

It got worse. In late 1994, when discussions about a potential match between Deep Blue and Garry Kasparov were initiated, the first version of the Deep Blue chess chip was still being designed. There was still no sign of the custom repetition detector from VLSI Technology after over a year. With time getting short, the decision was made to drop the custom repetition detector from the design. So the six months spent on designing the detector went down the drain as well. In total, the one bad decision to create a custom repetition detector delayed the project by one year. A pricey decision, not just in terms of the wasted time, but also in terms of a vastly weakened chess machine. While detecting repetition does not seem very important at first sight, as you will see later, it can have a very subtle influence on a chess program's positional play.

At about this time VLSI Technology decided to move the work to their Boston office. A few months later, when I delivered the first version of the complete netlist to VLSI's Boston office, *sans* the repetition detection logic, I saw the partial layout of the custom repetition detector. The layout was about five times bigger than I expected, with over 40 percent of the area occupied by two giant wire bundles crossing each other from one side to the other. An automatic tool would have caught the fact that the two halves could be interleaved like a comb, and the crossing wires should occupy very little area. So the custom layout somehow became much worse than an automatic layout. The engineer at VLSI's New Jersey office had been told that the wires should be interleaved, but somehow the information was never relayed to the layout technician. We never would have accepted the custom layout as it was, even if we had the time to wait for its completion.

Today, if I design another chess chip or any other chip, I would approach the chip vendor decision quite differently. The semiconductor industry has changed quite a bit since the late 1980s. Then, chip designers designed the circuit with schematics, often using chip vendor specific tools. From the early 1990s, chip designers turned to language-based logic synthesis tools, describing the chip in hardware description languages and relying on automatic logic synthesis tools to create the netlist. The chip could be designed without a specific chip vendor in mind. The designer could pick the chip vendor very late in the design process since there is only a small penalty to switch the chip vendor. Alas, when the chess project was started, I did not have this luxury. By the time synthesis tools became widely used, IBM was in serious financial trouble and there was no money to acquire the new tools. The Deep Blue chess chips were designed almost entirely using circuit schematics even though there were far better design tools available near the end of the project. We also did not have many choices on the chip technology front as a result of using vendor-specific tools. The 1997 rematch between Garry Kasparov and Deep Blue was played using 0.6-micron CMOS chips, even though the industry had already moved on to 0.35 micron CMOS technology and beyond [3]. Anyway, the reasons for choosing VLSI Technology over LSI Logic would no longer be valid today. In particular, I would also avoid any custom layout like the plague, unless I have full control over it.

At the time that we made the decision, choosing VLSI Technology was probably as good as any other choice. In the final count, VLSI delivered their end of the new agreement. So everything did turn out all right. There were better choices on the design tools later on, but we were in no position to make the choice, given the tight IBM budget at the time. By the time IBM's finances were back on track, the design was already close to completion and it was too late to change the tools.

Murphy's Law

Serious negotiations between IBM, Garry Kasparov, and the ACM (Association for Computing Machinery), which was the main sanctioning organization for the big match, were taking place in late 1994. The match was to be held in February 1996 to coincide with the celebration marking the 50th anniversary of ACM. The design of the Deep Blue chess chip was near completion, but there was still the huge task of verifying its correctness. Murray and Joe agreed to drop what they were doing and help with the chip verification. Deep Thought II was turned off and disconnected because we needed its host computer, which was our only machine with sufficient main memory to run the chip simulation. We were expecting to turn Deep Thought II back on for a few test games

---

[3] The chess chips would have been about twice as fast if we had had access to the better technology. The die area should reduce by about a factor of four, which would improve the chip yield quite dramatically.

when the new chess machine became operational; otherwise, as far as we were concerned, Deep Thought II was no more.

The ICCA (International Computer Chess Association) held a World Computer Chess Championship tournament triennially. They approached IBM to sponsor the event, to be held in Hong Kong in May 1995. We had won the event in 1989, but did not participate in 1992. If it had been entirely up to me, we probably would have skipped the event again. Murray, Joe and I were already swamped with the chip work as it seemed far more important to make sure that we would be ready for Garry Kasparov.

However, our manager, C J Tan, had a different idea. Seeing the championship as a chance to add publicity to the match with Garry, he arranged to get the funding for the championship and agreed to participate. There was a slim chance that the new chess chip might be available for the Hong Kong event, but it soon became clear that it would not even be ready for fabrication by then. The only other choice was to compete with Deep Thought II.

Jerry Present, our communications person at the time, wanted to use the name Deep Blue Prototype instead of Deep Thought II. I wanted to use the name Deep Thought II. My reasoning was as follows. Deep Blue, the new machine, would be at least 100 times faster than Deep Thought II in effective search speed, and furthermore, Deep Blue would have a far better grasp of positional concepts in chess. Comparing Deep Blue with Deep Thought II would be like comparing the sun with the moon. Well, I exaggerate a little bit, but the difference in computation power was roughly of the order of a thousand to one, taking into account the far more complicated chess evaluation computation carried out on the Deep Blue chess chips. I was proud of what had been done, and did not want anything to be linked to Deep Blue unless it did use the new chips. Deep Thought II was still using the chess chips that I designed back in 1985. As far as I was concerned, Deep Thought II was a dinosaur about to become extinct. It was not going to usurp the name of our new megaton solar blaster, even if only partially.

Jerry, however, persuaded C J to stick with the name Deep Blue Prototype. The Communications Department would like to be able to say that Deep Blue was the successor to the reigning World Computer Chess Champion, Deep Blue Prototype, at the time of the match with Garry Kasparov. In the "unlikely" case that Deep Thought II did not win the championship, then it was not really

Deep Blue playing anyway. The problem was that, given the Swiss tournament format of the championship, the "unlikely" was highly probable. Despite the fact that Deep Thought II beat our closest competitors by about a three to one margin (or 200 rating points difference in computer vs. computer play) in lab tests, our chance of winning the championship was only about 50–50. There were twenty-four competing teams, and only five rounds of games would be played. With so few rounds, luck played a very important part in winning the tournament. We were the strongest, but there were about five or six teams just one class below, and another three to five teams only slightly weaker than they. The team, Murray, Joe, and I, all knew about our real chances given the format. Randy Moulic, our first manager, also would have known about the odds, having gone through a 1990 ACM Championship that we did not win outright. But C J had only been through the 1994 ACM Championship with us. In that one event, Deep Thought II won the title outright, even though we forfeited one game when a sudden storm in New York knocked out the electric power to the lab [4].

Deep Thought II remained turned off until about a month before the Hong Kong event. Murray spent a small amount of time preparing it for the championship. The final verification work on the new chip was still going on, and we did not have much manpower to spare. We had to free up some of Murray's time, as he was the chess expert. We had never been so cavalier in our preparation for a computer chess event, save for ChipTest's first outing. Then, we did not care whether we won or not, and for this last outing of Deep Thought II, our main concern was keeping the date with Garry, nine months away.

It seems that things usually go wrong when you are least prepared. As Murphy's Law predicts, everything that could go wrong soon went wrong.

Murray and I, traveling with C J, flew to Hong Kong to be the on-site operators. Joe stayed behind to watch over Deep Thought II. It was the first time since the start of the chess project in 1985 that I had been back to Asia, it was also my first trip to Hong Kong.

The first hint of potential trouble exhibited itself when Murray and I went to the playing site, the Chinese University of Hong Kong. The Internet connection to the United States was not

---

4   This event will be described in the next chapter. The first discussions I had about the first Deep Blue match took place at the end of the event.

quite working; for that matter, neither was the connection to Europe. The three main universities in Hong Kong used a common carrier, which had a limited capacity, for all their Internet connections. Before the event, the teams with computers on remote sites had tried out Internet connections *into* Hong Kong from their home countries, and they appeared fine. But getting *out* of Hong Kong using an Internet connection was almost impossible, at least during the tournament. It looked as though the remote teams might have to pay very expensive long distance phone bills.

As it happened, the day before the championship IBM Hong Kong had announced an IBM Internet service for Hong Kong. This service was usable although the connection seemed to drop from time to time. It might have been a problem with the local phone service, since we were having problems when we dialed long distance as well. (In 1997, I was back in Hong Kong doing a Deep Blue demo via the IBM Internet connection, and it went smoothly. So the communication problem we had in 1995 might not be with the Internet connection at all.) The phone line problem became an important factor in the last game played by Deep Thought II.

Our first round opponent was Star Socrates, a parallel chess program from MIT, running on a multi-million-dollar supercomputer—a machine about a hundred times more expensive than the workstation that Deep Thought II ran on. Star Socrates was considered our most dangerous opponent. Its search speed was at least comparable to Deep Thought II. When Deep Thought II played Star Socrates the year before, I saw for the first time a program that actually "out-searched" Deep Thought II—it was reporting search depths larger than Deep Thought II's. Yet Deep Thought II had outclassed it easily. Would one year make a difference? Deep Thought II had been off line for over half a year, and the MIT folk were probably not sitting idle. In 1994, Deep Thought II had played a regular chess opening, but with only one month of opening preparation for the Hong Kong event, Murray opted to play an irregular opening to take both programs out of their opening books. The game became a contest of raw chess playing strength. I was not too happy with Murray's opening choice; we had White, and yet we had a slightly worse position out of the opening. Deep Thought II, however, soon overpowered Star Socrates.

For the next two rounds, Deep Thought II continued to play irregular openings; we won both games and led the field by one full game. I continued to mumble to Murray about the bad openings. In retrospect, I should have kept quiet. Murray chose to play irregular openings out of necessity—there was no time to do proper opening preparation. Deep Thought II was a better player than the rest of the field, and by taking other programs out of their opening books, Murray gave our opponents a longer rope with which to hang themselves.

Our fourth opponent was WChess, one of our tougher opponents. Deep Thought II played a normal opening this time. The position was even when both programs came out of their opening books. Deep Thought II soon found a way to win a pawn and had a winning position, but WChess had some counter play. Deep Thought II made one bad move and its position deteriorated. Almost immediately after this, Deep Thought II found that WChess had a way to draw the game. WChess did not see the draw at this point, but it played the right moves. Deep Thought II suddenly found its bishop was close to being trapped and it had to give up material to keep the bishop. WChess was about to go ahead in material. It was a fast turn of events. At this point WChess saw the draw, and soon also saw that it would be ahead. Luckily for us, Deep Thought II had enough pull before its bad move, and despite the bad move we were able to hold the draw. After this game, I was a little bit uneasy about our decision to drop the repetition detector from the design of the new chess chip. If Deep Thought II had had the ability to detect repetition in hardware, it would have found where the bad move would have led and played a better move instead.

Nonetheless, we still led the field by half a game, and our last round opponent was Fritz, an easy opponent for us. Fritz's strong point was its tactics, but Deep Thought II was a far better tactician; in fact, it won about nine out of ten games against Fritz in our pre-tournament tests back at IBM. I was exhausted on the way back to our hotel. The previous few days, I had been complaining about the bad openings. By this time, especially after the not so good result in round 4, I was of the opinion that the irregular opening approach had been a very good idea. Given the relatively weak positional sense of Fritz, an irregular opening should work really well. For once, I kept quiet when I should have spoken up. When I went to sleep that night, I was expecting Murray to cook up some irregular opening for Fritz. The next day brought a big surprise.

Murray went to the playing site early and chatted with some

of the other participants. One told him that Fritz had a horrible opening book, and had lost one of its games right out of the opening book. Murray took the comment seriously and decided to use a normal opening against Fritz. After all, if Fritz had been a piece of cake when we played irregular openings, it would be even easier if we played a real opening, especially given that Fritz had a bad opening book. Murray did not tell me about his decision before the game. Deep Thought II opened with a king pawn opening, and I gave Murray a quizzical glance. Fritz replied with a sharp line in the Sicilian Defense. A clever "transposition" (deliberate swapping of opening moves from their normal playing sequence) on the part of the author of the Fritz opening book took Deep Thought II, out of its own opening book. There were four main move choices for Deep Thought II, and two of them were castling moves that normally take the king out of the center into the safer wing positions. Both castling moves, probably by design of the author of the Fritz opening book, were bad in this position. Deep Thought II assessed the position as favorable for itself and wanted to castle. Murray's face turned white. The position looked precarious for us. It was the first move out of the opening book for Deep Thought II, and it was spending extra time on the move. Perhaps there was some hope that Deep Thought II would play a safer move. Suddenly we got disconnected. According to Joe, who was watching the game from our lab in Hawthorne, Deep Thought II did switch to an alternative move. But the new move never showed up on our screen in Hong Kong before the line drop, and we did not know about it until after the game.

The MIT Star Socrates team was using a program that allowed them to reconnect to their chess program without the need to restart. Had we used the same program, we would have reconnected, found the new move already played by Deep Thought II on its internal board, and played it on the real chessboard. As it was, we had to restart Deep Thought II, which now had less time to spend on the position. Compounded by the fact that it was started "cold" without the help of previous calculations and thus probably a factor of two slower effectively, Deep Thought II could no longer find the more reasonable alternative move.

After Fritz's next move, the evaluation of Deep Thought II dropped to a repetition draw. So it was a repetition detector problem as well! If Deep Thought II had had a hardware repetition detector, it would have avoided the bad castling move, with or without the line drop. I was feeling even worse about the decision to drop the hardware repetition detector from the new chip.

Our position against Fritz was getting bad, but it was not hopeless. We continued to have problems with the communication line. We muddled along, losing precious time on our clock, but we were not busted yet. Then it hit. Deep Thought II found the move that it wanted to play, was losing, and entered into the "panic time" state where it would spend extra time to find an alternative move. Grandmaster Robert Byrne, the *New York Times* chess columnist who was the honored guest of ICCA, dropped by and whispered that Deep Thought II had to play a certain move to keep the position alive. The move intended by Deep Thought II was not the move that Robert suggested. We watched helplessly as Deep Thought II spun its wheels, trying to find a good alternative. The search appeared to be exploding—Deep Thought II was suddenly searching a much larger tree. Several of the alternative moves were rejected. Would Robert's move be found in time? The clock was ticking. Time was up. Deep Thought II played its originally intended move as nothing better had come up. The game was effectively over. Fritz did not play the best attacking moves, but it was good enough to win the busted position, and we resigned for Deep Thought II. Fritz ended up winning the tournament after beating Star Socrates, when it self-destructed in their playoff game.

The tournament taught us several things. From my point of view, the most important was that if I ever got another chance to make a newer version of the chess chip, it must have a hardware repetition detector. There were other lessons too. We had to take opening preparations far more seriously, and we must have good backup plans whenever we played remotely. We should be able to reconnect to the chess program in the same way as the MIT team, and we should test out the communication lines thoroughly beforehand. We could not do anything for the hardware repetition detector problem before the match with Garry, but we certainly could do something about the communication issues.

The decision to use the name "Deep Blue Prototype" also came back to haunt us. Several computer chess vendors renamed "Deep Blue Prototype" to "Deep Blue" when describing their result from the Hong Kong event. One went as far as saying that their program beat both Garry Kasparov (in blitz games) and Deep Blue (it never played Deep Blue). Although, to be fair to them, the vendors probably would have done the same even if we had used the name Deep Thought II.

Four Hours to Spare

Although we dropped the plan to use the new chess chip for the Hong Kong tournament, there was another event where it would have to be used. IBM Research was planning to open a new research lab in Beijing, China, and we were invited to play a friendly match with Xie Jun, the Women's World Chess Champion, as a part of the opening celebration. The Beijing match was scheduled for late September 1995. A clause in the match contract with Garry Kasparov stated that IBM could terminate the match contract on or before 31 October 1995. The team was not told explicitly that we had to do well in the Beijing match but, given the time proximity, the link was clear.

In late August 1995, VLSI Technology gave us some disturbing news. None of the chips in the first batch passed the manufacturing test. They sent us some of the better behaving chips in early September. The Xie Jun match was scheduled for September 21, less than three weeks away. It was a very tight schedule even if the chips had passed.

At the time we got the news from VLSI Technology, Joe had started porting the Deep Thought II software to the new hardware. I had received the printed circuit boards for the new chips a few weeks earlier and had done the basic tests on them. Now, Joe and I were in for some fun time together.

The basic tests for the printed circuit boards simply checked whether the boards could be initialized properly. I had prepared more advanced tests for testing the chip with the board. None of the chips passed the simplest of the advanced tests that checked the connectivity of the bus wires to and from the chips. The problem could be with the board or it could be with the chips. The basic tests for the boards used only 8 bits of the 32-bit Microchannel bus in the IBM RS/6000 workstation. The advanced test used all 32 bits to check out the chip operations. It was possible that there were something wrong with the 24 untested bus bits. Using an ohmmeter[5], I checked the connections between the chips, and the Microchannel bus on the board, and found that physically the wires were connected, but somehow they were con-

---

5 An ohmmeter is an electric meter used to measure electrical resistance.

nected incorrectly. It turned out that the RS/6000 workstation interpreted the 32 bits differently from the printed circuit board. In technical terms, this is the so-called "byte swapping" problem. The 32 bits can be divided into 4 bytes, with each byte having 8 bits. The workstation assumed that the 4 bytes were ordered in a certain way, while the board assumed that the 4 bytes were ordered in a different way. Okay, this was not pleasant, but the problem could be bypassed by reinterpreting the 32 bits in software.

After the software change, the chips started to pass some of my tests, but they all failed on one of the simpler tests. Worse, even the same chip failed differently from one test run to another. So, the problem was probably not with VLSI Technology's manufacturing test setup. Something peculiar was going on inside the chip. I tried out all sorts of hypotheses. Since the chip worked during the pre-fabrication simulation, the most likely cause had to be some sort of electrical problem. The question was what type of electrical problem. In one of the trial tests, there seemed to be some pattern sensitivity in the chip's behavior. The chip appeared to behave differently depending on what was last read out from it. To test out whether there was indeed a pattern-specific sensitivity, I tried setting the last readout to be a 32-bit zero before doing a failed read operation from the chip. The chip now passed the test that it had previously failed. I then added a read operation that appeared to read out zeros reliably before every normal read operation, and the chip passed all the modified tests. I informed VLSI Technology about the finding and sent them the revised manufacturing test vectors, so that we could get factory prescreening on all the incoming chips as soon as possible.

There was still the problem of what was causing the chips' strange behavior. I tried setting the extra read operation to read out 32 bits of 1s, and again the chip worked. I now strongly suspected that the cause of the problem was some sort of "cross coupling" among the 32-bit output bus wires on the chip. When one of the bus wires switches, say, from 1 to 0, the adjacent wires could experience a spurious voltage drop due to *cross coupling* through the capacitances [6], between the switching wire and the adjacent wires.

---

[6] This is not strictly correct, but a high capacitance between two wires can be viewed as a small (imaginary) resistance during high frequency switching. So the voltage changes from one wire will be "conducted" through the capacitance to the other wire, especially when the capacitance is high.

The cross coupling effects were not too important in older chip technologies, but with the more advanced technologies the wire spacing was much smaller, and the capacitances between the wires went up to the point that cross coupling could not be ignored.

The engineer from VLSI Technology did not believe my cross coupling theory at first, but after going over the capacitance values for the output bus wires with me, he agreed that it was plausible.

What could be done to avoid the cross coupling problem? We could space the bus wires further apart to reduce the inter-wire coupling capacitance. Alternatively, shielding wires could be introduced between the bus wires. There were probably some other simple solutions. The software from VLSI Technology did not provide any ready answer. One solution at my disposal was to give the output bus more time to settle before reading the output value. Of course, that would require a modification to the circuit design, and re-fabricating the chips.

Anyway, feeling that all the chip problems were resolved, I sent an e-mail to the rest of the team summarizing my findings. The next morning, I received a message from Joe Hoane. When Joe inherited the Deep Thought II code, he added a massive amount of code for program self-testing. Using the self-testing code, Joe found a repeatable problem with the chip even after adding in the preread operation. After a long night, Joe meticulously pinned down the problem to something related to the *en passant* chess moves. The *en passant* rule is one of my least favorite rules in chess. Over half a year of my life was wasted fixing problems related to *en passant* in one chess machine after another. It took me half a day to understand the precise nature of the problem. I had made a subtle logic design error. The chip misbehaved under certain conditions when Black had an *en passant* move. The easiest temporary solution that I could think of was to use two chess chips simultaneously, one of the chips having the regular board, and the other having the board flipped by 180 degrees with White pieces becoming Black pieces, and vice versa. By comparing the two chips, the problems could be located on the fly and fixed in software. Adding the pre-read operation had already made the chess program far more complicated. The new board flipping operation, combined with the pre-read operation, probably increased the amount of code tenfold. Joe had about one week left to fix the software and find out whether there was any other showstopper before I was to hop on the plane to Beijing. Murray, who was creating the software for the new evaluation function hardware, also suddenly had some new tasks to perform. Using two chips simultaneously introduced several complications that had to be resolved in the evaluation software.

Joe uncovered some additional problems but no new major one with the chip. I quickly made changes to the chip design and gave the engineer at VLSI Technology the new netlist. We had just enough time to get a new batch of chips for the match in February 1996.

Joe worked very long hours during the entire week, and the new program was still not quite working. We made a tape containing a snapshot of the software. On 18 September, I got on the plane with the tape and a printed circuit board with two chess chips on it. Joe had about sixty-four hours left to create a program that used the new chips to play chess. Murray stayed behind in case Joe needed any help. C J Tan took the trip too, to help smooth things over in Beijing.

The plane trip was uneventful. I checked with Joe the morning after my arrival; the new program was still being worked on, but he had some things that he wanted me to look over. C J and I visited the IBM Beijing Research Lab during the day to do the preliminary setup. I tried to connect to the United States but the phone line only worked intermittently, and it was impossible to retrieve anything. The Beijing Lab was in a newly developed area that only a few years back was farmland. In fact there was still farmland nearby at the time of my visit. Apparently, the rapid economic development in Beijing had put serious strain on the phone line capacity, and the service in the outlying areas of the city suffered as a result.

After I got back to the hotel, I checked with Joe on the status of the new program. The match was to take place the next afternoon. Joe had something that almost worked, and he believed that he would be able to send a playing program to me in time for the match, via the IBM internal network. The next morning, an employee from IBM China Headquarters brought a floppy disk to the playing site. There were four hours left to the match. The program on the floppy disk was loaded onto the workstation hard disk, and I did some simple tests. Yes, the program appeared to be working. Joe had put in a heroic effort. Well, there was not much to do but wait and pray.

Xie Jun, a petite young lady in her early twenties, used to play Chinese chess before she received Chinese government sponsored training for "western" chess. She then burst onto the world chess scene, and surprised the chess establishment by winning the Women's World Chess Championship, becoming the first Asian to do so. As our match was a friendly one, Xie Jun got to choose the time control. I don't have a record of what time control was used, but it was probably twenty minutes for the game, with an additional twenty seconds after each move. No game score was kept which gave Xie Jun an opportunity to try out new opening ideas without worrying about revealing her secrets. We agreed beforehand to play two games. The audience sat in a nearby room linked to the playing room via a closed circuit video hookup. Xie Jun's coach gave a running commentary to the audience.

In the first game, Xie Jun apparently tried out one of her new openings. The 4-hour-old program got into trouble pretty quickly after the opening phase. On one of her moves, Xie Jun slowed down and studied the position. At this point the new program had a big score drop. There was a killer move for Xie Jun but she did not see it, and played a move that should have been good enough to win. It was, however, interesting to observe that she slowed down at the precise moment when there was a kill. After a few more moves, the new program crashed. There was an *en passant* possibility for Black that somehow crashed the program. When I tried to restart the program, I accidentally wiped out the internal score file that it kept. Xie Jun graciously agreed to play a new game. Precisely the same game got played. Once again, Xie Jun slowed down at the critical position. She must have sensed that there was a better move that she could play. With the short time control, she again missed the killer move, but her move was good enough. The program crashed again at the same point[7]. This time I somehow managed to get the program restarted. We played on a little while, then the program crashed again in a similar fashion. Since the program's position was getting pretty bad, we conceded the first game without trying to restart.

After the first game, Xie Jun mentioned that she must have missed a killer move in the critical position. I confirmed her suspicion and told her what the program had calculated it to be. After a short break, we started the second game. This time the new program played without any crashes. Xie Jun fell into a tactical bind,

[7] We never found the bug that caused the crashes in this version of the program. By the time that I got back from China, Joe had the program working properly.

and resigned as soon as the position became hopeless. I was relieved that she did not play on. The program could very well crash again if the game went on much longer.

So the Beijing match was tied at one to one, and our match date with Garry Kasparov was still on.

"No Computer Will Ever Beat Me"

When I was at Carnegie Mellon, the graduate student organization in the Computer Science Department operated a Coke machine that dispensed cheap bottled Coke for thirty-five cents a bottle. The proceeds were the main funding source for many of the TG parties in the Department. About a year or two into my stay at Carnegie Mellon, some graduate students and engineering staff got together and decided to make an electronic interface for the Coke machine. It then became possible to "finger" it electronically from the confines of one's office, and find out whether any cold bottles were left in the machine. In fact, you could finger the Coke machine in Pittsburgh, Pennsylvania from, say, Palo Alto, California, although this capability probably offered very little utility.

The Coke machine was located on the third floor of my building. My office was on the eighth floor so I fingered it a lot, until I found an alternative supply—one of the bigger offices on my floor had a large refrigerator that was used as an auxiliary Coke machine by a few students, who, in exchange for the privilege, would help load up the refrigerator from the storage room on the 3rd floor.

Jay Sipelstein was an occupant of this big office. Jay had received his Bachelor degree from Yale University and while he was there, he used to hang around the Yale Chess Club. One day, Jay mentioned to me that there was a Yale student—an International Master—who would give simultaneous exhibitions in the chess club and beat everybody. He said that someone had asked the International Master whether he thought any computer would ever beat him. The International Master answered, "No computer will ever beat me." At the time he made the boast, he probably had good reasons to be smug. A few years before, he had been on a television show slaughtering Cray Blitz in blitz games. He was also an up-and-comer. The year after the International Master graduated from Yale, he became a Grandmaster. The name of this new Grandmaster was Joel Benjamin.

The tied match against Xie Jun in Beijing kept the match against

Garry Kasparov alive. Xie Jun was a Grandmaster, but our friendly exhibition was played at a shortened time control, and we wanted to play some test matches under more serious conditions.

We did not have the full power of Deep Blue, which would be about thirty times faster than the machine we had, so playing at an even level with Grandmasters at a regulation tournament time control would be a satisfactory result. We scheduled to play in our lab, two games each, against three leading US Grandmasters. The Grandmasters were offered incentives to try to win the match or, failing that, to try to draw the match. We were also using the test matches to screen for a Grandmaster to help with the opening preparation for the match against Garry Kasparov, but none of the Grandmasters knew about the job opening. We always knew that we would need a Grandmaster on the team in the final match. Of course, the Hong Kong incident had also made that crystal clear.

Deep Blue Jr, the scaled down machine, won one of the matches, drew another, and lost one.

The winning Grandmaster was none other than Joel Benjamin. Deep Blue Jr was in the very early stages of its development, so losing one of the matches was not a big surprise. The way Joel won the match 2–0, however, was a big surprise.

The first game against Joel was a typical computer affair. Deep Blue Jr misjudged the endgame position, and Joel's positional judgment proved superior. We knew that there was lots of room for improvement in Deep Blue Jr's evaluation function, so there was nothing to be alarmed about.

The second game was a long one. It started in the afternoon and finished late at night. When the endgame phase was reached, it was clear that Joel was better but the position was probably drawn. The incentives offered were for winning or drawing the match, so the practical thing for Joel to do was to offer a draw, win the match, take the cheque, and say thank you. Joel pressed on. Murray and I were getting hungry by now. For a short while, it appeared that Joel was not making progress. But somehow he slowly and patiently tricked Deep Blue Jr into making one slight mistake after another, until he got complete control of the situation. He then pressured Deep Blue Jr to finally give up material, and shortly afterwards we resigned for the program.

After walking Joel out of the building, Murray and I were silent for a while. There was a lot of work ahead, but we also both knew that we had found the person to do the opening preparation for Deep Blue. Joel did not know it yet, but we had found the last piece of the puzzle. The question was whether we had enough time to create something that could beat Garry Kasparov in February 1996.

🐴 CHAPTER 10

A Living Mount Everest

At a Seaside Resort

I became aware of the ACM's interest in hosting a Kasparov vs. Deep Blue match under unusual circumstances, well before the Hong Kong event.

While I was working on the Deep Blue chess chip, I considered attending computer chess events a nuisance. Even if I had not been involved with the preparation for the event, I knew perfectly well that I would not be able to do any serious work on the chess chip for a few weeks—I could not stop myself from following our progress in the event.

When the 1994 ACM Computer Chess Championship came along, I was against going. The chess chip design work was entering the critical final phase, and given that the entire project hinged on the chip working, it seemed foolhardy to waste time on a tournament, albeit an important one. Monty Newborn, the organizer of the ACM event, and a good friend of C J Tan, persuaded him to enter Deep Thought II into the Championship, and I was overruled.

It turned out that both Murray and Joe had already scheduled their vacations around the time of the championship. Joe might be able to show up for the closing part of the championship, but would definitely miss the early part. I was the only person who could go to the ACM event and operate the program.

The championship was held in Cape May, a seaside resort town at the southern tip of New Jersey, about a four-hour drive from our lab in Hawthorne. Since there was not much I could do to avoid the "obligation" to go, I treated the trip as a vacation from the chip design work[1]. In that sense, the drive was quite pleasant—a scenic route, sun, fresh air, and lots of sea breeze. At the hotel, I bumped into several members of the other teams. Everyone was trying to feel each other out. Who would be dangerous this year? Star Socrates from MIT was attracting a lot of attention, as it would be the first program since Deep Thought II to cross over the one million positions per second mark.

On the first day of the tournament, the weather turned stormy. What I did not know was that the storm was much worse in Hawthorne. Our first round meeting was with Zarkov, a respectable opponent. Prior to the tournament, Murray had been experimenting with the King's Gambit opening. The King's Gambit is a violent opening dating back to the romantic age of chess in the 19th century. It is rarely seen these days at top-level chess events. It is also probably not a sound opening for White. Murray had found some opening innovations for White in the King's Gambit with the help of Deep Thought II, and wanted to try them out. Zarkov, however, was not cooperating. It played a line that led to a position which Murray had not examined and it was a good, possibly even a winning, position for Black. Deep Thought II was not too happy about the situation it found itself in, but there was no obvious kill for Black. All the other teams who came by our table thought that we were lost. To tell the truth, I was not too concerned, but I should have been. Ignorance is bliss. Had he been present, Murray would have been blaming himself. I had seen Deep Thought II win brilliantly using the King's Gambit, even though it usually did not like White's position out of the opening. I just did not know that the position on the chessboard gave us no counter chance, if Zarkov had known how to play it correctly. With Zarkov's unwitting help, Deep Thought II seized enough opportunities, and eventually John Stanback, the author of Zarkov, resigned for Zarkov as soon as the position became hopeless. Neither he nor I knew at the time that if the game had lasted for another half-hour, Deep Thought II would have had to forfeit.

While our game against Zarkov was going on, a sudden downpour took place in Hawthorne. Over two inches of rain fell within an hour, and the buildup of water shorted the transformer provid-

---

1   With the heavy pressure to complete the chip, I had not taken any real vacation days for years by then. IBM did not allow their employees to accumulate vacation days from one year to another. I ended up going to work on "vacation" days. It was a sacrifice that I will not make again.

ing power to the lab. For the last half-hour of the game against Zarkov, Deep Thought II was using the battery power of our UPS (Uninterruptible Power Supply) backup. The battery could last only an hour or so, and it ran out of power by the second round. I found that I could not connect to Deep Thought II at all, so I asked for a time-out from the tournament director to investigate what was going on. I phoned Jerry Brody, our support engineer [2], and the only person in the group not out of town, and asked him to get into the lab to find out what went wrong. Twenty minutes later, Jerry gave me the bad news. There was no power in the lab, and there was no estimate about when it would be back. With the consent of our opponent, the tournament director granted us more time. In computer chess events, there is usually a provision for unlimited communication time-out. Power failure was never explicitly covered in the rules, although an argument could be made that it was equivalent to a communication failure. By eleven pm, we still could not get the machine back. Our opponent was asked whether the game could be rescheduled to the next day; he declined and we forfeited the game without playing a single move. The machine was up and running at about one am, but it was too late. (Eighteen months later, during the first Kasparov vs. Deep Blue match, we informed the electric company about our power requirements. After seeing the front-page news that the match was making, the company made special arrangements to ensure a continuous supply of electric power to IBM Research Lab. They certainly did not like the prospect of getting worldwide notoriety for causing Deep Blue to lose a game due to a power failure on their part!)

Back to the tournament. The event was a five-round Swiss. For all practical purposes, losing one round by forfeit pretty much eliminated our chance of winning the tournament. The best we could do would be 4 points out of 5. Based on past experience, this was usually insufficient to win a tournament like this one. I was feeling miserable.

Our third round opponent was WChess which put up a stiff fight, but Deep Thought II won without too much trouble. The fourth round opponent was Star Socrates, whom we would face

---

2 Jerry had been with the team ever since we joined IBM. He did not really get involved with the technical work of Deep Blue, but was more of a provider of general support, including parts acquisition and order/contract processing.

again a year later in Hong Kong. During the game, the MIT team was very pleased to observe that Star Socrates was reporting "greater" search depth than Deep Thought II. At this stage of the tournament, Star Socrates was the only team with a perfect score. It also had White, so the MIT team must have felt that they had a great chance to win the event. Just as in Hong Kong a year later, Deep Thought II won the game relatively smoothly, even though there were anxious moments in both games. After all, anything that searches over a million positions per second is not something to be taken lightly, and Star Socrates was definitely a contender.

The fifth round pairing became very interesting. The only program that remained undefeated was Mchess, the second round opponent against whom we had forfeited. Mchess had conceded only one draw. Normally, in a Swiss tournament, you would not play any of your opponents twice in the same tournament. But Mchess and Deep Thought II never did really play each other, and Deep Thought II had already played all the other top programs, with the sole exception of Mchess. So Deep Thought II played Mchess again, this time for real, and won the game fairly quickly. The tournament now became a question of whether Star Socrates could win its last game against Zarkov, in which case it would tie for first. Star Socrates lost, and Deep Thought II won the title cleanly, despite the second round forfeit.

The next morning, I had a good breakfast in the hotel. The sun was shining. The beach looked enticing, and Deep Thought II had pulled off an impossible feat. I was in a very good mood. Monty Newborn, the tournament organizer, asked whether he and his friend could join me. Monty introduced his friend as Frank Friedman, a professor from Temple University near Philadelphia. Frank was also Monty's boss in the ACM organization. Monty and Frank asked me when the new chess chip would be ready, and I told them that it should be available some time the following year. Monty then broached the real subject. He asked, "Would IBM be interested in playing a match with Garry Kasparov during the ACM Annual Conference in 1996?" This was getting interesting. I answered, "I don't speak for IBM, but I would imagine so." Then I added, "The match would be quite expensive." Monty said that he expected the prize fund for the match to be something like $300,000 to $400,000. I told him I believed that the prize fund would have to be much higher, because the match would have greater historical importance than a regular World Chess

Championship match. The last World Chess Championship match had a prize fund of well over one million dollars. I told Monty and Frank, "I would be very surprised if Garry settles for anything less than a million dollars." Monty had some ideas of his own, "Well, if we only play, say, six games, then we could get the prize fund down." "Perhaps", I answered without much conviction. We concluded the conversation without making any real commitment. ACM would start talking with Garry and get his feedback. I placed their odds of getting Kasparov on board at 1 in 5.

The ACM people proved me wrong. Garry eventually agreed to play a six-game match against Deep Blue in Philadelphia for a total prize fund of $500,000, with $400,000 to the winner, and $100,000 to the loser. Garry was so confident of winning the match that he agreed to it without demanding more money. In fact, he wanted the match to be all or nothing with the loser getting nothing but was eventually talked out of the idea. IBM Research put up the prize fund. Deep Blue's share of the prize would go back to IBM to fund more research, not necessarily in computer chess. ACM was scheduling the match as part of its 50th anniversary celebration. 1996 was also the 50th anniversary for ENIAC, the first electronic computer, and ENIAC was built near Philadelphia. Therefore, ACM decided to kick off its year-long celebration in Philadelphia, and the Kasparov vs. Deep Blue match (10–17 February 1996) was the first event on the agenda. The match was to be played at the rate of one game per day, with one rest day following every two game days. The game days were 10, 11, 13, 14, 16 and 17 February.

Winter in Philadelphia

In December 1995, two months before the Philadelphia match, we received a small batch of the revised chess chips from VLSI Technology. The chips worked properly this time. There was no more need to do the pre-reading operation. There were no more problems with *en passant*, and no more chip mirroring. Grandmaster Joel Benjamin agreed to be Deep Blue's match second. The time remaining until the match was so short that his main function was limited to preparing the opening moves. Since most of the chips were still in VLSI's testing and packaging lines, Deep Blue did not really exist yet, and Joel did pretty much all his opening preparation on Deep Blue Jr, the scaled down workstation version of Deep Blue.

About two weeks before the match, the remainder of the chips arrived. It took the better half of a week to test them all out, and then two days or so to load them up into the IBM RS/6000 SP supercomputer, that was to be Deep Blue's host. We had barely enough time before the match to test out all the hardware, and do the basic software testing on the big machine. We also did not have as many chess chips as we would have liked.

Given our experience in Hong Kong, we decided to set up two backup machines at the playing site in Philadelphia, with the main RS/6000 SP supercomputer staying behind at the lab in Yorktown Heights, New York[3]. One backup machine was a regular IBM RS/6000 workstation running the Deep Blue Jr program. The other machine was a small four-way RS/6000 SP supercomputer, with four workstation nodes. The main machine was a thirty-six-way[4] RS/6000 SP supercomputer. Theoretically, with a thirty-six-way machine, the system could have up to 576 chess chips working together, with sixteen chess chips per workstation node. Due to the limited number of chess chips available, each node on the main machine only had six chips, for an aggregate of 216 chess chips total. The chess chips in this batch searched about 1.6 million positions per second, and the theoretical maximum search speed of this first Deep Blue was about 300 million positions per second. The observed search speed was about 100 million positions per second. The software overhead associated with running the search in parallel was quite high. We probably could have speeded up the machine by up to a factor of two, if we had had another six months to work on the software.

The chess chips evaluated the chess positions in far more detail than possibly any other chess program that had ever existed. Almost all the evaluation function terms were computed directly on chip[5]. As it was, to perform the same computation on a general purpose computer, as that done by the 1996 Deep Blue, would

---

3 We had moved from Hawthorne, New York to the main IBM Research lab in Yorktown Heights, New York.

4 This is the real number. At the time of the match, C J Tan gave out the number of host CPUs as 32. We were instructed to stick to the number 32 to avoid confusion. The 36-way machine consisted of two 16-CPU frames plus four workstations.

5 The software evaluation function assigned weights for the evaluation terms, instead of computing the evaluation function itself as in typical chess programs.

need at least a one trillion instructions per second general-purpose system [6]. It was the most powerful chess machine ever built. It had also never played a single chess game going into the Philadelphia match.

Philadelphia was sufficiently close that driving there made more sense than taking a commercial flight. On 8 February 1996, Murray, Joe, Jerry Brody, and I finished the last pre-match testing and drove to Philadelphia while Grandmaster Joel Benjamin took the train. I don't know how Joel felt during his trip but in our car, the atmosphere was a little bit somber. We had come so far, and yet we were still a long way from where we wanted to be. Deep Blue was still a two-week old baby. It was a very powerful baby, but a baby nonetheless. Would it be the baby Hercules that strangled the two serpents sent by the Goddess Hera? Or were we sending a helpless baby up as a tribute to placate the sea monster Cetus, but without the aid of Perseus? We were afraid that it would be the latter.

We arrived at the Philadelphia Marriott Hotel in the late afternoon. The conference and the match were to be held in the Philadelphia Convention Center right across the street. An enclosed walking bridge connected the hotel directly to the center. The entrance hall at the convention center end of the bridge was decorated with several high towers that reminded me of chess rooks. While checking into the hotel, we were greeted by Terrie Phoenix, the ACM director of public relations, and Marcy Holle, the communications person from IBM Research in charge of press relations for the chess project. Marcy had replaced Jerry Present a few months back when he retired. Terrie and Marcy were on their way somewhere else, but they informed us about the press conference to be held the next day.

A small contingent of IBMers had arrived several days earlier to deal with all the logistics, video setup, web content distribution, and so on. We met with some of them for dinner. They told us some of the surprises that they encountered.

When the match contract was signed, it was decided that the match would be played in a large theater in the convention center,

---

[6] Put it in another way. Each chess chip was roughly equivalent to a multi-million-dollar general purpose supercomputer. In particular, a single chess chip was actually more powerful for chess processing than the host RS/6000 SP supercomputer we used for Deep Blue.

to accommodate spectators who wanted to see the match directly. However, the person in charge of making the arrangements left ACM before the deposit had been put down. By the time ACM got back to it, the theater had already been rented out. A lecture room was found to serve as the match room, with an adjoining room reserved as Garry's dressing room. Matt Thoennes was the IBMer in charge of making the whole arrangement work. A raised stage was set up in the lecture room, and several video cameras were brought in to provide video feeds to the audience. There was enough space for about seven or eight rows of spectator seats. When Garry's mother, Clara Kasparova, inspected the match site, she objected to the idea of having rows of spectators. A partitioning wall was added leaving just one row of seats for Garry's entourage, ACM officials, and IBM personnel. The paying audience would stay in the commentary room. Another interesting request by Clara, at least from Matt's point of view, was for a port-a-john (portable toilet) in Garry's dressing room. Matt asked someone at the ACM how to get a port-a-john, and was surprised to receive a catalog of all sorts of them, from the most basic to fancy executive models with luxurious amenities. Besides the port-a-john, food and drink (including Toblerone chocolate, apparently one of Garry's favorites) were provided.

The morning after our arrival, while we were having breakfast in the hotel restaurant, Clara and Garry's coach Yuri Dohokian were at another table. It was the first time that I had seen either of them. Yuri was stout looking and young. Clara was elegant in her demeanor, but you could sense that here was a woman who had seen both good times and bad. It took great inner strength for a young widow to raise Garry to the great success that he became. Garry is a strong-willed person, and Clara probably had a strong hand in shaping his personality. Clara was friendly, but she also commanded respect. Throughout Garry's career, whenever there was a big match situation, she was always there to lend her support. For the Philadelphia match, Clara proved to have a calming influence on Garry.

The press turnout at the pre-match press conference was decent, with around twenty reporters showing up. The playing color was decided with Deep Blue having White in the first game. At the press conference Garry predicted a win for himself but did not guess at the final score. Most were predicting an easy win for Garry; David Levy went so far as to predict a 6–0 wipeout win.

Privately, I believed that David's result was highly improbable, but it was not out of the question that we could lose the match very badly. No one outside IBM knew at the time that our machine was only two weeks old. We were nowhere near ready for the match.

The first match game began with a lot of anxiety for the Deep Blue team. We had never seen Deep Blue play a single game ourselves, and had no idea what to expect. Compounding this, we had some early glitches in starting the game owing to computer network problems in the Yorktown Lab.

At Carnegie Mellon, during public games we isolated the Deep Thought workstation from the departmental local network to avoid the occasional network outage, which could render the machine unusable. Originally, we also planned to isolate the RS/6000 SP running Deep Blue from the rest of the Research lab local network. But the plan was not workable—the machine was semi-public for the entire lab, and it could not be isolated because of the way that it was set up. As a result of the occasional network problems, Deep Blue took a little while to start up for the first game. Mike Valvo, the match arbiter, started Deep Blue's clock while we were still waiting for Deep Blue to start up.

Deep Blue opened the first game with e4, moving the pawn in front of the king by two squares. Garry responded with c5, moving the queen bishop pawn forward two squares. This was the Sicilian defense, Garry's favorite defense against e4. Before the match, we had some debate about whether he would play it. Joel's opinion was that Garry was very disciplined in opening selection and he fully expected him to play the Sicilian. There were many good move choices for White after Garry's c5 but, unfortunately, most of them had reams of associated analysis. Joel only had months to prepare Deep Blue's opening book, so we chose to play less traveled opening lines. Deep Blue answered c3, moving the queen bishop pawn forward one square. This is a sound, but somewhat irregular, opening for White. The advantage was that the c3 Sicilian was rarely played at the Grandmaster level and above [7], and as a result there was no need to do extensive opening preparation. The disadvantage was that the opening was a little bit dry, and did not seem to offer much in terms of winning chances for White. At least, that was my

---

[7] The c3 Sicilian was actually quite common in computer chess play. Most programmers did not have a lot of time to prepare their opening books.

opinion based on my past experience with Deep Thought and Deep Thought II, playing both sides of the c3 Sicilian. Joel had a different opinion.

The c3 Sicilian frequently leads to the so-called "isolated queen pawn" position, where White's queen pawn ends up with no friendly pawn on the adjacent files. The isolated queen pawn is usually a handicap in endgames, but in middle games it offers dynamic attacking chances for White. The problem was that most chess programs were usually good reactionary defenders, but not good proactive attackers. Joel spent a significant amount of time coaching Deep Blue Jr how to attack from the positions arising out of the c3 Sicilian. There was one nagging problem. Deep Blue Jr did not like White's positions, and assessed the position to be better for Black. Usually, Deep Blue would still play the right attacking moves, but occasionally it would allow Black to repeat the position since it expected Black to avoid the repetition draw. What happened was that the 1996 version of Deep Blue did not have full grasp of the idea of attacking potential, and hence made the wrong assessment.

The fact that Deep Blue did not expect Black to repeat the position created an intriguing situation in the first game. On move ten, Garry produced a new move that took Deep Blue out of its opening book. Three moves later, Deep Blue presented Garry with an unexpected choice. When I played move 13, Nb5 for Deep Blue attacking his queen, he was taken aback.

Garry looked at the board intently for a moment, then raised his eyebrows and stole a glance at me. I could not help but smile momentarily on seeing his expression. Deep Blue did not really "enjoy" its position, and yet Garry was taking the position very seriously. My smile faded the moment I realized that I was smiling. I don't know how he interpreted my fleeting smile but he spent a long time on his reply. One of his choices was to undo his last move, Qd6, by moving his queen back to d8. In this case, Deep Blue would have undone its own last move by playing Nc3 and repeating the position, effectively offering a draw. Deep Blue played 13. Nb5, in part because it was willing to settle for a draw. Garry did not move his queen back to d8, either he did not want an early draw, or he did not realize that Deep Blue would have taken an early draw. Garry finally placed his queen on e7, a square that Deep Blue considered somewhat awkward, as one of Garry's knights was soon pinned against his queen. From then on, his position steadily went downhill and became desperate.

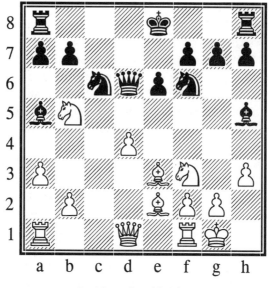

Position after 13. Nb5.

From there, Garry proceeded to whip up a nasty looking attack that surely would have unnerved any carbon-based chess player. Deep Blue totally ignored his attack, and merrily snatched up queenside pawns. Garry's attack, meanwhile, was looking more dangerous as time went on. All that he needed was one free move, and the game would be all over in his favor. At this point, Deep Blue unleashed its own attack. Garry could beat back the attack but would lose most of his material and see his attack dissipated. For the last few moves of the game, he knew that his position was hopeless, and yet Deep Blue, with over an hour of time left on its clock, was still taking time to calculate its best move. After Deep Blue's move 37, Garry had had enough, offered his hand, and resigned. Garry had about five minutes left on his clock for his next four moves, while Deep Blue had about an hour left for its next three moves. It was the first win ever by a computer over a World Chess Champion under regulation time control. History was made!

After shaking hands with me, the first question that Garry asked was, "Why did it take so long to play its moves? A PC program would have seen that it was winning instantaneously." I shrugged my shoulders and told him that Deep Blue simply had too much time left on its clock. Next, he asked with a pained look, "Where could I have played better?" This question took me by surprise. I could barely play chess and the greatest chess mind *ever* was asking me where he could have improved his play. Of course, Garry's question really was "Where did Deep Blue think that I could have played better?" I tried to answer his question as best as I could from what I remembered of Deep Blue's analysis. Sensing that I was not seeing the game on the same level as he and Deep Blue, Garry gave up after a few minutes, and quickly left the building without talking to anyone outside of his entourage.

It did not really hit me how momentous the occasion was until Joel Benjamin came up to the stage to shake my hand. Joel said, with a broad smile, "I dreamt about beating Kasparov myself and shaking his hand," adding, "This is almost as good." Throughout the entire game I had been reining in my emotion. I now felt both elated and relieved. Murray and Joe were ecstatic as well. A reporter came by to get a quick quote and then rushed out to file the copy. There weren't that many reporters around then, but that changed very quickly in the next few days.

The IBM match web site was swamped during the first game. The newspaper *USA Today,* carried a front page article stating that IBM's Deep Blue was doing well but the web site was not. Apparently the web master had thought that only a few thousand surfers would be visiting the site during the game. Had we been asked, we could have told the web master to expect at least tens of thousands visitors and possibly hundreds of thousands [8]. One of the web visitors was Jonathan Schaeffer, trying to connect from the University of Alberta in Edmonton, Canada. Unable to get through, Jonathan scanned the news service and found a Reuters story erroneously saying that Garry was White. Our friend Dap Hartmann, was in Boston and had problems connecting as well. He and Jonathan agreed to both try and access the IBM site periodically and keep each other posted. They were able to follow the game by getting the board position from time to time. The web display for the board position did not state which player had what color so Jonathan and Dap "watched" Garry score a nice win as White. As predicted. End of story. It was twenty-four hours later that Jonathan found out that Garry had lost. Jonathan's situation was probably quite typical for a lot of web visitors on the first day.

---

8 Contrary to the web master's initial expectation, the IBM match web site turned into *the* most popular web site up to that point in time, exceeding even the Superbowl web site and the swim suite edition web site of *Sports Illustrated.*

IBM started mobilizing the web team during the first game. An IBM RS/6000 SP supercomputer, the same type of machine as Deep Blue's host computer, was enlisted as the new web server to handle the workload. After game 2, *USA Today* carried another front page article, this time stating that IBM had fixed the web site.

That night after game one, the IBM team had a celebration dinner. No matter what happened in the remainder of the match, we had made our point. The Kasparov camp apparently was in a crisis. According to Frederic Friedel, who was serving as Garry's computer consultant, Garry went for a late night walk on the Philadelphia streets in below freezing temperatures. During the walk, he asked, "Frederic, what if this thing is invincible?"

Quality from Quantity

Joel and Murray worked together on Deep Blue's opening moves for game two during the night and the next morning. I was present during part of the opening preparation session. Test positions related to the opening were entered into a test file by hand, and Deep Blue analyzed the positions in the test file overnight for human analysis the next morning. We all agreed that if there was ever going to be another match, we would need to automate the opening preparation process, both to speed it up, and to reduce the chance for human error. We had no idea how prophetic our observation was. After the opening preparation session, Murray uploaded the opening file, which was prepared on his IBM Thinkpad laptop computer, to Deep Blue in our Yorktown lab. Or so he thought.

Game two started innocently enough. On the second move, Deep Blue was out of its opening book. I did not know it at the time, but something had gone wrong when the opening file was uploaded, and Deep Blue did not have the new opening book. Since we never did use the new opening book, the opening prepared for game two ended up being played in game four. Deep Blue was only out of the opening book superficially, however. Ever since Deep Thought II, Murray had created what we called the "extended book", which tried to capture the human concept of "opening theory". When Deep Blue was out of the opening book in the traditional sense, it started to use statistics from games played by Grandmasters to help it decide which move to play. If a move in a particular position had been played by strong Grandmasters with great results, then the move would be given a bonus, proportional to how good the results were. This gave Deep Blue a bias to play the "known good lines", but still allowed it a chance to play unexpected moves that, in its assessment, appeared to give better chances.

Murray's human error in transferring the file was not the first in this game. On move six, two pawn captures were possible for Deep Blue. I mistakenly played the wrong pawn capture on the official chessboard. Murray rushed in to inform Valvo, the arbiter, and me about the mistake. It was soon corrected, and time was added back to Garry's clock. The extended book worked quite well in this game. By the time that Deep Blue left known opening theory, Garry had only a slight advantage. Murray's human error, ironically, in combination with his earlier work on the extended book, produced a very playable position for Deep Blue.

On move eighteen, Garry offered a sham pawn sacrifice and Deep Blue declined. Taking the pawn would have given him a strong attack. On the next move, he offered a real pawn sacrifice. Post-game analysis indicated that Garry's pawn sacrifice should have led to a draw if Deep Blue had played the best moves. After the game, while trying to analyze what went wrong, we found an evaluation software "bug" in Deep Blue. The Deep Blue chess chip contained a piece of hardware that recognized minor pieces (bishops and knights) on so-called "outpost" squares, squares on which they were protected by friendly pawn(s) and could no longer be attacked by the opponent's pawns. The chess chip further identified whether the minor pieces could no longer be challenged by (or exchanged with) the opponent's minor piece. It is well known in chess lore that if an outposted knight can no longer be challenged, then it can be as valuable as a rook. However, unchallengeable outposted bishops are perhaps no better than regular outposted bishops. Unfortunately, the software code that assigned the values, wrongly assigned unchallengeable bishops the same values as unchallengeable outposted knights. This gross error in the software evaluation plagued Deep Blue's play for the remainder of game two. If we had had more time for preparation, as we did in the Deep Blue rematch, this fairly obvious "bug" would have been discovered during test games long beforehand.

A sequence of piece exchanges ensued after Garry's pawn sacrifice. Deep Blue had at least two chances for relatively easy draws during the sequence. The first one it missed because of its desire to park its "unchallengeable" outposted bishop. The second one it missed because of a bias placed into the program to avoid trading queens. Going into the 1996 match, we believed that Garry was definitely the stronger player, and to increase our tactical chances, we gave Deep Blue a large penalty for trading the queens. The queen trade avoidance bias backfired in this game. Garry, after observing the bias first hand, exploited it masterfully in later games.

After the dust settled, Garry had a clear edge, but Deep Blue still had drawing chances. He then allowed his most dangerous pawn to be traded for one of Deep Blue's weak pawns, unnecessarily, according to Deep Blue. An ending with each side having a queen and a bishop, with the bishops on opposite colored squares, appeared on the board. The ending was probably drawn, but Deep Blue's position was very difficult to hold [9]. Garry initiated a long and subtle maneuver that netted him a pawn. With the pawn deficit, Deep Blue's position began to crumble. On move 73, Murray, who had replaced me as the operator after the first time control, resigned for Deep Blue.

Garry was exultant, went immediately to the commentary room, and spoke to the audience for over thirty minutes. Clara signaled him to cut it short, but in his excited state he went into a detailed post mortem analysis of the game, and gave a summary of the match so far. The audience thoroughly enjoyed it. During the summary, he said, "I congratulate the researchers at IBM for a fantastic achievement. They have succeeded in converting quantity into quality." That helped reduce the sting from the loss that we just suffered. The next praise took us by surprise. "In certain kinds of position, it sees so deeply that it plays like God."

That night, we went over the game carefully trying to find out what went wrong. When Murray discovered the problem with the outposted bishop, we were all shocked. The surprise was not from the fact that we had a serious bug—we expected many more bugs, given the little time that we had to prepare for the match. The big surprise was how close we had been to possibly winning the match. Without the bug, Deep Blue might very well have drawn game two. Garry already had lots of self-doubt after game one. A

---

[9] After the game, Garry showed a possible drawing line that entailed Deep Blue sacrificing a pawn immediately. Deep Blue did not understand his drawing line at all.

drawn game two could have tilted the match odds heavily in our favor, not just because we would remain up by one game, but also because of the psychological pressure that would be placed on Garry.

The next day, February 12, was in theory a "rest" day although we, and probably they, were hard at work. Two members of Garry's camp did get some rest. Terrie Phoenix took Clara Kasparova and Frederic Friedel shopping. During the 1996 match, the two teams maintained a cordial relationship, and Terrie probably played the major role in smoothing things along. Terrie left ACM before the 1997 rematch. The relationship between the teams was more competitive at the 1997 rematch, in part because of the very real possibility of Deep Blue winning the match, but the absence of someone like Terrie most likely played a part as well.

The Deep Blue team quickly settled into a routine for this rest day. Murray and Joel had the most stressful work, preparing the opening for the next two games. I spent my time running tests, which sometimes revealed problems in the chess program. The program itself was sufficiently stable, and most of the problems were endgame related. Joe acted beyond the call of duty as the fire fighter who fixed up the problems as they came along. He had another task during rest days—speeding up the program. The parallel chess program on the IBM RS/6000 SP was quite a bit more complicated than Deep Blue Jr, which ran on a single RS/6000 workstation. It was also a fairly new program, and there was lots of room for improvement. Some of the improvement was done throughout the match, but most of it came during the rest days.

Once in a while, I would remove myself from the testing and join Murray and Joel in their discussions about our opening choices. Deep Blue won the first game, but neither Joel nor Murray was happy with how the opening went; Garry could have had an easy repetition draw. In a short match, you have to try to win every time that you have White. We needed something better. Murray and Joel worked late into the night on the opening problems. Joe also stayed late on his own task. I decided to take a break and joined the rest of the people from IBM for a nice dinner. I like to eat, and no work was going to stop me from enjoying a good meal.

Murray and Joel did not come up with a good solution to our opening problems during the rest day. But the morning before the third game of the match, Joel declared that he had had an inspiration during the night. Deep Blue would deviate early from the moves it played in game one. There were several possible continuations that could be played by Garry. We checked out a few, and they looked good for Deep Blue. In some of them, Deep Blue found clearly winning lines for itself. This was looking great! There was not enough time to check everything out but we did as much as we could and put in the new opening lines.

Everything went as expected; Garry played into our prepared opening lines. After move twelve, Deep Blue was out of our checked book lines, but was still in one of our expected sequences. On move eighteen, Joel expected Deep Blue to play 18. Be5, and set up a potential attack. Deep Blue refused to play 18. Be5, and moved one of its rooks instead. It turned out that Garry had a strong refutation against 18. Be5, and he had seen the refutation several moves back at the board. Without 18. Be5, Deep Blue had no attack but several weak pawns that had to be defended immediately, or at least that was the way it looked. While Deep Blue's position looked optically grim, it was an illusion. After several inhuman looking moves, it became clear that Deep Blue was not losing, and might even be slightly ahead. On move 39, both sides agreed that there was no point in playing on, and a draw was agreed. It was an impressive game by both Garry and Deep Blue, but we had wasted one of our Whites.

Since the opening prepared for game two was never played, there was no opening preparation session in the morning before game four. This time, Deep Blue played a Slav defense. Deep Blue's position after leaving its opening book turned out to be less favorable than the one it reached on its own in game two. On move fifteen, Garry had a chance to make a speculative sacrifice, but decided against it. After the match, Garry visited IBM Research and analyzed the position with Deep Blue. Deep Blue assessed the sacrifice as sound, but there was no clear win for him. After seeing some of the attacking and defensive moves that Deep Blue came up with, Garry was glad that he did not make the sacrifice. However, he said that he would still have played the sacrifice against any other opponent, human or electronic. Deep Blue would have played the sacrifice itself, given Garry's position at move fifteen.

After making Deep Blue's move 21, I left the playing table and rushed to the rest room. The match rules specified that the operators could leave or return to the table only when Deep Blue was on move, or it had just moved. This was somewhat unusual. In human vs. human games, either player can leave the table at any time. We did not consider the concession too great when the contract was negotiated, and had agreed to the term. Anyway, by the time I rushed back to the game room, Garry was still thinking and I was not allowed back to the table. He thought for a long time on his twenty-second move, and I waited until he made the move. As a result of what happened next, we tried to change the rules for the 1997 rematch to allow operators to come and go quietly. The rules were changed initially, but somehow the old rules were adopted in the end.

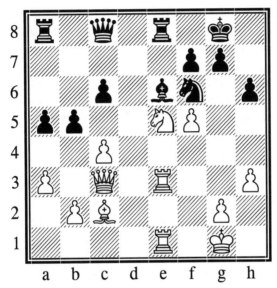

Position after Garry Kasparov's move 22. f5.

When I got back to the table, my computer screen had entered into a blank "screen saver" mode. I typed in Garry's move f5, and Deep Blue crashed. The screen saver mode interpreted the 'f' in f5 as a wakeup character, and Deep Blue received a '5' instead of the full move f5. Joe had been working on the Deep Blue parallel chess program, and had added some testing commands to the program to help him with his work. Unfortunately, '5' was one of the testing commands telling workstation number 5 to listen to the next command. Needless to say, the command '5' would cause an immediate program crash when not executed in the program-testing mode.

Garry was on his way to take a break. The program crash made it necessary for me to restart Deep Blue, with our clock ticking away. I informed the arbiter, and started typing as fast as I could. Murray and Joe rushed into the game room to find out what went wrong. Garry saw the activities, got flustered, and complained to the arbiter. Clara, who was in the game room throughout the entire match, shouted something in Russian to Garry, and he calmed down, perhaps realizing that Deep Blue's clock had been ticking. (Someone told me afterwards that Clara had shouted "shut up".) After coming back from the crash, Deep Blue quickly answered Bxc4. Garry had expected Bxf5, after which he had prepared to play Nxf7, sacrificing his knight for two pawns. One report asserted that Garry claimed the knight sacrifice would have led to a winning position for White beyond Deep Blue's search horizon. Judging from the faulty analyses given in chess books on the match, the knight sacrifice would certainly have won against human opposition. Post-game analyses with Deep Blue suggested stronger defensive moves for Black than the ones given in the books, and some of the attacking moves given in chess books appear to lose outright for White. Personally, I believe the sacrifice would have led to a draw with best play by both sides as there were enough counterbalancing factors. During Garry's visit to IBM Research after the match, he also wanted to see Deep Blue's analysis after his f5. The 1996 Deep Blue preferred Bxc4 slightly over Bxf5. The 1997 version of Deep Blue preferred Bxf5. If Nxf7 does not work after Bxf5 as I suspect, then both Bxc4 and Bxf5 are playable.

By the time Deep Blue played Bxc4 in response to f5, most of Garry's opening advantage had dissipated. Even so, Deep Blue's position looked tenuous. After Garry's move 34, Deep Blue pushed its weak c pawn forward one square and suddenly it was threatening checkmate. Garry had less than one minute per move left before the time control at move 40. For the next few moves, both sides made at least one mistake. Garry made his because he was short on game time, and Deep Blue's because we were short on program development time. At the time of the match, only one third of the positional features recognized by the chess chip were in use by the chess program. One key endgame feature for this game was, that if all the pawns are on the same half of the chessboard, the game is more likely to be drawn. The chess chip could recognize this important endgame feature, but the software did not make use of this ability. Deep Blue made a move that allowed Garry to remove its last queenside pawn. Deep Blue still had the better position, but he had no problem finding the best way out and sacrificed his rook for Deep Blue's strong knight. On move 50, a draw was agreed. After four games, the match was tied at two points each.

During the next rest day, I saw Frederic Friedel in the hotel elevator. He described what happened to Garry, "He went back to the hotel room, stripped to his underpants, and stared at the ceiling for a long time."

Garry, however, would soon recover.

A Mount Everest That Grows

The quest to create a computer that could beat the World Chess Champion in a match, was one of the oldest holy grails in computer science. The quest could be traced back to the 18th century, before Charles Babbage's mechanical computers in the 19th century, and well before ENIAC, the first programmable electronic computer. In 1949, three years after the creation of ENIAC, Claude Shannon, the father of information theory, re-ignited the fire for the quest and described how a computer could be made to play chess. The holy grail remained hidden for nearly 50 years after Claude's seminal work. To a computer scientist, the quest to beat the World Chess Champion had taken on the same significance as climbing Mount Everest to a mountain climber.

One slight difference. The World Chess Champion is a living being. We are talking about a Mount Everest that grows.

The first four games of the 1996 match gave computer scientists a glimpse of the holy grail. We could see the top of Mount Everest; the problem was, that this Mount Everest would soon grow a few hundred feet taller, right in front of the eyes of the world.

On 15 February, the last rest day of the match, Joel and Murray continued their search for an opening line for White that could give us another win. By the afternoon, we had found a line that appeared to give Deep Blue good chances against Garry's Sicilian defense. Still smarting from the debacle in game three, this time we started checking the new line during the rest day. The next morning, going over Deep Blue's analyses of the possible continuations, we found and patched a few holes.

Deep Blue played the same opening move as it did in game one and game three, e4. Garry instantly replied e5. I did a double take. No Sicilian! We had gotten him to abandon his Sicilian defense! Was he afraid of our treatment of the c3 Sicilian? Calm down. This also meant that our opening preparations for the last day and half were wasted. Both teams were in new territory now. Or in the case of Deep Blue, two-month old territory[10]. Two months before the match, Murray spent a few hours putting in some alternative book lines, just in case that Garry played something else. Very little testing had been done with these alternative lines since.

The game followed with Nf3 and Nf6. Garry wanted to play the Petroff defense, also known as the Russian opening. Petroff is known to be somewhat drawish. Deep Blue avoided the Petroff and went into the Four Knights Scotch opening. The fact that we had never tested the opening showed in the way Deep Blue played the game. By move 23, Garry had gained a slight advantage; after making it, he offered a draw.

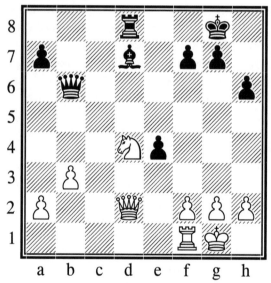

Position after Garry Kasparov's move 23.

I was the operator at the board. The Deep Blue team had agreed before the match that a draw offer would be relayed to the rest of the team in the back room, and the decision would be made

---

[10] Garry had a very odd comment about Deep Blue's immediate book response to his opening choice in game five. "How could you know that I would play this?" he exclaimed. Garry rarely played this opening line, but what he played was perfectly normal in Grandmaster play. He seemed to believe that we would only prepare for the opening lines that he usually played.

from there [11]. No one on the Deep Blue team was expecting a draw to be offered at this early stage. The two earlier draws had been played until clearly drawn positions were reached. I rang the back room and told the gang about the offer.

Deep Blue assessed the position as slightly better for Garry. I was a little nervous about the position on the board. Garry had one extra pawn on the king wing, and it was cramping Deep Blue's position. Back in the Deep Thought II days, I once played through a game where one side had such a kingside pawn majority, and launched a deadly attack using the extra pawn to great effect. Deep Thought II had serious problems understanding the value of the kingside pawn majority in attacks against the king. Deep Blue had the potential to understand the position on the chessboard, but I suspected that the software coding had not been done yet. With Garry looking on, I could not voice my concern to the team. The rest of the team would have to make the decision. Besides, accepting a draw this early, when there was still a lot of play left in the game, seemed like the wrong thing to do. It was not every day that you get to sit across from the World Chess Champion in a serious game. No decision came from the back room. Meanwhile, Deep Blue had made up its mind on what it wanted to play, unaware of the draw offer. Mike Valvo, the arbiter, made a snap ruling insisting that we either had to accept the draw offer immediately or make Deep Blue's intended move. Mike's sudden ruling came as a shock, and even today I consider it somewhat questionable. In chess games between human players, the draw offer stands until it is declined or until a move is made on the chessboard. No move had been made on the chessboard, and the match rule explicitly stated that the operator could accept the draw offer with *or* without consulting Deep Blue. In other words, when the draw offer was made, the decision was no longer Deep Blue's, and the fact that Deep Blue had made up its mind on the move to play, should not have affected how or when the operator made the decision. Mike Valvo's ruling forced us to make up our mind immediately, and the draw offer was declined.

What then followed was not pretty, unless you were Garry.

---

11 The match rules did not explicitly allow this arrangement. All parties involved, including the Kasparov team and the match arbiter, recognized it beforehand as the only practical solution, given the operators' relatively weak chess playing strength.

Deep Blue showed several weaknesses as the game unfolded. Some of the weaknesses could be fixed by simply activating the unused hardware evaluation terms on the chess chip. Others required adding new evaluation terms either in hardware or in software. On move 47, twenty-four moves after Kasparov's draw offer, we resigned for Deep Blue. At the time the resignation took place, Clara Kasparova gave a visible sigh of relief. Garry just needed one draw for the last game to win the match, and he would have White.

That night and the next morning, Murray and Joel worked hard. To draw the match, we would have to win the last game with Black. It was a tall order. Garry lost very few games as White in his career. Moreover, our opening system for Black had been prepared under the premise of trying to draw as Black. No opening was ever prepared to handle the case of having to win as Black. The opening we played in game four was barely adequate to try to hold the draw. We needed something else, something that was riskier but held some chance to win. Murray and Joel settled on the idea of playing the Semi-Slav defense. They tried to enter as many possible variations as possible, and did whatever tests they could in the short time available.

Game six followed a normal line for the Semi-Slav defense. Then Garry deliberately transposed his moves to take Deep Blue out of its opening book. The fact that we had never let Deep Blue Jr play this opening became immediately obvious. Deep Blue was supposed to develop its light-squared bishop to the b7 square, but after being taken out of the opening book by Garry's transposition, it moved the bishop to the d7 square instead. Deep Blue liked to put its bishops on open diagonals, diagonals no longer impeded by pawns, and it did not understand that sometimes it is acceptable to put the bishop on a closed diagonal, as long as the option to open the diagonal existed. It was possible to fix the problem to some extent in software, but a complete solution would require modifying the chess chip. The modifications, implemented as a result of this game, to the chess chip to improve the handling of the bishops and, similarly, the rooks turned out to be critical in the 1997 rematch.

Today, whenever I look at the remainder of the game six, especially with the help of the newer version of Deep Blue, I cannot help but wonder, "How the hell did the old Deep Blue manage to tie the match after four games?" The old Deep Blue made many positional mistakes in the game, and Garry, sometimes cajoling, sometimes pressuring, had everything to do with causing the mistakes. The last major positional mistake by Deep Blue was to move its bishop to b8 on move thirty, trapping both the bishop on b8 and the rook on a8. The chess chip was able to detect the bishop being trapped. Unfortunately, or perhaps fortunately in the sense of shortening our torment, there was very little penalty levied by the evaluation software for getting the bishop trapped. After Garry's move 43, we had suffered enough and resigned for Deep Blue. He had won the match by the score of 4 to 2.

In the first four games, Deep Blue was treading familiar ground and was able to avoid making overt positional mistakes, most of the time. In the last two games, Garry forced Deep Blue into unknown territory, probed for its weaknesses, exploited them, and played Deep Blue as if he were a virtuoso conductor. Mount Everest grew a thousand feet.

Deep Blue 1 chess chip, as used in the 1996 match.

♜ CHAPTER 11

Retooling

Picking up the Pieces

The drive back from Philadelphia was unusually quiet. Everybody was exhausted, both physically and mentally. I was not in the best of moods, but I was feeling much better than during the drive to the match. Losing is never pleasant, but I knew in my heart that we would get another shot at Garry.

What we had achieved in Philadelphia exceeded the expectations of almost everybody, including ourselves. After the first four games, we had tied the match with possibly the best chess player ever. We could easily have drawn game two if we had more time to test the program thoroughly. In game four, Garry had a precarious ending that he managed to draw with Deep Blue's help [1]. Deep Blue could have been ahead after the first four games. If we had been leading then, who knows what would have happened [2]? The publicity generated from the match was tremendous; the match news was on the front pages of the *New York Times*, *USA Today*, and possibly every newspaper in the United States. The *'Tonight'* show, the *'Late Night with David Letterman'* show, and the *'Saturday Night Live'* show all carried spoofs of the match in their late night TV segments. I did not know it at the time, but over one billion "impressions" [3] were recorded worldwide during the match. The

---

[1] The 1997 version of Deep Blue would have treated the ending differently, and had a decent chance to win.

[2] On the other hand, the last two games of the match did show that there was still a gap, and the 1996 Deep Blue, as we suspected, did not really deserve to win. Looking back, I am glad that we lost the Philadelphia match. The better player won.

equivalent advertising value for the US market alone was worth over $100,000,000. We were within striking distance of beating Garry and making history. The event could only get bigger. There was no way in hell that IBM would not want a rematch.

I took a day off, and then went back to the office out of inertia. Murray and Joe took a week off. Each had a newborn baby at home, and much catching up to do. Joel's contract with IBM had expired, and he returned to the life he knew before his short stint on the Deep Blue team. I was really in no condition to work, and was merely doing things that did not require much thinking. Before the Philadelphia match, I wrote a software evaluation function that used all the evaluation features available on the chess chip. This was written to do experiments on automatic adjustment of the evaluation weights, also known as evaluation tuning, for the hardware evaluation features. The program measured how well the program's moves, obtained from very shallow searches, matched Grandmasters' choices in positions from their games. The basic assumption was that the greater the matching rate, the better the evaluation function, and the stronger the chess program. Running the experiments did not require a lot of thinking, and since there was ample machine time available after the Philadelphia match, I spent all my days chewing up machine cycles to run the experiments.

These experiments on evaluation tuning uncovered some surprising facts. In particular, the weights assigned to "rooks on open files" by human Grandmasters, appeared to be much lower than the ones traditionally used in chess programs. I knew about this before the Philadelphia match, but I thought the result an artifact of some software bugs that I had introduced somewhere. Closer examination after the match indicated that the result was real. It was not that human Grandmasters attached lower weights to "rooks on open files", but that they were far more discriminating about when "rooks on open files" were important. In other words, there were far more contexts used by the human Grandmasters, either consciously or unconsciously, than by typical chess programs. After this discovery, I went through the entire set of

---

3 "Impression" is a term used in advertising. Just hearing, seeing or reading the advertising message does not count as an impression. Only after the message is registered in the mind of the potential customer does the "impression" count. Each impression usually requires several exposures to the message.

hardware evaluation features, and located all the features that had low evaluation weights according to the tuning program. All these features might be in need of improvement.

Murray, Joe, and I had a meeting after they got back from their vacations. We examined what went wrong in the match, and reached three conclusions. The first was that Deep Blue's search speed appeared to be adequate. Garry was outplaying Deep Blue positionally, but not tactically. This brought us to our second conclusion, which was that Deep Blue was grossly inadequate in the amount of chess knowledge that it had, compared to the World Champion. The chess chip was too new for us to learn how to use the hardware evaluation features effectively in the short time available. During the Philadelphia match, only about one-third of the hardware evaluation features were really in use. There was a lot of room for improvement by creative use of the existing chess hardware. The third conclusion was that the team, the humans, had to be better prepared. We were not prepared when Garry made his draw offer in game five. For game six, we did not have an opening ready to try to win as Black. Psychologically and procedurally, we were not ready for the big match, period. The team had gone through a lot together, but none of us really had any big match experience.

We had no idea when we would get another shot at Garry. Joe had some doubt whether we would get another chance at all, but after talking with Murray and me, he was convinced and relieved that we would probably have another go. The question was what we could do to increase our odds next time. We could improve the search speed of the program, but that probably would not help much. The software evaluation function could certainly be improved. We could also improve the chess hardware, but that would be possible only if there was enough time before the rematch, and there was enough money allocated to make a new chip release. We would need to do whatever we could to convince the management to schedule the rematch as late as possible, and to allocate an adequate budget to allow for the release of a second-generation chess chip. Murray and Joe were not too thrilled about the prospect of going through the gyration of creating a new chess chip, and all the new software to go with it. But I persuaded them to at least make sure that we had adequate time and funding just in case. We all agreed on what the last set of tasks should be. We needed to build tools for match preparation. Garry won the

Philadelphia match in part because he could adapt faster than Deep Blue. It was difficult to make Deep Blue as adaptive as a human being, but we could help by working as a well-oiled team. In Indy 500 car races, after going around the laps several times the cars need to get their tires replaced at the pit stop. The pit-stop mechanics, by working as a team, and with the proper tools, can replace the tires in less than eleven seconds. We did not need to be as fast as pit-stop mechanics, but we could adopt the same approach. We needed to create sets of tools for everyone involved: a set of tools for the programmers (us), and a different set for the Grandmasters. We also needed to make sure that all members of the team knew what their responsibilities were.

Before the new tools were created, however, I got into a debate with Murray and Joe on whether there should be a new chip, and then on what should go into the new chip. This debate lasted several months.

Another Six Months

For some unknown reason, I seem to be able to concentrate well after a long overseas trip. In 1985, after my trip to Taiwan, I was able to pour in the energy needed to finish the move generator chip, in six months. In 1996, about a month after the Philadelphia match, I was asked to give a talk about Deep Blue at the IBM Tokyo Research Lab. IBM Research was having its own fiftieth anniversary celebration, and the Tokyo Lab was hosting a one-day conference on parallel processing as part of the celebration. My talk was one of the sessions in the conference. For the next six months after this Tokyo trip, I worked harder than I ever had in my entire life, harder even than when I designed my first chess chip.

In 1985, there was no question over whether the chess move generator would be fabricated, as the MOSIS service was effectively free. In 1996, I began work on the new version of the Deep Blue chess chip without knowing whether there would be money to build it. Besides working on the new chip, I also had to wear the hat of an advocate, first persuading the rest of the team, and then our manager, that the new chip was desirable and necessary.

Given all the uncertainty, I took a staged approach, both in the chip design and in my attempt to persuade everyone. New functions were added to the chess chip in stages, always maintaining a new "working" version in the process. This meant I could stop the new design at any point, and have something that was ready for fabrication on very short notice. The chip design process was relatively straightforward, I just had to put in the work; the task of being an advocate was much harder.

Originally, money had been set aside only for fabricating more of the same chess chips that were used in the 1996 match. It took some doing, but I managed to convince the rest of the team that we should at least add a repetition detector to the chess chip before going through another chip run. Murray, Joe and I, had observed Deep Blue Jr playing strange moves that appeared to result from the "horizon effect" related to the lack of repetition detection in the chess hardware. Deep Blue Jr would sometimes try to repeat a position that it liked by pushing the position into the part of the search tree beyond its "repetition detection horizon", which was the "horizon" for the software search tree that did have repetition detection. While this behavior had a definitely detrimental effect, neither Murray nor Joe was willing to endorse the addition without clear evidence that it was necessary. The disasters that we had in Hong Kong turned out to be the persuasion that I needed. The draw given up to WChess could have been avoided. Many other things went wrong simultaneously in our loss to Fritz, but with a hardware repetition detector, the machine would have avoided the problem line in the first place. It was conceivable that Deep Thought II might have won the Hong Kong event with a perfect score; in other words, its performance would have been more than 200 rating points higher. This final argument got both Murray's and Joe's attention, and they agreed to endorse the idea. This took place before my visit to Tokyo.

Some time before the Philadelphia match, I realized that there was a better way to implement the evaluation function that would reduce the chip area significantly. During the flights to and from Tokyo, it dawned on me that this implementation also made it possible for the evaluation function to be far more comprehensive. The problem was that this would entail a wholesale change to roughly two-thirds of the chess chip. The change was highly desirable, but it was also very risky. I believed that this change had to be done if we wanted to beat Garry, and I *really* wanted to win.

We had a team meeting with C J after my trip to Tokyo; Murray and Joe helped me persuade him that the detector had to be included in the new chip. But all three balked at the idea of creating a brand-new evaluation function. In the end, it was agreed that I would design two versions of the chess chip, both with the hardware repetition detector, but one with the old evaluation function, and one with the new. My first priority was to create the version with the *old* evaluation function. I could spend time on the version with the *new* evaluation function, but I would not be getting any help from Murray or Joe—they had two sets of match preparation tools to create. Of the two new chips, only one would be fabricated. To get the new evaluation function, I would have to complete the design of the repetition detector, *and* the new evaluation function, as well as having the entire chip thoroughly verified, all by myself. I had four months until we would decide which version to use. I agreed to the extra workload as it provided another chance to create a chess machine that was strong enough to beat the World Chess Champion, and I was going to do everything within my power to make that happen.

The first month was relatively easy, and mostly spent designing and verifying the repetition detector. By the end of the first month, I had the first new version ready. There were three months left for the even newer version that I really wanted. Based on the experience from the first Deep Blue chess chip, Murray and Joe surmised that it would have taken at least a solid year even *with* their help. There were several reasons why I believed that I could pull it off. First, there were quite a number of software tools left over from the design of the first Deep Blue chess chip, and I could leverage the old work to save some time. Second, I was rested and I could pour in longer hours if necessary. Third, being the sole designer, I had the full picture of what was in the design, and I would have much shorter cycles of finding problems and fixing them. Finally, above all, I wanted to win.

The second month was spent redesigning the new evaluation function. Since it was a wholesale change, I could not tell whether anything was working until the new design was partially completed, about two weeks into the second month. I was thrilled that the new circuit passed my initial test—the new design worked in principle. Now came the hard part. A software model had to be created, and the design and the software model had to match each other. The software model had to be created based on the design intent, not based on what was in the design, to avoid perpetuating any design error. This software model was almost completely new, as the new evaluation function was quite different from the old one. Pieces from the software model for the old chip were used, but mainly as building blocks. For the next month and half, until the end of the third month, I was working close to 100 hours per week. There were no weekends. Every night when I drove home from the lab late at night, I would tell myself repeatedly, "I want to win." After I got home, I would check my circuit simulation to make sure it was still running. If I woke up during the night, I would check the simulation again, and if necessary, fix my software model or whatever before restarting the simulation.

By the end of the third month, I had the new evaluation function reasonably verified. Of course, this would have not been possible without the software tools left over from the old chip. I was starting to get ambitious. The software model, and the hardware were matching quite well, and I no longer had to wake up in the middle of the night to check things. Since I was ahead of schedule, I figured that I might as well look for whatever other improvements I could make. Before the first Deep Blue chess chip was fabricated, my original design had a complicated chess move generator that could "prune" away provably useless chess moves, which theoretically could effectively speed up the chess chip by three to five times. The plan for the complicated move generator was dropped in the first Deep Blue chess chip, as the correctness of the computation involved was quite difficult to verify. There was not enough time to do the original move generator that I planned earlier. It was far too complicated. But I could do something intermediate in complexity if I was willing to drop the "correctness" requirements on how I pruned away the chess moves. I found a pruning scheme that I was happy with, went ahead and implemented the new move generator, without telling either the rest of the team or our manager. To be on the safe side, I added to the new move generator a mode that allowed it to behave the same way as the old move generator. Eventually, *after* it was completed and tested, I did inform Murray and Joe. They were not thrilled.

The new move generator, along with some improvements in other areas, was designed and verified in the fourth month. As the end of the fourth month drew near, it became clear to Murray and Joe that my new design was ready and we made the conscious decision to tailor all the new software development to the new design. The new evaluation function offered so many powerful new features that both Murray and Joe decided that making the switch would be worthwhile. Even if there were some minor problems with the new chip, the advantages provided by it were overwhelming.

It turned out that there were two more months to go before the design had to be delivered to VLSI Technology. I used the time to make small incremental changes.

Meanwhile, after we made the decision to use the new evaluation function, Murray took its software model, added a graphical interface, and created a powerful analysis tool. This new piece of software became an important tool during the program development, and during the rematch itself. Joel rejoined the group at about this time, and was introduced to the tool. Quite likely, the most important new evaluation features on the new chess chip were added as a result of our interactions with him.

One day, while I was going over a new evaluation feature that I just added, a very excited Joe Hoane came into my office. He said, "There is something that you should see", and took me to Joel's office. Murray was already there. Apparently, Joel had been talking with Murray and Joe about some problems that Deep Blue Jr had in a game Joel had just played against it. He had seen similar problems before, but could not pinpoint the exact source until he got the new analysis tool for the evaluation function.

Deep Blue Jr, as well as most of the other modern chess programs, understands the importance of putting rooks on open files, files that are no longer impeded by pawns, so that the rooks can exert the greatest influence. The problem was that, at the time, along with any other chess programs that I knew of, Deep Blue Jr did not know that rooks could be profitably placed on files where it had the *option* of "opening up" the files. That is, the option of removing the pawns impeding the rooks, usually by making a pawn capture. In the game that Joel just played, Deep Blue Jr could have piled up its rooks on such a *potentially open* file and exerted long term pressure indirectly. Instead, Deep Blue Jr opened up the file prematurely and then placed its rooks on the resultant open file. But this action gave Joel the chance to challenge the open file with his own rooks, which then were traded off along the open file. With all the rooks gone, Deep Blue Jr's positional advantage dissipated into thin air. Joel suggested that the right way to play the position was to just pile up the rooks on the *potentially open* file, and wait for the most opportune moment before opening it. Similarly, the same concept also shows up in the relationship between the bishops and the diagonals. Game six in the first match was a prime example of Deep Blue's incorrect treatment of bishops on diagonals. After some discussion, we came up with rules for recognizing the relevant features. That very afternoon, I put in and tested the new features which was a relatively easy modification. This new feature showed up in the critical game two of the 1997 rematch when Deep Blue pinned down Garry's heavy pieces to his back rank as a result of a *potentially open* file. Without the new feature, it was very unlikely that Deep Blue would have won. Not bad for an afternoon's work.

Other major new evaluation features were also added during the last two months of chip design. The first Deep Blue chess chip had a fairly comprehensive evaluation for king safety, but the 1996 match provided ample evidence that still more work was needed. A massive redesign of the king safety evaluation logic took place during the last two months of chip design, with the help of the evaluation function analysis tool. This redesign positively influenced Deep Blue's play in games five and six of the rematch. Undoubtedly, it also altered the course of the other games at one point or another, for better or for worse.

The Phantom Queen
The netlist for the new chess chip was sent out in September 1997 to a design firm contracted by VLSI Technology to do the physical design. Fabrication for the new chips started in late December 1996. The printed circuit boards for the new chess chips were designed in parallel, and became available before the new chips were shipped back in February 1997, less than three months before the rematch. After long negotiations with Garry, the rematch had been scheduled to take place in May. The amount of time left for preparation for the rematch was only slightly better than the time left for the first match. However, the software was in much better shape this time. We already had working software based on the old chips, and we had the new software evaluation function in pretty good shape before we ever laid eyes on the new chips.

The initial integration of the new chess hardware with the new software went smoothly, but then we started to hit snags. Joe, who was doing the bulk of work for the software integration, did the integration methodically. He started with the common features of the old and the new software, then added new features one at a time. He first ported the old software to the new chess hardware, and it went fine. He then simplified the software interface to the chess hardware, as the new chess hardware allowed a simpler interface. This also went well. The next step Joe took was to activate the hardware repetition detector where he soon ran into problems.

The design software that I used to simulate the new chess chip was somewhat limited. Ideally, we would have liked to be able to run the chess software on top of the simulated chess chip, so that any problems with integrating the chess software with the chip could be discovered before the chips were fabricated. There were two obstacles that faced us. First, there was no easy way to do it. The design software did not have a simple mechanism that allowed us to drive the simulated chess chip directly from the chess software. Second, the simulated chess chip was over a million times slower than the real chess chip, and *one minute* of running time on the real chip would have cost us over *two years* of simulation time. There was only just slightly over one year of time between the 1996 and the 1997 match. Usually, it would take at least several *hours* of running time on the real chip to uncover all the problems associated with the system integration. So the new chess chip was never really verified to my complete satisfaction before it was submitted for fabrication. More advanced design software was already available, but there was no time to convert the design to run with the newer design software. Besides, it cost big bucks to get the newer design software.

The hardware repetition detector was thoroughly tested, or so I thought.

In 1992, when I transferred the control of the chess software to Joe, I wrote the chess program in a certain way. All my testing of the hardware repetition detector was based on how I interfaced the Deep Thought II software with the chess hardware. Joe had changed and improved the software substantially in the intervening four years. By early 1996, his new program for the search part alone had grown to well over 100,000 lines of code, or about 20 times the size of the code that I gave him in 1992. Needless to say, Joe accessed the chess hardware in a more complicated fashion, and used the full set of all possible operations. I simulated and tested the hardware repetition detector based on how I wrote the chess program, but with Joe's code, it did not work properly. Some of the chip operations that were not tested in my simulation, but were used by Joe in his code, had the side effect of giving false data to the hardware repetition detector.

The problem was not fatal, and the solution was relatively easy, as long as you didn't have to write the code. He modified the chess program to use the smaller set of chip operations that worked properly with the hardware repetition detector. This cost us about a week but Joe got it working in the end.

The next problem that he uncovered, however, had no pleasant solution. One of the big questions about the new chip was how
well the hardware search pruning really worked. After Joe enabled
the hardware search pruning, the early results were fairly good.
The pruning appeared to speed up the search by a factor of 5 to 10,
more or less in line with my estimate. Then Joe found something
peculiar. In one of the positions that he was testing, an extra White
queen showed up on the a1 square (lower left corner) of the chip's
internal chessboard after the search was completed. The problem
was repeatable no matter which chip was used. It was almost certain that I had introduced a logic design error somewhere. The
immediate questions were what and where?

Joe located a position where the phantom queen showed up
in a three-ply search. It took about one day of simulation to repli-
cate the error. My least favorite chess rule came back to haunt me.
The phantom queen only showed up when *en passant* was possible
in the position. So it was *en passant* yet again. Under certain rare
conditions, either a White queen on a1, or a Black queen on a8
could materialize out of thin air. The phantom queens, however,
would not show up if we disabled the hardware search pruning.

We had three ways to solve the phantom queen problem.

The simplest was to just disable the hardware search pruning,
giving up the five- to ten-fold speedup from the pruning. This was
adequate as a short-term solution to get something running immediately.

The second approach, which I preferred, was not feasible
time-wise. It was a hardware solution. The new chess chip was
designed to be controllable externally with an FPGA (Field
Programmable Gate Array), costing around $20. The external FPGA
could monitor the hardware search and remove the phantom
queens as they showed up. This approach would also give us the
option of adding additional evaluation features inside the FPGA,
without going through the costly redesign of the chess chip.
Another advantage of the hardware approach was that the software
remained essentially the same. There were slightly over two
months left before the rematch. This hardware solution required a
new batch of printed circuit boards, and our regular printed circuit
board supplier said that at best they could supply the boards about
two weeks before the rematch. Two weeks was too tight even for
my taste. We might have been able to find a new supplier who
could supply the boards faster, but it was too risky a proposition.

The third approach required massive software changes, and I was of the opinion that we were better off sticking with the simplest solution of the first approach. I was not comfortable with making such changes right before the match. This approach was based on the observation that whenever the phantom queen appeared after the hardware search, the positional evaluation almost always changed slightly. The proposal was to enable the hardware search pruning before the search as the default, and when a change in evaluation was observed after the default search, remove the phantom queen(s), disable the hardware pruning, and re-search the position. Normally, less than one in ten positions given to the chess chips needed to be re-searched. The effective speed was thus about thirty to one-hundred percent slower than the design speed, but much faster than the speed provided by the simplest software fix. There were two correctness problems with this approach. First, there was no guarantee that a positional evaluation change would be observed when a phantom queen did show up after hardware search. Second, the phantom queen, given the right conditions, could show up during the search, but then get overwritten before completing the search, and thus cause a false search result yet without any indication of the fault. In other words, the search could not be completely trusted because of the phantom queen problem, if the third approach was adopted. It was an intellectually interesting solution, which was probably why Joe decided to spend about a month getting it to work.

There were no other hardware errors uncovered after the phantom queen problem. The problem ended up costing us about one month of Joe's time, and probably made the software less stable as a result. The last known software bug caused by the phantom queen problem was not fixed until two weeks before the 1997 rematch. In the end, everything worked out all right, but things did look bad for a while.

Quality before Quantity

During the 1996 match, Garry congratulated the team for succeeding in "converting quantity into quality". What he did not realize at the time was that Deep Blue never had just quantity. In particular, in the drawn game three, some of the new evaluation features in the chess chip came prominently into play. Some of the "inhuman" moves were not the result of deep searches at all, but of Deep Blue evaluating Garry's rook getting close to being trapped.

For the 1997 rematch, the main emphasis of our match preparation was to improve the underlying quality of Deep Blue's chess knowledge. This time, we wanted the quality to go in before the quantity.

Creating the new chess chip was just the first step in our quest for quality.

Going into the 1996 match, Deep Blue had only existed for two weeks. It was a baby. It was a very powerful and very talented baby; otherwise it could not have possibly beaten Garry in its very first game. But the result of the 1996 match also made it painfully clear that the baby needed to be taught the tricks of the trade. By September 1996, it was certain that the rematch would take place, and Joel Benjamin was invited back to IBM Research to be the headmaster of a chess school with only a single pupil, namely, Deep Blue. (In reality, most of the time, the pupil was actually Deep Blue Jr, since we did not have full access to the IBM RS6000 SP supercomputer that Deep Blue ran on.)

A typical school day started with Joel playing "take-back" chess with Deep Blue Jr; sometimes this continued in the early afternoon. Deep Blue Jr was probably already of Super Grandmaster (2600+ international rating) strength even in the early days, so Joel allowed himself to take back his own moves when the position started to look bad for him. By going back repeatedly to positions where he still had chances, he found lots of positions that caused Deep Blue Jr serious problems. After the "take-back" chess sessions, he would tell us about the mistakes made by Deep Blue Jr. We would then either make changes to Deep Blue Jr or, in some circumstances, make sure that the problems were dealt with in the new chess chip. The next day, the whole process started again, usually with some surprises waiting for Joel. The newly improved Deep Blue Jr would frequently play moves that it would not have played the previous day.

Most of the daily changes were in its evaluation function.

Up to this point in time, the Deep Blue team acted as a troika with each team member responsible for a disjointed area of expertise. Murray was responsible for the evaluation function and the opening book, Joe had all the rest of the main program, including the very complicated parallel search code, and I was responsible for the hardware and the test programs. The team was set up so that no one person had the role of the team leader but all were equal. Usually, everyone kept to his own area of expertise.

On two occasions, however, we joined in to help one of us who was in need. The first time was when the first Deep Blue chess chip was near completion. Murray and Joe chipped in to help me. Now, with the constant stream of evaluation problems uncovered by Joel, and a new evaluation function to complete, Murray could not handle the workload all by himself. I was still spending most of my time on the new chess chip, so Joe provided the much-needed help. Murray and Joe complemented each other extremely well.

Murray and Joe had quite different programming styles. Murray liked to think things through before he wrote a program. This meant that he tended to make steady but slower progress. This fact, in conjunction with the short time that we had, was why only about one-third of the hardware evaluation features were in use at the time of the 1996 match. Joe was more an experimentalist. He would write code very fast, try it out and see how it worked. With all the new evaluation features suddenly available, Murray was overwhelmed with riches. Joe took it upon himself to work on the evaluation function codes for the new features, and quickly came up with new stuff on top of what Murray had already written. Joe was a much weaker chess player than Murray, but the evaluation weighting he put in the code turned out to be pretty good. Murray's work on the evaluation function became more fine-tuning than coding. We ended up getting the combination of both Joe's speed and Murray's thoughtful care.

When the new chess chips came back from VLSI Technology, we had a fairly good evaluation function in place. Not all the evaluation features were used to their full potential even up to the end of the rematch itself, but the function was already in much better shape than what we had at the time of the 1996 match. Murray played the first few games with the new software, using the new chess chip, against two of the top commercial PC programs. At the time, the new software used only one chess chip, running at a slowed down clock rate. Furthermore, because of the phantom queen problem, the hardware search pruning was disabled, slowing down the new software by another factor of five to ten. The "Pico" Deep Blue Jr was thus running at effectively only 100,000 to 300,000 positions per second, or roughly the same search speed as the fastest commercial chess program running on, say, a high end Pentium Pro-based personal computer. The biggest difference between the programs would be in the evaluation function; that is, the chess knowledge encapsulated in the programs or, in the case of "Pico" Deep Blue Jr, in the chess hardware.

Murray played the first few games with the "Pico" Deep Blue Jr without telling anybody. One day, he mentioned that he had played a few games against the top commercial chess programs, and asked me to guess the outcome. Given that Pico did not really have an edge in search speed, and the new evaluation function was still not tuned, I answered, "About 50–50." Then Murray dropped the bombshell. Pico had won all the games. I wanted to see the evidence. Murray showed me fragments of the games from memory. The reason for the domination by Pico became obvious. In our quest to improve Deep Blue's chess knowledge, we had created something way beyond what had been done in commercial chess programs. In each game fragment that I saw, the relative chess knowledge deficiency of the commercial programs became crystal clear, and I could tell precisely what hardware evaluation features were at play in each game.

Murray played a few more games afterwards. Pico kept on winning. On the eleventh game, Murray decided to give a two to one time odds to one of the commercial programs. Pico lost the game. The other program's relative tactical strength became too much for Pico's better evaluation function to compensate. Shortly thereafter, Joe completed the first version of the new Deep Blue Jr software that used multiple chess chips. We decided that it was the time for the new Deep Blue Jr to attend Grandmaster Joel's Excellent Little Chess School. At the time when Murray abandoned the games against the commercial chess programs, the 10–0 record by Pico (excluding the game with time odds) indicated that, in computer vs. computer play, Pico was at least 200 rating points stronger than the best commercial chess programs, with roughly ninety-five percent certainty.

The Communication Department in IBM Research started the media kickoff for the rematch in early February, at roughly the same time we received the new chess chips. One of the kickoff events was the first game between the old Deep Blue Jr and the new Deep Blue Jr in late February.

The reporters witnessing the one-game informal private match, between the old and the new, were from the ABC *'Nightline'* show and *Time* magazine. We were expecting the new version to win, but nothing could be taken for granted. After all, we only just had the new program working. The game started roughly equal, but then the new Deep Blue Jr initiated what looked like a promising attack. The old Deep Blue Jr was unconcerned, and was in fact quite optimistic about its own chances. The new Deep Blue Jr was also getting optimistic. Both could not be right. Then, suddenly, the new Deep Blue Jr saw the win of material. The old version still saw the position as about equal but was definitely wrong. It played a move unexpected by the new version. Now, it was all over; the new version declared that it would win massive material. After the move of the new program, the old program saw the doom as well. The game lasted only about twenty moves. Everyone was amazed. I would not have believed that any chess playing entity could do this to the old Deep Blue Jr. All the chip work on improving the king safety evaluation, and all the new software work to exploit the hardware evaluation features, had paid off handsomely. The reporter from *Time* commented that the moves played by the new Deep Blue Jr had a distinctly human-like quality to them. Garry would be playing a vastly different program from the one he played in 1996.

So the new program was dominating other computer programs, including the old version of Deep Blue. It was a good sign, but one question remained to be answered. How strong would the new Deep Blue be against human Grandmasters?

Grandmaster Miguel Illescas was an up-and-coming chess star from Spain. In the last ten years or so Spain has become a major chess country. The strongest chess tournament in the world took place annually in Linares, Spain, with Miguel being one of the frequent participants. As a result, he became quite familiar with the top chess players. We had our first contact with Miguel in 1995 when Deep Thought II lost a two-game match to him. We invited him to help with Deep Blue's opening preparations for the 1996 match, and he did it remotely from Spain. For the rematch, Miguel had a two-week time slot, in March 1997, in which he could travel to the United States, and we took the opportunity and invited him over.

Miguel spent the two weeks working with Joel on the opening preparation, but every once in a while he would play a few casual games with Deep Blue Jr. He lost most of the games. This was another good sign but casual games cannot be taken too seriously.

Joel and Miguel worked very well together. Joel had intimate knowledge of how Deep Blue behaved, while Miguel was in the top chess echelon. When Joel had some difficult opening problems,

Miguel sometimes would come up with what the top players had discussed among themselves about the very same problems. When Miguel had questions about Deep Blue, Joel would tell him the answers in the common chess language among the Grandmasters.

After Miguel's visit, Grandmasters Nick DeFirmian and John Fedorowicz were invited to help with specific opening systems that Deep Blue might use during the match. We kept these meetings a closely guarded secret until the start of the rematch to avoid signaling Garry which openings Deep Blue might play, giving him a dangerous edge. There was no point in preparing for over a year, painstakingly improving the program, only to get slaughtered by Garry's renowned home opening preparations. We were going into the match to play Garry, not his home preparations. Just like Miguel, Nick and John also played casual games against Deep Blue Jr and lost most of them. Again, a good sign. But to be certain, we would need to play against other Grandmasters in serious training matches.

We scheduled two training matches for Deep Blue Jr in April 1996. The first was against Grandmaster Larry Christiansen, and the second against Grandmaster Michael Rohde both of whom had extensive experience playing against computers.

John and Nick were both looking forward to seeing the training matches in person. In John's words, "I would like to see them suffer." Larry and Michael were close friends of his. To avoid any possible leaks of their involvement before the rematch, it was decided that they would work at home.

Larry played the first of the two two-game training matches. In the first game, Deep Blue Jr set up a promising position, and then suddenly gave up a pawn for no apparent chess reason. It turned out to be a software bug causing it to play a random move. Shades of ChipTest's first outing where ChipTest played the first move from the move generator, whether good or bad. The Deep Blue Jr bug was related to how time control was handled. The bug had been fairly recently introduced and Joe had been trying to track it down for a while. He thought that it was fixed, but apparently it was still there. The position looked hopeless, but somehow Deep Blue Jr whipped up some tactical magic and it was a repetition draw. Joe located the bug and fixed it before the game on the second day. Deep Blue Jr won the second game, and won the match by the score of 1.5 to 0.5. No bug showed up in the match against Michael, which again was won by Deep Blue Jr by the score of 1.5 to 0.5.

The performance of Deep Blue Jr against the two Grandmasters in games played under regulation time control was in the high 2700s, or within about 50 rating points of Garry Kasparov. There were too few games to take the performance seriously, but Deep Blue itself would be five to ten times faster than Deep Blue Jr, and possibly 100 to 200 rating points stronger. If Deep Blue was not yet stronger than Garry, it was well within striking distance.

The Deep Blue 2 chip used in the 1997 final match.

♟ CHAPTER 12

The Holy Grail

The Chinks in the Armor

Leading up to the 1997 rematch, we sensed a quite different atmosphere several months before the event itself. We felt good about our chances. Garry Kasparov was strong, but he was not invincible, and Deep Blue was closing in. We were making fast and steady progress. Our own assessment right before the rematch was that, if Deep Blue was not already stronger than Garry, it was close enough and he would not be able to win by more than one game. On the other hand, he was sufficiently strong that we seriously doubted that we could win the match by more than one game. There was a fairly good chance that the match would be drawn as well. From our point of view, this would be a perfectly good result. If we had, say, six more months to prepare, and if we could maintain our rate of improvement, it was conceivable that Deep Blue would be able to win the match by more than one game. But, of course, we did not have six more months. Whatever we came up with would have to do, and it looked as though the new Deep Blue might be good enough.

Publicly, we kept quiet until about three months before the rematch. The new chess chips were kept under wraps, and since we were not absolutely sure that they would work out, their existence was not publicly known until the match was under way. We had a contingency plan to revert to the old chess chips if we discovered something terribly wrong before the rematch.

Garry, meanwhile, was apparently getting nervous. In late February 1997, Michael Krantz, the same *Time* reporter who had witnessed the one-game match between the two versions of Deep Blue Jr, interviewed him. Michael mentioned to Garry that he had seen the game and been quite impressed with the human-like quality of the moves played by the new program. Garry became quite agitated. First, he asked Michael for the game score. When he replied that he did not have it, Garry asked whether he remembered what opening was played. Garry was quite disappointed when he found out that Michael did not have any idea what the opening was called [1]. What Garry did not realize at the time was that *ABC Nightline* had a complete video tape of the game, and in fact, had broadcast segments of the game earlier on air. Did Garry ever find out about the *ABC Nightline* tape? I don't know. But if he did, he would have known that he indeed had something to worry about.

Shortly after Garry had his *Time* interview, we received an e-mail from Frederic Friedel asking if he could visit IBM Research with a reporter from Germany. We had a friendly relationship with Frederic, but we were concerned he might have the side mission of probing for information relevant to Garry's match preparation. We would be very polite but alert, to avoid giving Garry an edge. Frederic visited the lab in early March 1997, and both the visit, and the interview went fine. At the end of his visit, Frederic made an unusual comment, "Garry would win easily if he should play anti-computer chess. But he will never do it." In anti-computer chess, the human player deliberately plays sub-optimal moves to get to positions that they think are difficult for the computer to handle. In this sense, Garry had already played anti-computer chess in the 1996 match. We did not give Frederic's comment much thought. We had prepared extensively for the possibility of playing against anti-computer chess already. We had no idea how far Garry would actually go in the coming rematch. One of Frederic's questions was, not surprisingly, whether we thought Deep Blue could win the match. He did not look too pleased when we gave him the straight answer that Deep Blue had a very real chance of winning. I did not tell him that I believed Deep Blue would have a better than fifty percent chance of at least drawing the match.

As the rematch drew near, Garry started making various requests through his agents either outside of, or in conflict with, what was in the already signed match contract. Some of Garry's requests were quite reasonable, but others were less so.

---

[1] For the curious, the opening line played in that game was the Tarrasch variation of the Queen's Gambit opening.

One request was to use a new chess clock, based on Garry's specifications and custom designed by Audemars Piguet, a Swiss watchmaker that Garry endorsed in advertisements. Another one, related to the new chess clock, was to use an entirely new and irregular time control that Garry had recently dreamt up. The match contract already specified that the regulation time control was to be used, just as in the 1995 Kasparov vs. Anand World Championship Match. In the end, Garry's new clock was adopted, but not his new time control. This new time control was exceedingly complicated, and even the new clock did not work with it. More seriously, even if Garry's clock could handle his new time control, the Deep Blue team had neither the time nor the energy to modify the program to deal with his late request.

Garry was not handling the request himself, so he was not wasting his time or energy on it. But if we had agreed to it, we would have had to spend valuable time, which we did not really have, to code the new time control and do extensive testing which could have cost us weeks of preparation time. Remember that we had less than 12 weeks to bring up the new Deep Blue for the rematch. We did, out of good will, spend time looking over the new chess clock and the document for the new time control. It was the team's opinion that there was no way we could program in the new time control and finish the match preparation in time. However, George Paul from IBM Research was asked to evaluate the new chess clock, and see whether there was any way that both of Garry's requests could be satisfied. We were relieved when, after spending days examining the clock, he reported that it had enough problems handling even the regular time control. After George's report, Audemars Piguet fixed the clock in time for the rematch, with a regular time control.

Early in the contract negotiation for the rematch, it was agreed that, if Garry offered a draw, the operator would be allowed to tell Deep Blue of the offer. If the team decided to decline the draw offer, Deep Blue would then be told that the draw offer had been declined. The purpose of this rule was to prevent the repeat of the situation in the 1996 match where Mike Valvo forced the Deep Blue team to make a rash decision after Deep Blue had come up with a move, without knowing that a draw offer was being deliberated. As far as we were concerned, the ability to be able to override Deep Blue, and accept draw offers, was a courtesy out of respect for the human player. Chess has too many exceptions, and it is not possible to program the computer to understand that a position is drawn in each and every circumstance. Without the ability of the programmers to override, the human opponents might be forced to needlessly play out drawn endings, which would serve no useful purpose other than tiring them. As the rematch drew near, Garry had second thoughts, and before agreeing to the new rule, wanted to add another rule that the Deep Blue team would not be allowed to see how Deep Blue assessed the position while deliberating on the draw offer. This was asking for too much as our deliberation would then be made without any input from Deep Blue the player. The match was supposed to be between Garry and Deep Blue, after all. What if Deep Blue finds a brilliant win that no human being would see? The match rule for draw offers was never resolved to anyone's satisfaction. Internally, the Deep Blue team made the simple decision that we would not accept any draw offers in unclear positions. In the rematch, he did not offer draws in unclear positions, so the problem never came up.

Since our first ACM game in 1986, ChipTest and its successors had played over one-hundred formal tournament or match games in public, and Garry had or could have had access to every one of them. The match contract explicitly obliged the Deep Blue team to provide, when requested, the scores of all our public tournament games. These scores were readily available, as we were at the top of the computer chess food chain, and our games were always carefully scrutinized. But, in my recollection, Garry never bothered to request the game scores. This, however, did not stop him from repeatedly complaining that he had no access to *any* Deep Blue games. True, he did not have access to games played by the newest version of the program, but usually neither would he have had access to games played by, say, the new and improved Anand during the months of training before their world title match. One might argue that the newer version of the program was vastly different from the old one, so Garry should have been given a chance to study it. This is a backward argument. The newer version was vastly different only because we had put a tremendous amount of work into it, just as Anand and Garry himself would have done. Should Anand be forced to give Garry sample games just because he had improved himself from six months of training? If he had asked Anand to give him sample games to study, any reasonable person would have considered the request ludicrous. Why should he be the only one to have secret weapons for the match?

We wanted to be fair, but to give Garry games from our pre-match training would have placed us at a serious disadvantage. In the exhibition match between him and Deep Thought in 1989, he had unleashed a devastating new opening line that busted Deep Thought's opening in game two. Deep Thought was dead on arrival when it found itself out of its opening book. If Garry had some idea of what openings Deep Blue would play, who is to say that history would not be repeated? We wanted to play the World Champion, not his home preparation against our openings. Could we have given him some token game scores nonetheless? Theoretically, yes. But there would have been some serious complications. If he had not been able to take advantage of the game scores, then we would have been accused of deliberately misleading him. If he had been able to make use of the game scores, then, in order to make the match a fair one, we would have had to make substantial changes to the opening books, change the program, and possibly even build a new machine (so that it could play new openings well)[2]. Garry would then ask for new games. Back to square one.

Garry had made similar complaints during the 1996 match, but they were not quite of the same intensity. Why did he still complain now, when he had already played against Deep Thought twice and Deep Blue six times, that he did not have *any* Deep Blue game to study? One possible reason was that, in his mind, he deserved to have new games to study, even though it was not a right that he would have against a human opponent. There was another possibility. During Frederic Friedel's visit to IBM Research, he made an interesting remark that might shed some light. Before the 1997 rematch, Garry had had great success in top-level chess tournaments against other top human players, and appeared to be at the peak of his career. One of the secrets of this great success, according to Frederic, was that he was revamping his entire opening repertoire with the help of commercial chess programs. These programs were used to point out potential problems in his repertoire, and to find new moves to surprise his opponents. Deep Blue was a far more powerful chess machine than any program that

---

[2] To play certain openings well may require a program to recognize chess positional evaluation features that no other chess programs, including Deep Blue, recognize. In that case, we would need to add new hardware, or at least new software, so that the machine can play the openings well.

Garry had access to. If he could use commercial chess programs in his opening preparations to great effect, a group of Grandmasters working together with the help of Deep Blue surely would produce some great opening surprises. Was Garry, one of the greatest chess opening theorists ever, actually afraid of *our* home opening preparations?

Garry's problems going into the rematch went beyond just general nervousness. For someone nervous about his own chances, he, surprisingly, grossly underestimated Deep Blue's strength. In the pre-match press conference, a reporter asked him how strong he thought Deep Blue was relative to the commercial chess programs. He answered that he expected Deep Blue to win eight out of ten games against the best commercial chess programs. "Pico" Deep Blue Jr, which was about one-thousand times slower than Deep Blue, probably would win at least eight out of ten games against the best commercial programs, based on the experimental data we had. A ten-fold difference in speed between two identical programs would very likely produce a winning ratio of 8 to 2, and we are talking about a base program that was already capable of winning eight out of ten games, speeded up a thousand times ... When I heard Garry's statement, I said to myself, "Boy, Kasparov is in for some shock."

Before the 1996 match, Garry looked untouchable, and at the end of the 1996 match, he *was* untouchable. Before the 1997 rematch, however, chinks were already showing up in his armor. I liked our chances.

Setting Up Shop

The rematch took place on the Manhattan Island of New York City, roughly half an hour drive from our lab. In theory, we could have commuted from our homes, but most of us stayed in Manhattan throughout the entire match. Joel lived in lower Manhattan, but stayed with the rest of us in the Michelangelo Hotel, which was just across the street from the Equitable Building, the match site, in upper Manhattan. Miguel, who arrived from Spain just before the match, also stayed in the Michelangelo with his wife. Miguel, Nick, and John served as Grandmaster commentators for the reporters in the pressroom. Miguel was also serving as our second when Joel had to give interviews to reporters during the games. Nick and John, having fewer responsibilities and being native New Yorkers, went home every night. All the Grandmasters were involved in the opening preparation sessions between games. IBM set up a customer hosting area in the Michelangelo Hotel, with a microwave video feed from the match site. The invited IBM customers could watch the games and the live commentaries in a comfortable and relaxed setting. Food and wine were served continuously. Nick and John, both with a taste for fine wine, were frequently sighted at the customer hosting area. After the match, Garry made the outrageous claim that they had played for Deep Blue from the Michelangelo. Nick and John were just there to enjoy the food and the wine, taking care of their gastronomic delight, and rubbing shoulders with the IBM customers.

The decision to host the rematch in New York City created some difficult problems early on. The match negotiation started more than a year beforehand, but it was already quite difficult to find a venue that was of the right size, had adequate facilities, and proper vacant time slot. At first, the Millennium Hotel was declared as the match site but after the rematch announcement, the hotel said that a wedding ceremony was booked for the last weekend of the rematch, and wanted IBM to pay an additional fee so that the ceremony could be rescheduled. It so happened that IBM CEO Lou Gerstner usually hosted his stock analyst meetings at the Equitable Building, and quite a number of IBMers were familiar with the site. The Equitable Building, the headquarters of Equitable Insurance, is a modern building with all the necessary wiring for video connections between floors already in place. After an extensive examination, the new site was decided to be the better venue, and the Millennium Hotel booking was cancelled. I wonder how the managers of the Millennium Hotel felt after seeing the massive publicity, once the rematch got under way?

The Equitable Building was an imposing skyscraper, as befits the headquarters of a big corporation like Equitable Insurance. The Broadway Theater district was close by, and during one of the rest days, show tickets were secured for the IBM team producing the off-Broadway chess show. None of us on the Deep Blue team went to the show, though. Joe, Murray, and I had worked for nearly three decades, combined, on the project, and we intended to keep our eyes on the ball. Broadway shows could wait a while.

Within walking distance was the Rockefeller Center. The Saturday morning before game five, some enterprising IBMers, led by Matt Thoennes, pushed the "life-size" Deep Blue model, which normally was on the stage at the match auditorium, into the street right next to the live broadcast of the NBC's *'Today'* show in the Rockefeller Center. The *'Today'* hosts were quite surprised to find the big black box outside their window.

The main entrance for the Equitable Building was on seventh Avenue. After passing through the main entrance, the spectators arrived in a majestic marble lobby, three stories high, with daylight coming in through the glass ceiling. Directly facing them on the far wall was a giant painting by Roy Lichtenstein. As a result of security concerns following the Oklahoma City and the World Trade Center bombings, the audience was asked to pass through metal detectors and a security check. They then had to go one flight down to the 480-seat auditorium, which served as the commentary room. Not all the seats were available to the general public. IBM, ACM, and Garry all had some reserve tickets. Some of the IBM tickets were given to the United States Chess Federation for their guests, and most of the others went to lucky school children. A small number of IBM tickets were reserved for invited customers who wanted to see the auditorium first hand. Reporters were allowed into the auditorium when the fire safety capacity was not exceeded.

At the front of the auditorium, three giant projection screens displayed live video feeds of the chessboard, the game room, and the computer analysis board used by the commentators. The projection equipment was provided gratis by AmPro, the company who provided the same service in Philadelphia. There had been talks earlier with Matsushita. Had the talks worked out, video walls would have been used instead of projection screens, and live match video would have been shown on the giant Panasonic/NBC TV screen in Time Square. However, some personnel changes took place at Matsushita, and the talks broke down.

Below the projection screens, on the right side of the stage, stood a "life-size" model of one *frame* of an RS/6000 SP supercomputer. The frame was a refrigerator-sized box well over six feet high. Garry himself could have fitted nicely into it. A real frame would house up to 16 RS/6000 workstations. The frame on the stage was actually just a wooden box model of the real machine. After the match, this wood model was shipped to California on a charter plane for TV commercial shoots.

Mike Valvo, the match arbiter for the 1996 match, was serving as one of the three main commentators in the auditorium. The main commentators from the 1996 match, GM Yasser Seirawan

and IM Maurice Ashley, were the other two. Of the three commentators, I thought Yasser was decidedly pro-Kasparov, while
both Maurice and Mike were relatively neutral. Yasser was the first
American player to become a World Championship Candidate
after Robert Byrne (USA) lost to Boris Spassky (USSR) in 1974. If I
am right about this bias, it was kind of interesting, especially considering that Garry refused to share the same stage with him
during the 1997 match. Yasser and Garry used to be close friends
in the late 1980s, but chess politics got in the way of friendship.
Maurice first became well known when Raging Rooks, a Harlem
junior high school chess team he coached, won the US Junior High
School Chess Championship in 1991. The first time I met him was
when his team visited IBM Research shortly after winning the title.
Besides his coaching activities, one thing that really impressed me
about him was his stated desire to become the first Grandmaster of
African descent. Not long after the rematch, his dream became
reality. Good things do happen to good people.

The thirty-fifth floor of the Equitable Building, where the games
took place, was off limit to the spectators. Only one regular elevator goes up there, and only people on a restricted list were allowed
by the security guard to enter it. After taking the elevator, you
would be greeted by another security guard, who would check your
name against the list. Since very few people were allowed, after a
few days the security guard would recognize your face and greet
you with a smile.

    To get to the game room, guests and reporters alike passed
through a storage room that was connected to the game room by
a winding temporary corridor. The corridor was constructed with
sound proofing material to cut off the noise from the storage room
air conditioner. The game room had many high-power lamps and
video equipment that generated lots of heat. The storage room air
conditioner provided much-needed air conditioning for the game
room and had to run continuously. On entering the game room,
you would see a single row of chairs. One of the chairs—ornate yet
comfortable—looked quite inviting. This was Clara's chair that she
had personally chosen. Clara was always present during the games,
and it was simple courtesy for IBM to make sure that she was as
comfortable as possible. Beyond the chairs, you could see a partitioned area that occupied roughly a quarter of the game room. This
was Garry's rest area, furnished with a sofa, table, fruits and bottled

water. He liked bananas, and every day, fresh, unblemished bananas would be delivered to the table. Another soundproof room was provided for him on the same floor, stuffed with more goodies. There was no port-a-john in his room this time, possibly because of the difficulty of bringing one in. He shared the same rest room as the rest of the crew on the thirty-fifth floor, except that he had the highest priority. Nobody, including members of the Deep Blue team, was allowed to use the rest room while he was in it.

Beyond Garry's resting area in the game room was another door, usually closed. It was actually the first of two soundproofed doors leading to the sound control room. It was also Garry's private entrance. Beyond the two doors was a draped corridor. Whenever he opened the first of the double doors, the video crew and the IBM team were informed to stay away. The draped corridor led to both Garry's private room and the common rest room. The only way from the Deep Blue operational room to the common rest room was also through the draped corridor. As he again had highest priority, this meant that no one on the IBM team was allowed to go to the rest room whenever he was out of the game room, even when he was not using it.

The front half of the game room was the playing area. Compared to the sterile environment of the 1996 match, it looked almost homely. The room was really a TV studio used by senior executives of Equitable Insurance for broadcasting and recording corporate messages, and was set up to look like the study of an aristocrat or perhaps a rich lawyer. In the center of the front wall was a big poster for the rematch. If there was a painting behind the poster, it probably had a medieval scene, perhaps of a knight rescuing a damsel in distress, or maybe a portrait of the patriarch of the family in full battle regalia. Several paintings of medieval scenes adorned the walls. The bookshelves were full of old law books. On the shelves was a ship model as well as several wooden duck decoys. Potted plants livened up the well-lit room.

The lighting was a little too bright for Garry but he compromised since he wanted to look good on the video. The lighting above the playing table had to be adjusted several times until he was finally satisfied that there was no more shadow around his queen. The playing table was custom made, with a forty-five-degree bend at the rear toward the Deep Blue operator on the right. A black, $5000 IBM flat panel display sat on this part of the table.

To the left, Garry sat on a studded leather armchair of the exact firmness he liked. On the right, the Deep Blue operator sat on a similar chair. The match arbiter, Carol Jarecki, sat at a desk to the right. Murray, Joe and I rotated as the operator from game to game, with occasional substitution during long games. The match rules forbade the operator from leaving the chair while Garry was thinking, so the operator was usually fairly uncomfortable after staying at the table a long while.

Deep Blue itself was also on the thirty-fifth floor. A few months before the rematch, IBM RS/6000 division announced the availability of a new RS/6000 SP, which had CPUs (Central Processing Units) that were about twice as fast as the CPUs in the model we used for the 1996 match. The demand for the new one was outstripping the supply. The only way that we could have access was to get one that was being tested on the factory floor prior to being shipped to the customer. Instead of the usual, the RS/6000 SP in question would be doing the floor testing on the thirty-fifth floor of the Equitable Building, in front of the eyes of the world.

The RS/6000 SP arrived at the Equitable Building a week before the rematch, with all the chess cards in place. It had two frames, each frame housing 15 RS/6000 nodes for a total of 30 nodes, or 30 RS/6000 workstations. Each SP node contained two chess cards, with eight chips per card. The total number of chess chips in the system was 480. Theoretical maximum search speed was about one billion positions per second. This is the speed guaranteed-not-to-be-exceeded by the system. The actual maximum speed was around 200 million positions per second. Before the move, the people handling the logistics told us that there would not be any external phone access to the Deep Blue RS/6000 SP. So we all moved into the Michelangelo Hotel the day after the machine was moved, since there was no way for us to access the machine from our offices in Yorktown, or our homes.

When we went up to the thirty-fifth floor of the Equitable Building, we found Deep Blue ensconced in a small closet-sized space at a far corner of the building. There was a dedicated air conditioner for the machine, but the space around it was quite warm. The adjacent space was a little bit cooler, and a few days later we installed a floor fan to circulate this air to help reduce the temperature. The whole machine area was too warm even for someone wearing a short-sleeve T-shirt and shorts. We did not have access to other parts of the thirty-fifth floor at the time, and it was quite difficult to work for a long period on Deep Blue, as we were forced to stay in the machine area. For a couple of days, I ran extensive tests of the system when Joe was not running his own test on the search efficiency of the parallel program. Some of the chess cards appeared to have been damaged in transport, or perhaps suffered from the effect of the high heat, and had to be replaced. The machine area and the game room were separated by three other rooms, and had different air conditioning systems. It was therefore quite funny to hear Garry complaining in public, a year after the rematch, that the air conditioner was adjusted for Deep Blue's comfort instead of his own. During the rematch, Kasparov did complain that his resting area in the game room was too cold. It turned out that there was an air vent right above his resting area and a deflecting surface for the airflow was installed afterwards.

Besides the final testing, there was still some work ongoing in both the evaluation function and the opening book for Deep Blue. A hotel suite was supposedly reserved at the Michelangelo so that we could work on the opening book with the Grandmasters. IBM had made block reservations at the hotel, and we were quite surprised to find that our suite had already been taken. For several days, we had nowhere to do the opening preparation except on a coffee table in a small room next to Deep Blue's room. Finally, we figured out what happened to our suite. When IBM was making the hotel reservations, Garry wanted to stay in a hotel closer to Central Park, so his entourage was all booked into the Plaza Hotel. A suite was also reserved for the Kasparov camp at the Michelangelo for the duration of the rematch, but not before. Garry's new manager, Owen Williams, arrived at the Michelangelo a week early, and accidentally took the suite that we had reserved. We got our suite when the one reserved for the Kasparov camp became available.

Three days before the rematch, we were finally allowed to move into the operations room, which was to become our home base. The operations room was probably normally used as an editing room as there were panels for switching sound tracks and video channels on one side. The room was cramped and during the games normally no more than six people could crowd in. Ken Thompson, of UNIX and Belle fame, was always present. He was serving as the impartial observer for both the camps. During the games, Ken was the only person outside IBM who got to see Deep

Blue's running log, besides the Grandmasters and the occasional reporter. The running log detailed Deep Blue's "thinking" process, namely, what it planned to do in various circumstances. At least one of the three Deep Blue team members was always present, ready to swap positions with the operator at the table. Either Joel or Miguel was always around, depending on which one of them was in the pressroom. A couple of other IBMers went in and out from time to time. Every once in a while, a reporter from a major media outlet would be escorted in for an impromptu interview. A chair in the operations room was probably the best seat in the house during the games. There were video feeds from the game room and from the auditorium, so you would not miss anything important happening in the building. (It would have been nice to have had a video feed from the pressroom, but none was available.) You had at least one Grandmaster on hand for chess discussion, and at least two experts (Ken and one or two of the three Deep Blue team members) for computer chess discussion. More importantly, you got to see what the best chess

The Deep Blue group in the game room
before the start of the 1997 match.
Standing from left to right: *Jerry Brody, Feng-hsiung Hsu,*
Joe Hoane, Joel Benjamin, and C J Tan. Sitting: *Murray Campbell.*

playing entity in the world was "thinking" while all the discussion was going on.

We were ready for the show.

It Saw the Mates!

Two days before game one, a press conference was held on the forty-ninth floor of the Equitable Building. It was originally estimated that about one-hundred journalists would show up but in the end over two-hundred arrived. The room was completely packed. ABC, CBS, NBC, CNN, Fox, BBC and a few other European TV networks sent their crews. After the press conference, I had a chat with an IBM old-timer who had been involved in the product launch for the IBM 360 computer in 1964, arguably the most important launch in IBM corporate history. He exclaimed, "This is far bigger than the IBM 360 launch. There is nothing in IBM history comparable to this." As the match progressed, more and more reporters showed up to cover it. Eventually, there were simply too many reporters, and the pressroom was moved to a much bigger room on the fiftieth floor, with a spectacular view of the city.

In both Deep Blue matches, photographers were allowed to take pictures at the start of each game. Now, there were too many photographers, and they had to be divided into two batches for each game. First one group was allowed to cram into the room, and take a few pictures. Then they were ushered out and the second group allowed in. Some photographers were caught trying to stay on for the second session; there were even some cases of violence as the photographers jockeyed to get the best shots. At the start of game one, a security guard hired by IBM was punched by a photographer who subsequently had his press pass revoked.

Garry and I smiled broadly and shook hands before we sat down for the first game. The rematch had a total prize fund of $1.1 million, with $700,000 for the winner, and $400,000 for the runner-up. At the moment that we shook hands, he was probably smiling about *his* $700,000. I was wondering what would happen when he received *his* $400,000 check. We would not get to share the $700,000 winner's check—Deep Blue's share would go back to IBM. But seeing our dream finally coming to fruition would be more than enough. We would all be on cloud nine. All the personal sacrifices would be justified. Would some of us shed tears of joy? Would I?

Despite Frederic's claim during his visit that Garry would win easily if he played anti-computer chess, but would never do it—he did just that. For the entire first game, his pieces never left his half of the board.

After the first nine moves, Garry and Deep Blue arrived at a well-known position that had been played many times at the Grandmaster level. The position was closed and highly positional, exactly the type of position that was supposedly hard for a computer. Garry next played an unusual move, 10. e3, moving his e-file pawn forward one square. A more normal move was to move the e-file pawn forward two squares, offering a pawn trade. He wanted to keep the position closed for a little bit longer. With the move e3, he revealed his strategy for the entire match—play anti-computer chess. We were about to see one of the strangest chess matches played at the highest level. Why did he decide to adopt this strategy? How and for how long did he prepare for this style of play? I have a theory.

Frederic believed that Garry would win easily if he played anti-computer chess. Frederic and Garry were close friends, so he must have known about this opinion. We had told Frederic during his visit that Deep Blue had a good chance of winning the match and it is reasonable to assume that he relayed this information to his friend. I don't know whether Garry had begun his match preparations before receiving this information; he was not particularly forward about things related to his training. Before the start of the rematch, he had stated publicly that he had prepared seriously for it. Afterwards, he stated that he had not prepared for it. I believe that he did prepare for the rematch, at least in the sense of preparing to play anti-computer chess. Furthermore, I believe that Frederic's visit to Yorktown might have triggered Garry's decision to play in this way. One possible scenario was that the prematch confidence of the Deep Blue team might have caused him to wonder whether we had prepared some killer opening lines. Well, our team of Grandmasters, together with Deep Blue, found quite a few opening innovations, but they were not necessarily killer lines [3]. However, Garry did have reason to be cautious. The easiest way for

---

[3] Deep Blue found some of the new lines, including one that was rejected by the Grandmasters. In the Queen's Gambit Accepted opening, it found a pawn sacrifice (e4) for White that it liked. The Grandmasters thought that Deep Blue's move was too ambitious as the compensations for the pawn seemed to be tenuous. A few months after the rematch, the same move was played at the Grandmaster level, and with good results.

him to avoid our new opening lines was to play anti-computer chess by abandoning normal openings altogether.

Assuming that Garry decided to adopt the anti-computer style of play after Frederic's visit to Yorktown, then he had just over two months to prepare the new style. Since he did not have access to Deep Blue, the commercial chess programs were most likely his sparring partners. Given his statement at the press conference that Deep Blue should beat the commercial programs by 8 to 2, my guess is that his success rate against the commercial program must have been better than 8 to 2. Of course, he was quite wrong in his assessment of the relative playing strength of Deep Blue and the commercial programs.

After Garry's e3, Deep Blue seemed to be in a like mind, and moved its h-file pawn one square. It was a slight error but, considering his last move, it was playable. A better move would have been to develop the queen. This move and Deep Blue's next move, which placed its queen in an awkward position, pointed out a problem that Deep Blue had. When the new chess chip was being designed, little design effort was put in the chess hardware on how to position the queen. The chess books that I had, only gave cursory treatments on the positional play of the queen. After this game, Joe wrote some simple code on where the queen should be placed.

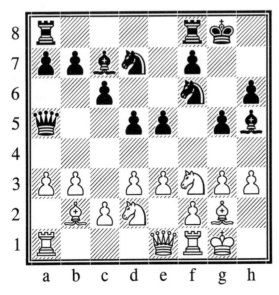

Position after move 14.

For the next few moves, Deep Blue played some other questionable moves, but given the fact that Kasparov was playing suboptimal moves himself, Deep Blue's position was still tenable.

After move fourteen, Deep Blue advanced both the g-file pawn, which was in front of its own king, and the e-file pawn to the fifth rank. Deep Blue's king was almost completely devoid of pawn protection. The f5 square now became a weak square—it could no longer be guarded by the adjacent e-pawn and g-pawn. The position looked horrible even to my eyes. The question was whether Garry could exploit the f5 square easily. When I looked more closely at the position, it dawned on me that maybe Deep Blue's treatment of the position was fine, even though it was certainly not one that would be chosen by a human player. For the next ten moves or so, Garry tried very hard to get a knight to the f5 square, to no avail. In the 1996 match, even though Deep Blue won the first game, I had the distinct feeling that Garry was the one calling the shots. As I watched this game unfold, I had a completely different feeling. It felt more like a negotiation. He was trying to execute his plan, and Deep Blue kept on finding moves to thwart it. He then found a new way to continue his plan, and Deep Blue came back with another counter plan. Neither side was getting what it wanted. Deep Blue, however, would never get frustrated. I had no idea how the game would end, but I did know that if every game where Garry had White was going to be like this one, he would be in deep trouble.

Deep Blue's move 22. ... g4, which resulted in its g-file pawn being traded with Garry's h-file pawn, was controversial. Some analysts considered it justified in that Deep Blue gained better piece activity; since Garry did not get a clearly winning position as a result, it was hard to say for sure that it was a bad move. The move was the result of a bug we had introduced just before the rematch. An automatic tuning run for the evaluation function pointed out to us that the weighting for one class of king safety terms should be increased. When we increased the weights of the terms, Deep Blue appeared to play better, and we left the new weights in. What we did not realize was that, in extreme cases, the new weights reached the maximum allowed value, and became saturated. In other words, Deep Blue no longer distinguished between a very bad position, and an even worse position. Tossing away the g-file pawn therefore meant nothing to Deep Blue, as long as it eliminated Garry's h pawn. We found the bug only after

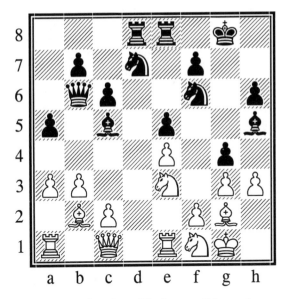

Position after Deep Blue's move 22. ... g4.

game four, when a similar problem showed up. In both cases, it was far from certain that the moves were bad.

Deep Blue's move 28. ... f5 put the game into a crucial phase. At the board, both Garry and I were taking it calmly. He was probably expecting it, even though the move was played at the exact

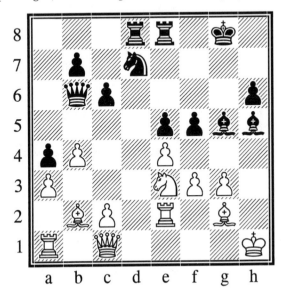

Position after Deep Blue's move 28. ... f5.

instant of his twenty-eighth move. In the auditorium, the commentators were shocked—none of them expected it. It was
probably the best move in the position, and Garry had the choice
of whether to make an exchange sacrifice (giving up a rook for a
bishop or a knight) or not. Deep Blue was expecting him to make
the exchange sacrifice, although it assessed the position after the
sacrifice to be much better for Garry. Post mortem analysis indicated that he would have been much worse off if he had not made
the sacrifice.

As it was, Deep Blue did not like its position. Usually, this
meant that I would be feeling miserable, but I wasn't—the position
was messy and yet we would have our chances. In the auditorium
and at the pressroom, people were starting to talk about an upset
win for Deep Blue, but they were not seeing Deep Blue's output.
Garry quickly made the move that initiated the exchange sacrifice.
The next few moves all went as Deep Blue expected. Both Garry
and Deep Blue apparently had seen all the ramifications.

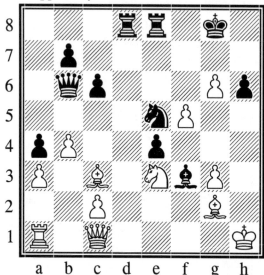

Position before Deep Blue's move 33. ... Qb5.

When the dust settled, however, Deep Blue played a questionable move, 33. ... Qb5, which allowed Garry to play Qf1 to
trade off the queens. Deep Blue was willing to trade the queens
because its king was less safe. But Garry also had two *connected
passed* pawns (the f5 pawn and the g6 pawn) that could become
very valuable in the endgame phase *if the queens left the board*. The

ability to express this endgame feature existed in the chess hardware but was not in use. Joe wrote the code to use this hardware ability after game one, but the new code was not active until we had a rest day after game two to check it out. Afterwards, Deep Blue played 33. ... h5 instead.

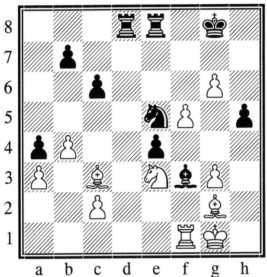

Position before 36. ... Kf8. 36. ... Ng4 was the last chance to draw.

The move 33. ... Qb5 was probably bad, but it was not necessarily losing, as Deep Blue had a drawing move later on move thirty-six. Instead of 36. ... Kf8?, 36. ... Ng4! appears to draw. Post mortem analysis with Deep Blue suggested that Deep Blue might have played 36. ... Ng4 if it could have searched one more ply, which would have required roughly a six-fold increase in search speed.

Without 36. ... Ng4, Deep Blue's position quickly went downhill. By move forty-four, we were close to resigning for it. Then it suffered the same bug that caused Deep Blue Jr to toss a pawn against Christiansen in its training match. Instead of playing 44. ... Rf5 and prolonging the game as it intended, it played the instantly losing move 44. ... Rd1, and after Garry's reply, we immediately resigned. That night, Joe worked late and finally fixed the bug that had haunted us for over a month.

After the game, we knew we had work to do, but the team was in high spirits. We had Black, and yet Garry's anti-computer chess experiment almost backfired on him. Deep Blue mishandled the position once the position became double edged but, if this scenario continued, we would have our share of wins as Black. For a group of people who had just lost the first game of a six-game match, we must have looked surprisingly cheerful to the reporters.

Garry, meanwhile, apparently was puzzled by Deep Blue's last move in the game. The day after game two was a rest day, and when I surfed the web to catch up on the match news, I came across an article written by Frederic Friedel about what happened in the Kasparov camp after game one. Garry was perplexed by the move 44. ... Rd1. Deep Blue played it as a result of a bug but Garry did not know that. So the whole Kasparov camp went into a very deep analysis on why the alternative move 44. ... Rf5 was no good. In the end, they concluded that the reason why Deep Blue did not play 44. ... Rf5 was "It probably saw mates in twenty or more [moves]." I could not help but burst out laughing [4].

A Bad Move That Wins

The morning before game two, the team debated whether we should make changes to Deep Blue's evaluation function. Joe had already fixed the bug responsible for the last move in game one, but there were two other changes that we needed to look at. The proposed change to the passed pawn evaluation was too drastic, and we decided to leave it out for game two. Joe's change to the queen evaluation was relatively minor, and we decided to keep it in the program. The program that played game two was essentially the same program that played game one.

Murray was the starting operator for the day, so I spent time in the operations room during the early part of the game. Deep Blue opened with 1. e4. Garry, instead of replying with his normal Sicilian 1. ... c5, played 1. ... e5, just as he did in game five of the 1996 match. Had Garry played 1. ... c5, we would have been ready to battle him with the main lines of the Sicilian instead of the c3 variation that we played in 1996.

The game quickly became a Ruy Lopez opening (also known as the Spanish Torture), named after a 15th-century Spanish priest. Nick and Joel, rather than Miguel our Spanish contingent, had prepared the basic lines for the Ruy Lopez. As the opening quickly unfolded, Joel was in an unusually upbeat mood. He had played

---

[4] One report stated that the Kasparov team also burst out laughing when they finished their analysis on why 44. ... Rf5 was no good.

many games in the Ruy Lopez against Deep Blue Jr and was quite confident of Deep Blue's ability to handle the position.

Meanwhile, in the auditorium, the commentators were saying how terrible Deep Blue's opening preparation was. Deep Blue had allowed Garry to achieve a closed position. The commentators had written off Deep Blue even before the opening phase of the game was completed. It was not said, but it was clear that they were expecting Deep Blue to lose the game.

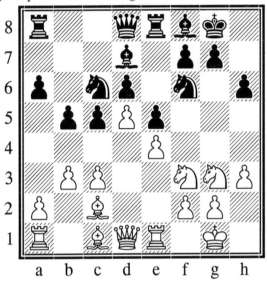

Position after Deep Blue's move 16. d5.

Garry was probably quite happy when Deep Blue played 16. d5, blocking up the center, ostensibly giving him the closed position that he so desired. Joel was also quite happy. Garry's opening selection had given Deep Blue a significant advantage in space that could haunt Garry for the rest of the game. Joel had been on the receiving end of many punishing games with the same theme. In the operations room, slowly but surely we saw Deep Blue's assessment of its positional edge creeping up. The commentators in the auditorium continued to say that Deep Blue was in trouble. Grandmaster Yasser Seirawan: "This isn't the kind of position that the computer can play very well." International Master Mike Valvo: "From the computer's point of view, there's nothing really clear in this kind of position."

Joel, possibly sensing a chance to needle Yasser, whom he had known for years, asked to be excused from the operations room so that he could get to the auditorium stage to defend Deep Blue's opening preparation. Almost immediately after he left, the commentators, having had more time to digest the board position and seeing Garry shaking his head a little bit, had a change of heart. Yasser was starting to say that he liked White.

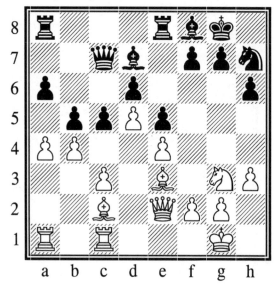

Position after Deep Blue's move 24. Rec1.

Deep Blue's "human-like" move 24. Rec1 forced its opponent to make a hard decision. Garry's 24. ... c4 closing up the c file was criticized after the game as removing his own last chance of counter play. Deep Blue was ready to play c4 itself and bust the whole position wide open and Garry's move at least stopped that. Garry probably did not want to allow the complications and, given the fact that Deep Blue had the more active pieces, it was an understandable decision.

Joel reached the auditorium stage at this point, a little too late to needle Yasser. Joel's first remarks were, "Well, I was following your commentary from upstairs, and you were talking about how closed the position was for so long. I was wondering when you guys were going to get around to the fact that the position was better for White, and you eventually did." The audience laughed.

In the operations room, Joe and I exchanged a look when Deep Blue doubled up its rooks on the a-file, and yet refused to open up the a-file immediately. Both of us were thinking about what happened many months ago after Joe knocked on my door.

The new evaluation feature about rooks on potential open files was in play here. I smiled and said to Joe, "Not bad for an afternoon's work." The two White rooks on the *potential* open a-file tied down Garry's heavy pieces to his back rank, and forced him to be completely passive.

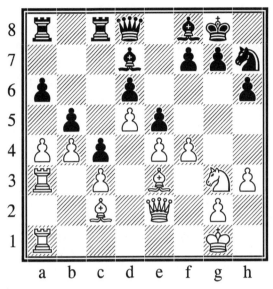

Position after Deep Blue's move 26. f4.

Deep Blue's 26. f4, opening up a second front on the king side, was probably partially a result of the new evaluation feature. Anatoly Karpov was watching the game live in one of the Internet chess clubs. He was making quite a few comments early in the game, and was fairly dismissive of Deep Blue's play. Deep Blue's 26. f4 did not escape his criticism; although, to the best of my knowledge, none of the other Grandmasters shared his view—in fact, they universally praised the move. As the game progressed, Anatoly made fewer and fewer comments, and towards the end fell silent.

In the game room, Murray signaled that he needed a replacement. Garry was still at the board thinking, so I took the long tortuous route through the normal entrance into the game room. I sat down with the other spectators and waited for Garry's move before making the switch with Murray. When I was in the operations room, Garry looked unhappy but otherwise normal on the video monitor. I was taken aback when I looked at him in the game room. He looked like someone who had just woken up from a bad nightmare. Part of his face was visibly red as if he had slept on that side for a while.

Soon after I took over as the operator, Deep Blue played the two moves that would cause Garry a lot of grief for the rest of the match. They were the moves 36. axb5 and 37. Be4. Right before axb5, it played the move Bxd6, which was followed by Garry's own Bxd6. While computing for the move Bxd6, Deep Blue's evaluation dropped. As a result, it went into the panic mode and ended up spending just slightly less than 15 minutes on its move thirty-five. As you will see later, Bxd6, which was an obvious move, used up more computation time than the next two moves combined, despite Garry's later claim that Deep Blue spent more time on 36. axb5 than any other move played in the match. (He might have meant 37. Be4, but Deep Blue spent only a normal amount of time on it.)

While writing the previous paragraph, I saw the log[5] for the move Bxd6 for the first time since the match itself, and it showed something quite interesting.

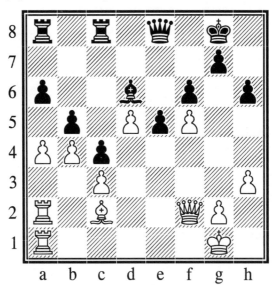

Position before Deep Blue's move 36. axb5.

5 At the time of this writing, you can find the game logs by following the links to the Deep Blue match site and then to the individual games from the web site www.chess.ibm.com. It is possible that IBM may not keep the site up indefinitely.

First, when Deep Blue finished the panic mode search for Bxd6, it was planning to play 36. Qb6 as the follow-up to Bxd6, but only barely, because it already saw hints that Garry might be able to do something nasty.

Before Deep Blue went into the panic mode for Bxd6, it had come up with an unusual principal variation when it finished its 9-ply search. The main line it gave was 15-ply deep. This number, however, was only the search depth on the master workstation, and did not include the additional search depths on the slave workstations (2+ plies), and on the chess chips (4+ plies). The main line was really at least 21-ply deep and maybe well over 30-ply deep, since there were additional search extensions on the work-stations and on the chips. Deep Blue was expecting Garry to give up two pawns and push his e-file pawn for a potential attack. The score was, however, only slightly more than a pawn up for Deep Blue, signifying that it thought Garry would have slightly less than a pawn worth of positional compensation.

At the end of its 10-ply search, it was expecting Garry to sac-rifice *three* pawns, but its score had dropped further to only a pawn up. At the eleventh ply, the score for Bxd6 dropped again, which then triggered Deep Blue to go into the panic mode. The principal variation once again had the three-pawn sacrifice by Garry, but it now showed him recapturing a pawn in the process. The line it gave was now 18-ply deep, or was really at least 24-ply deep and maybe even over 40-ply deep along the deepest line. I remembered that I was saying to myself at this point during the game, "Perhaps Be4 blocking the e-file pawn would have been a good move some-where around here."

Meanwhile, unbeknownst to me, Yasser gave the two-pawn sacrifice line to the audience at the auditorium and over the Internet. Deep Blue had discovered the same sacrifice line during its 9-ply search but had since rejected it as an inferior line for Black.

After Garry made his move thirty-five, all the other comput-ers in the world and the audience in the auditorium were expecting Deep Blue to play 36. Qb6, winning a pawn in the process. But now Deep Blue even more disliked the compensation that Black could get against Qb6. This time it went into the panic mode in a different way. When its normal search time was up at the start of the 11-ply search, the expected principal variation was falling apart somewhere deep down in the search. It entered a temporary panic mode that forced it to resolve the score for move

Qb6. When this search was completed, the score had dropped to 48 points (slight less than half a pawn) [6]. Since this score was more than 15 points lower than the expected score 74, Deep Blue continued to stay in panic mode to examine the alternative moves. The next move completed was axb5, which had a score of 63. This score was good enough, so Deep Blue immediately played 36. axb5, spending about 6.5 minutes on the move. It was still planning to play Qb6 on the next move. Garry replied with axb5.

On the thirty-seventh move, the score for Qb6 at the eleventh ply dropped to 32 points, 84 seconds into the search. After 126 seconds into the search, Be4 was scored as 37 points and replaced Qb6 as the best move. The 11-ply search was completed after 182 seconds. The search was terminated at its normal time after 199 seconds. Deep Blue did not go into panic mode on its 37th move, it just spent its normal allocation of time. As mentioned earlier, this last fact would become interesting, as later events showed.

It is hard to say with any certainty what causes a chess machine that searches two-hundred million positions per second to play a particular move. For the moves in question, I believe that two things came into play. Deep Blue was searching very deep along the critical lines, and its king safety evaluation had much greater weight than in other programs.

For 36. axb5, the decision was made because of very deep calculations. It turns out that 36. Qb6 might be objectively the better move, as White reserves the option of getting back into positions similar to the game continuation, while giving Black a chance to lose immediately. Based on the post game comments given by Garry, it was possible that Qb6 would have ended the game almost instantly since he did not see the strongest line. But then we would not have the very interesting finish of game two.

---

6 For the chess enthusiasts, the three-pawn sacrifice line starts as follows: 36. Qb6!? Qe7! (the alternative two-pawn sacrifice move Rd8 is refuted by 37. Be4!) 37. ab5 Rab8. And now the best line for White is 38. Qe3! ab5 39. Be4, spurning the three-pawn sacrifice to reach a position similar to the game. If White decides to accept the three-pawn sacrifice, then we have 38. Qa6 e4! 39. Be4 (39. Re1 Qe5 40. Re4 Qh2 41. Kf2 Bg3 42. Kf3 Bd6 draw) Qe5 40. Bf3 Rd8 and Black would get significant compensation. For example, if 41. Qa3, Re8 42. Re2 Qh2 43. Kf1 Re2 44. Be2 Re8 45. Bh5 Qf4 46. Bf3 Re3 47. Qb2 Qh2 draws. If 41. Ra3, Qe3 42. Kf1 Qd3 43. Be2 Qf5 44. Kg1 Qe5 45. Kf1 (45. Bf3 Re8) Re8 46. Bf3 Bc7! 47. d6 Bb6 48. d7 Red8 49. Re1 Qd6, and Black might be winning.

There was some evidence that the king safety evaluation was involved in the move decision for move 37 Be4, which was more a positional than a tactical decision. After game four, we found and fixed the king safety bug that occurred earlier in game one. Deep Blue stopped playing Be4 after Joe made the first bug fix, which effectively toned down the king safety term. When it was turned up again, Deep Blue again played Be4. Since everyone seemed to think that Be4 was a great move, Joe decided to use the second bug fix, which had the king safety evaluation roughly back at the same level as in game two, for games five and six.

I was not really too happy about the situation when Be4 was played. Deep Blue assessed the position as only slightly advantageous. It was a good thing that Garry did not seem able to read my face. My mood improved somewhat when, over Garry's next few moves, Deep Blue's evaluation started to creep upward. I was expecting the game to last quite a while. Then, suddenly, after Deep Blue's forty-fifth move, Garry offered his hand and said, "I resign." I was surprised as it seemed a little early to resign, but he apparently had had enough Spanish torture for one day. Deep Blue scored the position as about 160 points up. It was a winning edge, but the game was not really over. Garry probably started the game in an optimistic mood, especially when Deep Blue closed up the center. From then on, he had been forced to play defensive moves. The pressure just kept on building, and finally he could not take it any longer.

Garry did not say anything else after he resigned; there was no post-mortem discussion this time. He left the building quickly with his entourage. We went on to the auditorium stage to a round of applause. We were exuberant. Our labor for the last year had finally been recognized by the world. Murray, Joe and I had argued from time to time in the past, but for the last year or so we had put aside our differences and worked on the common goal. We had come together with the Grandmasters to be a real team, and all the teamwork had finally paid off. Personally, it was a very satisfying moment. The six months of work that I had spent on the new chess chip was completely justified. For those six months, I had poured my body and soul into the project. Having no weekends for six whole months, driving home late at night and waking up several times a night to check the simulation had all suddenly become worthwhile. We were happy. We felt like proud parents who had just seen their new baby taking the first significant step.

Yasser was not giving Deep Blue much credit at the beginning of Game two but by the end he changed his mind: "I would be proud to have this one." Maurice Ashley: "It's a gorgeous game." Joel Benjamin had the following to say: "This is a game that any human grandmaster would be proud to have played for White. This was not a computer-type game. This was real chess." It was the best game ever played by a computer.

Yet, there was a fly in the ointment.

I woke up early the next day, which happened to be a rest day. Still excited from the last game, I went into the operations room to catch up on the Internet news. One of the sites that I visited was Mark Crowther's "The Week In Chess". I had had some communication with Mark a few years back. He felt that computers would destroy chess, and a loss by the World Chess Champion to a computer would be very bad for the game. I suggested that man-machine chess matches could be a great boon to chess, and the eventual loss by the World Chess Champion to a computer would actually be a great opportunity for the chess world. The huge publicity would draw people to the game, and if the chess world could respond positively and take advantage of the publicity to promote the fun and enjoyment of chess to the new audience, there could be a massive increase in the game's popularity. Mark was not completely convinced. Perhaps he agreed with my logic but was not sure about how the chess world would react.

The first statement on Mark's web site about game two surprised me. He made a blanket statement that game two should be a draw. My first reaction was, "Mark is in denial." I took a cursory glance at Mark's analysis of the final position in game two, and went on to other news items before I went back to the hotel. Over breakfast, I mentioned to Murray that Mark was claiming that game two should be a draw. While talking with Murray, a thought occurred to me, "What if I am the one in denial?" I decided to double-check the analysis given on the web after breakfast.

I went back to the operations room and tried out the variations given on the web with Deep Blue Jr, as Deep Blue was being used to test out our opening preparations. Within twenty minutes, I was in shock. Yes, it looked like the position might be a draw with best play by Garry. There was a way for White to avoid an outright repetition draw, but the resulting ending, even though better for White, might not be winning. Deep Blue's last two moves in the game turned out to be mistakes.

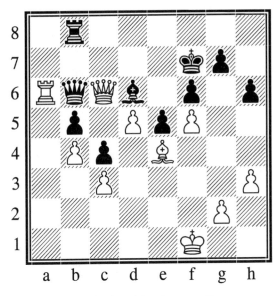

The final position in game 2.

Move 44. Kf1, moving king from g1 to f1 in response to Garry's Qb6+, even though still winning, made life tougher. A better move would have been 44. Kh1, which wins easily as there was no chance of a repetition draw for Black afterwards. Deep Blue played 44. Kf1 because it thought that it could force the queens off the board, and the ending would have been better with the White king closer to the center. The real culprit was the last move of the game, 45. Ra6, which allowed Black to either get a slightly inferior ending or a very deep repetition draw. I later discovered that the drawing line was first found by painstaking group efforts involving both human chess players and computer chess programs. Black's best move is 45. ... Qe3, which is fairly easy to see from a human perspective, but some of the follow-up moves for Black are not so easy for human beings. Garry obviously did not see the follow-up moves and hence the resignation.

After 45. ... Qe3, White could play either 46. Qd7+ or 46. Qxd6. To refute either of the moves, you need to do fairly deep and tricky analyses. Deep Blue Jr had the critical moves in its main line within minutes, but to sort out all the ramifications took close to an hour. The deepest line was about 30 plies deep. Deep Blue, in theory, should be able to cover 30 plies of forcing lines in real time. But there was one huge complication. Deep Blue, like most other chess programs, used the so-called *transposition table*. The transposition table allows a chess program to avoid searching the "same" position twice when the new position is a repeat of an old position already searched. The problem is that the new position is not really the same as the old one. They have different move histories. Normally, this fact does not matter, but when repetitions are involved, a program could either miss a repetition or find a false repetition because of the use of the transposition table. Sometimes, when the program searches deeper, the problem eventually goes away, and sometimes, the problem never goes away. Anyway, either Deep Blue was not searching deep enough, or it was sidetracked by the transposition table from seeing the potential repetition draw.

From the pure chess point of view, Deep Blue's last move in game 2, Ra6, deserves to be annotated with a "??" mark (this means a highly dubious move), as it could have allowed a win to be turned into a draw. However, from the psychological point of view, the move deserves to be annotated with a "??!!" mark (!! means an excellent move. ??!! would mean something like "a highly dubious but excellent move"). It did win the game, and in light of what happened subsequently in the match, some might even say that the move won the match.

Tempest in a Teacup

I phoned Murray the moment I realized that game two could have been a draw. We both felt a letdown. On the other hand, a win is a win, and it would be quite interesting to see how Garry would respond to the news. I knew that I would not want to be the one to tell him. As for the Deep Blue team, we had it easy. Our silicon-based player could not care less.

Frederic Friedel wrote an article on how the Kasparov camp found out about the potential drawing lines and how Garry responded to the news. Frederic had a flare for the dramatic so I always took what he said with a pinch of salt, especially when it was related to Fritz, a commercial chess program that he sold. Anyway, his account did suggest a few things that were missed by other reports.

According to the article, Frederic worked late after game two using Fritz to go down the potential drawing line and analyze the resulting positions. He found the drawing moves with the help of Fritz, but without knowing what had already transpired over the

Internet. However, at this point he was not too sure whether the position was indeed a draw. This was not a big surprise. The lines that lead to repetition draws were simply too deep, and Fritz, not surprisingly, could not see the repetitions starting from the final position of game two [7].

The next morning, he asked Yuri Dohokian, Garry's match second, to come to his room to look at the analysis. Frederic: "Yuri drew a sharp breath at 46. ... Re8 and said, 'We didn't look at this move.' He started checking my analysis and after some time came to the shocking conclusion: this move really draws." It is not clear from the above statement whether Yuri's "we" included Garry himself. But suffice it to say that Garry missed at least one critical drawing move during the game and possibly during his own postmortem analysis when he had all the time that he needed.

Of Garry's reaction, Frederic wrote, "Garry clutched his head and froze in the middle of the Fifth Avenue. There were no expletives, no cursing, just stunned silence." They were on their way to an Italian restaurant and Frederic described what happened in the restaurant, "... it must have been a miserable meal. It wasn't. And he's amazing. After about ten or fifteen minutes, he suddenly was fired up and started telling us about some Russian movie." So, according to Frederic, Garry took the news well.

While the news of the potential draw created a crisis in the Kasparov camp, among the Deep Blue team members, the main topic before game three was whether Garry would continue to play anti-computer chess. Our first feeling was that he would start to play normal chess because his anti-computer chess tactics were not doing too well. He did win game one, but Deep Blue could have secured a draw close to the end of the game. From our point of view, Garry was a little lucky that Deep Blue did not mix it up further and possibly even win the game. Game two was an outright disaster for him. He could have secured a draw as well but, like Deep Blue in game one, he did not see the drawing line either. Anyhow, the seed of Garry's game two loss was clearly his desire to play anti-computer chess, which led him to reach awful positions that were supposedly good against other computers, but turned out to be dismal against Deep Blue. But this was an analysis based

---

7 It is not out of the question that some other program might claim that it sees the repetitions, but chances are that if it does, it would be due to false repetition claims resulting from the use of the transposition table.

on pure chess merit. Our amateur psychological analysis of Garry's mental state led to a very different conclusion. He had a very strong will; most people would even say that he could be stubborn at times. He came to the match with a set plan, and that apparently was to play anti-computer chess. It was most likely that he would not change his plan unless it proved to be a complete failure. A good question to ask, now that we are looking back, is what would have happened if he had played normal chess for the entire rematch? I don't know the answer, but I do believe that it would have been a close match as well, and I would not be too surprised by a Deep Blue match win.

By the time game three started, the entire Deep Blue team believed that Garry would stick with anti-computer chess no matter what. So when he played 1. d3, it came as no surprise to us. Joe was the first operator for this game. The move 1. d3 probably had never been played at the highest level of chess. Ironically, it was a move that we had used against another chess program back in Deep Thought days. The commentators in the auditorium were quite shocked by the move. Mike Valvo: "Oh, my God." Maurice Ashley: "A cagey move. A shock of shocks in this match. This match has everything." Yasser Seirawan: "I think we have a new opening move."

During the first few moves, Garry appeared to be trying to

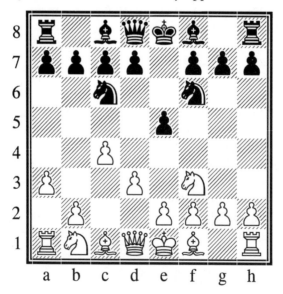

The position before 4. ... d6.

trick Deep Blue into playing the White side of the Sicilian defense, but, with him having an extra move, which could be critical in some of the Sicilian lines. Deep Blue's 4. ... d6, instead of the risky d5, sidestepped this possibility.

After Garry's 5. Nc3, the game had transposed back into a known English opening position. In this position, British Grandmaster Michael Adams once played Be7 as Black. Deep Blue was given a hefty bias to play 5. ... Be7 as a result of this one single game played by Michael. Many commentators criticized the move as a little bit passive. After this game, Murray changed the code used to compute the move bias in known positions. Michael was a very good chess player, but giving Be7 a hefty bias just because he had played it once, seemed excessive.

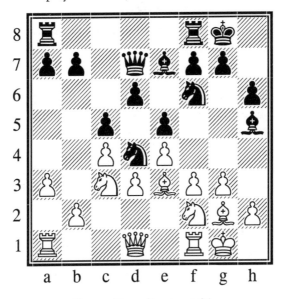

The position after move 14.

After Deep Blue's 14. ... c5, Garry had a slight edge but, according to the Grandmasters who had had time to think about the position after the game, Deep Blue's position appeared to be solid. Some Grandmasters had the first impression that the position clearly favored Garry. The British Grandmaster John Nunn commented, "True, Deep Blue has played the opening in a way which appears very odd to human eyes, because it doesn't fit any of the normal patterns for playing with the English opening. Ideally, White would like to set his kingside pawn in motion, but

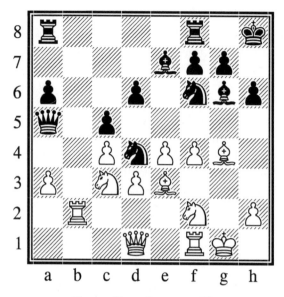

The position after move 22.

it isn't easy to achieve this." Sometimes, searching two-hundred million positions per second produces unusual new solutions.

The first critical moment of the game came after Deep Blue played 22. ... Qa5, and Garry replied 23. Bd2. At this point, Deep Blue had two choices, to play Qxa3 or Nxg4. The machine at first preferred to play Nxg4, but apparently Garry would get too much play, so it played Qxa3. This move wins a pawn, but in exchange, Garry obtained serious compensation.

The second critical moment of the game came when Deep Blue played 26. ... Bh7, allowing Garry to shut out its light square bishop for most of the rest of the game. We were not too happy with this move decision, nor were we happy about how Deep Blue was assessing the position as being in its favor. At best, the position was about equal. The penalty for bishops being shut out from the game was increased after this game. The alternative move, Bh5, appeared to be playable, but that would have been a different game with chances for both sides. Our main purpose in increasing the penalty was to encourage Deep Blue to try to activate the bishop whenever the opportunity presented itself.

The rest of the game was not too remarkable. Deep Blue's move 40. ... Bc7, returning the pawn, was the last difficult move. I had replaced Joe as the operator in the middle of the game. Garry was not too happy during the last few moves in this game. Deep

The position before 26. ... Bh7.

Blue was in the slightly worse position, but it had set up an unbreakable fortress. For the last five moves, Deep Blue just shuffled its king back and forth, and there was nothing constructive that Garry could do. He knew it was a draw, I knew it was a draw, and the rest of the world knew it was a draw but after what hap-

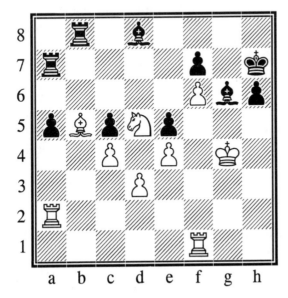

The position before 40. ... Bc7.

pened in game two, Garry could not bring himself to offer a draw immediately. What if there was a win? I felt sorry for him when he deliberated long and hard before he was absolutely, positively sure and offered the draw.

I was quite excited after this game. It was the first time we had ever played into a fortress draw in a serious game. I was not ready for Garry's outburst when we got down to the auditorium.

He first complained that Deep Blue spent the longest amount of time in all their games when it rejected the move Qb6 in game two. None of us were sure what Garry was saying but in any case, his recollection was wrong. Deep Blue rejected Qb6 twice in game two, at the time when it made 36. axb5 and 37. Be4. It spent about 6.5 minutes at move 36. axb5, which was far shorter than the fifteen minutes or so it spent on 35. Bxd6, the move right before axb5. Furthermore, I am almost certain that Deep Blue had spent more than fifteen minutes on other moves in earlier games against Garry. The second time Deep Blue rejected Qb6, it spent just over three minutes, which was its regular allocated time. It was not clear whether Garry was referring to 36. axb5 or 37. Be4. Some of his remarks during the match seemed to indicate that he was more concerned about 37. Be4, which, however, was just a positional move and was certainly not played at a slower pace. After the match, several computer chess programmers indicated that their programs would play 37. Be4 with slight changes in their evaluation function. Garry's next remark seemed to indicate that 36. axb5 surprised him.

He then said, "I sacrificed two pawns and I had some chances. I don't think that these chances are enough." I had no idea what he was saying at the time. Now, looking back, it all made sense. He had seen the two-pawn sacrifice line that Yasser was talking about in the auditorium. That line did not quite work. At the time, none of us realized that the line Deep Blue had was an entirely different sacrifice. Garry then described that he tried out the lines on his computers, but none of them saw any way for Black to save the game in the two-pawn sacrifice line.

He followed, "This machine missed, from a computer point of view, an elementary draw." When I heard this, I said to myself, "Huh?" The potential draw at the end of game two was hardly an elementary draw for a computer. Either he was getting very bad advice about what computers could do, or he genuinely did not understand chess computers. Both explanations were hard to believe. He did have good computer chess people working with him, and had he tried to get Fritz to find the draw, he would have known that the draw was far from easy. If Deep Blue missed the draw, the draw obviously could not be an elementary one, unless we had a bug. Garry's remark just did not make sense.

Joel was given the microphone and explained what had happened in a straightforward way. I thought that he did a good job explaining everything in laymen's terms.

Garry, however, continued to complain about how much time Deep Blue had spent on rejecting Qb6 (it spent only 6.5 minutes), how simple the draw was, and how the computer should not have been able to miss the elementary draw, and yet have been able to reject the Qb6 move. He also wanted to see move variations.

At this point, Maurice Ashley said, "If I am reading you correctly, Kasparov, or maybe I'm speaking out of turn. Do you think that there may have been some kind of human intervention during this game?"

Garry said, "It reminds me of the famous goal which Maradona scored against England in 1986. He said it was the Hand of God." Maradona knocked the soccer ball into the net with his hand and the referee mistakenly allowed the goal to count. It seemed to me that Garry was apparently accusing us of cheating, although very obliquely. Every one of us was fuming. I was tempted to grab the microphone, go to the Deep Blue model on the stage, and say, "Well, shall we open up this box and see whether Bobby (Fischer) is inside?" Over the years, Garry had been almost like a friend to me. He was as close as possible to being a friend without being one. The competition between the Deep Blue team and the Kasparov camp had been very good for both sides. Suddenly, I felt that I no longer wanted to have anything to do with him.

Joel could not take it any more, "After the match, we'll be happy to share exactly what it saw in this case. But I think that it's definitely a mistake for Garry to give a position to Fritz or any other computer and say, 'This is computer behavior and this is what Deep Blue must be thinking or what Deep Blue would do.' I think he's seen from the games that he's played against Deep Blue that it is no ordinary computer and plays at an entirely different level from any computer that he's seen. So maybe he should come to grips with the fact that Deep Blue can do a lot of things that he did not think were possible."

Joel could have been a little bit more diplomatic. Garry never did come to grips, not even after he was given Deep Blue's log for the two moves in question, after the match. I think part of the problem was that he asked for the log of the wrong moves. He should have asked for the log of move 35. Bxd6 in game two. Had he seen the 35. Bxd6 log, he would have realized that Deep Blue had already seen the three-pawn sacrifice when it finished its 10-ply search for Bxd6.

The other part of Garry's problem was indeed that he did not know what Deep Blue was capable of. The decision to avoid Qb6 on move 36 was mostly tactical, and involved mainly calculations. If he had really studied Deep Thought or Deep Thought II games, he would have realized that Deep Blue's predecessors were already capable of producing tactics way beyond the capabilities of other computers, even if the others had been scaled up to Deep Thought or Deep Thought II's search speed. And Deep Blue was close to a thousand times faster than either Deep Thought or Deep Thought II.

Last, but not least, the three-pawn sacrifice is quite hard, at least for other computers, and, it seems, for Garry as well. Pierre Nolot, a French chess journalist, once collected eleven chess positions that he said were unsolvable by any computer in reasonable time. Deep Thought II solved several of them in tournament time, and maybe eight or nine of them within a day. Some of those positions that Deep Thought II solved are probably still beyond the best commercial chess programs[8], even when given a full year of time. The three-pawn sacrifice that could arise after 36. Qb6 might be in the same class of complexity.

A Narrow Escape

Before the start of game four, there was some serious doubt as to whether Garry would show up at all. His manager, Owen Williams, was on the phone for a while, and everyone was relieved when the report came that Garry was on his way.

The Deep Blue team was mostly in the dark about what was happening until months later. The following is a reconstruction from interviewing the people involved.

According to Ken Thompson, who was on the appeals com-

---

[8] This may change by the time you read this. A few amateur programs were doing well on the Nolot position after adding in singular extensions. Some commercial programmers may very well decide to adopt the idea as well.

mittee, the night after game two he received a request from Garry. He wanted him to go over the game two log and verify that everything was above board. Ken had seen the log in real time and was well aware of what happened, but wanted to see it again to refresh his memory before he reported back to Garry.

Ken then asked C J for a printout of the log on the rest day and C J readily agreed to the request. Ken informed Garry that the request had been accepted. Later, C J promised to give Ken the game two log in question around noon the next day. Ken apparently told the other members of the appeals committee that the problem was taken care of. According to C J's recollection, someone from the appeals committee, probably Monty Newborn, then told him that the problem was resolved. Unfortunately, this led to Ken not getting the log at the specified time, as C J thought that the problem no longer mattered. Somewhere around this time, someone in the Kasparov camp told C J that Garry wanted to see the log for himself. Owen Williams was later quoted as saying IBM had agreed to let Garry have access to all the game logs during the match but then reneged on the promise. As far as I know, no one from IBM had ever agreed that he could have access to the game logs while the match was still going on. One possibility was that people in the Kasparov camp might have misinterpreted what Ken told them.

If it were up to the Deep Blue team, we would never have agreed to give Garry access to the game logs during the match. Deep Blue's game logs contained its "inner thoughts" on how the games would proceed, what it would have done given hypothetical moves that did not show up in the games, what it thought Garry's best moves should be, and so on. If he had the logs, he would have a complete road map on how Deep Blue would behave, rightly or wrongly, in various circumstances. Even a rank beginner, armed with the game logs, a very good memory, and the help of a good team of Grandmasters, would be able to beat Deep Blue consistently by merely memorizing the winning lines. Garry, besides being possibly the strongest Grandmaster ever, has a phenomenal memory. Granting him direct access to Deep Blue's game logs would be equivalent to giving him Deep Blue's silicon head on a silver platter, with $700,000 on the side.

Anyway, when Ken asked C J minutes before game three about the log, C J probably thought that he was asking whether Garry would be given the log, and gave a flat "no". Ken then told

Garry that the request was turned down. Garry was most likely already not in the best frame of mind after discovering that the final position in game two could be a draw. The fact that he had White in game three and that game ended a draw probably did not help his mood either. No wonder he lashed out at the Deep Blue team after the game. This whole sequence of events did not make his outburst completely excusable in my mind, but did make it more understandable.

By the morning of the day for game four, Ken was starting to get angry with C J, and said that he would not come to the operations room unless the printout was produced. A phone call was placed by IBM security to Ken, who was in his office in New Jersey, that the printout would be available for him when he came back. Meanwhile, Owen was saying that Garry would not play. Garry later said that he never said he would not play. The whole thing was up in the air until close to game time, when it was reported that Garry was on his way. Ken finally got the log and informed Garry about its receipt ten minutes before game four.

Now, back to the game itself.

During game four, Yasser made the comment, "It looks to me like Deep Blue is in deep doo-doo", which filled the auditorium with laughter. Game four gave me the most anxious moment of the match, even though Deep Blue did manage to draw. It was also a game full of richness. Garry played a profound pawn sacrifice that Deep Blue had a hard time fully appreciating. Afterwards we also found the king safety evaluation bug that had shown up in game one. I am certain that if I look deeper into the game, I will find many new ideas to improve Deep Blue.

Garry answered Deep Blue's 1. e4 with 1. ... c6 this time, the Caro Kann defense. Once again, he did not play his pet Sicilian defense, although by now this was no longer a surprise. We were fully expecting him to continue to play strange stuff. Garry's next move, 2. ... d6, however, had the commentators in the auditorium and the pressroom scratching their heads, "What do we call this thing?"

Grandmaster Miguel Illescas was in the operations room for this game. I was also in the operations room for the early part. Miguel is one of the most cheerful people that I have ever met. He almost always found some good things to say about Deep Blue's moves. He was a great person to have around when we needed cheering up, and in this game we needed cheering up.

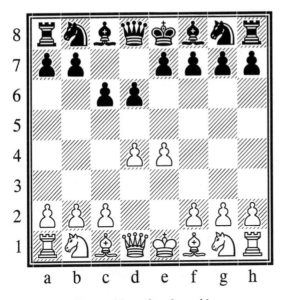

The position after 2. ... d6.

Miguel was quite optimistic about Deep Blue's chances early on. By move twenty, the machine seemed to have all the opening problems solved and was ready to start some real action. Right at this point, Garry unleashed an amazing pawn sacrifice 20.... e5. When Miguel saw this move, he instinctively called it a good sac-

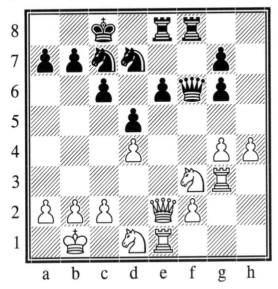

The position before Kasparov's 20. ... e5!.

rifice. Deep Blue would not play the move but assessed the sacrifice as sound.

Next, Deep Blue played some moves that were quite strange
to human eyes. 26. b5 was both panned and praised by different
commentators. Garry himself spoke highly of the move. We did
not like the move, and it triggered an evaluation software bug hunt
the next day. Joe was the one who finally found and fixed the bug
relating to this move and the corresponding move from game one.
Deep Blue's strange moves right before playing b5 appeared to be
caused by the same bug.

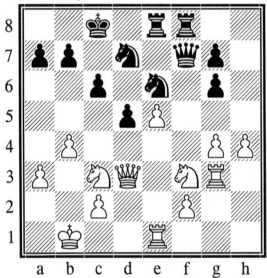

The position before Deep Blue's 26. ... b5.

As the position started to clarify after Deep Blue's strange b5,
Miguel was having second thoughts. The position continued to
deteriorate, and even Miguel was getting worried. Deep Blue was
starting to evaluate the position as better for Garry. The day had
started brightly for us, with two Whites for three games, but now
things were looking bad.

At this juncture, we had a surprise guest in the operations
room. IBM Chairman and CEO, Lou Gerstner, had decided to pay
the team a visit. *New York Times* reporter Bruce Weber happened to
be in the room. Lou's dramatic comment on the match was printed in the *New York Times* the next day: "I just think we should look
at this as a chess match between the world's greatest chess player
and ...", a short pause, "Garry Kasparov."

After this, none of us was willing to spoil the moment and tell Lou that Deep Blue might be in trouble. Lou stayed for about five minutes and then left.

When Miguel had time to look at the board position again, he became quite pessimistic, the most pessimistic that I ever saw him in the entire match. He thought that Deep Blue would not be able to survive the ending, which looked unfavorable. Deep Blue's assessment of the position, however, never got below half a pawn down. Murray was operating Deep Blue at the time. If Miguel was so unhappy about the position, Murray must have been feeling even worse.

On Garry's move forty-three, Deep Blue self-terminated. Before the match, Joe added in a piece of code that monitored the efficiency of the parallel search and terminated the program itself if the efficiency dropped too low[9]. Joe's idea was that a fresh start would be preferable in this case. This instance was one of the two times during the entire rematch that the self-termination code got executed. In game three, Deep Blue also self-terminated, but it was very early in the game, right after Deep Blue's move eight, and while Garry was still thinking about his move. We had to wait until he made his move before restarting the program on our own time in that game.

I took over as the operator after Deep Blue's game four self-termination. Garry asked briefly what happened and was satisfied when I told him that the program had to be restarted. Garry's move forty-three happened to give Deep Blue only one legal reply, so he knew precisely what the machine would play when it came back. Our problem gave him free time to think on the position, meanwhile, Deep Blue's clock was ticking. After the rematch, we had heard that Garry was upset that Deep Blue "crashed" numerous times and that he may have suggested that the "crashes" were distracting and suspicious. Personally, I would have preferred that Joe did not use a mechanism like the self-termination code, but I was not in Joe's shoes. However, I strongly doubted that Garry was really distracted by the two instances of self-termination and there was certainly nothing to be suspicious about, especially in the case of game four. You cannot violate the chess rules and play an illegal move.

---

9 For the readers who are also computer scientists, the efficiency could drop too low when there is a deadlock in the parallel system. Also, things can go wrong for other unknown reasons.

I was expecting a disaster when I left the operations room, but by the time Deep Blue was restarted, the position looked much better. Previously, I was just hearing Miguel saying that it was hopeless. Now I was examining Deep Blue's lines for myself, and those coming up seemed to point to a draw. The position on the board was a rook ending. The chess chip contains endgame ROMs (Read Only Memory) that encapsulate a lot of the relevant rook ending knowledge. Deep Blue also had access to the five-piece rook ending database on line, although in this game the database did not matter. After Deep Blue's move fifty-six, the position had reached a clear draw. Garry opened up his hands and said, before making any move, "Draw?" This draw offer was unorthodox. Normally, one offers a draw *right after* making a move. I immediately accepted the offer.

Did Garry have a win somewhere in the endgame phase? It is unclear. Many analysts claimed that they found winning lines, but on closer examination none of them works.

The match was all tied up with two points each after four games.

After a Drink or Two

Game four was followed by two rest days. In the Philadelphia match, there was only one rest day between game four and game five but during the negotiation for the rematch, Garry explicitly requested the extra rest day. The extra day probably cost IBM at least $100,000 more, in leases alone, for the venue and the equipment.

Of course, rest days were not really "rest" days for the Deep Blue team. The three of us, along with the Grandmasters, were hard at work trying to resolve problems that showed up in the match games, or finding potential problems in practice games or test positions. The critical evaluation bugs got fixed up by Joe. One of the match games triggered Murray to make a conceptual change to the evaluation function. We were learning from Garry himself. I ran Deep Blue Jr through a vast set of test positions and located a few bugs, which Joe promptly fixed. The Grandmasters worked on the openings, although it was clear by now that Deep Blue's opening preparations probably would not be tested. When we completed the bug fixes, the Grandmasters played a few test games against Deep Blue Jr to make sure that the modified program was indeed an improvement. This went on for most of the two rest days.

In game five, Garry reverted to the basic setup he played in game one, but with a slight deviation. On move four, Deep Blue decided to trade off its bishop for his knight, giving him the advantage of the bishop pair. But in exchange for the bishop pair, Deep Blue would have better piece development. In the operations room, we could see this from Deep Blue's main line. Giving up the bishop was a perfectly reasonable choice. None of us on the Deep Blue team thought much about the move. It was just a move. But we also knew that Garry might have problems with it. Some comments from Kasparov's camp indicated that they had a very simplistic view of Deep Blue's evaluation function. After game one, the Kasparov camp (as did Yasser Seirawan) apparently thought Deep Blue valued the bishop much higher than the knight, and it would go through serious contortions to preserve it. Garry's remark at the post-match press conference indicated that he was indeed surprised by Deep Blue's decision to trade off the bishop for the knight. I wondered whether he considered the possibility that Deep Blue might, indeed, be far more sophisticated than he gave it credit for.

Several members of the press apparently had taken up Garry's simplistic view about how Deep Blue evaluated a position. During this game, I went to the pressroom to give a few interviews, and was surprised by repeated questions about whether we had adjust-

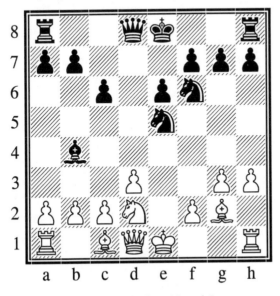

The position before 11. ... h5.

ed the relative values of bishop and knight before the game. The reporters meant well, but the questions felt like being asked, "You used your left hand to pick up the book just now. Did you change the relative values of your left hand and your right hand?"

After Garry's eleventh move, Deep Blue had a significant lead in piece development. At this point, Deep Blue produced the move h5, pushing its h-file pawn two squares. Garry started to jot down the move on his score sheet, then he took a double take and glanced at Murray, who was operating for Deep Blue. Murray gave Garry a slight nod, indicating that Deep Blue did play the move. Garry was surprised. So were all of us in the operations room. Joel's first reaction was, "I don't like the move. But I can't say what is wrong with it." In the auditorium, the immediate response from Maurice Ashley was "No!" Yasser: "Garry is a happy camper! Who's been programming this machine?" Maurice: "I mean we've seen some strange moves and we've seen some strange moves. That's a strange move!" Miguel apparently did not quite like the move at first either but after a moment's thought, he said, "Well, maybe one or two of the top ten players would play it, but only after a drink or two." I never did ask Miguel what he meant. But I was interpreting his comment the following way. The move h5 was signaling to Garry, "If you castle king side, I will attack you." Normally, even a top-ten player would not dare to be so aggressive. Deep Blue obviously had no idea that it was playing Garry Kasparov. Garry's post match comment indicated that he was quite shocked by the move, "No computer plays h5!" It was quite interesting that, during the game, the reaction in the pressroom was that h5 was a computer move, with some people inserting "stupid" before "computer". Analysts of the game later praised the move as a sophisticated positional idea.

Two years later, the move h5 was at the center of a controversy over the Internet. When I first heard Garry's post-match comment that "no computer plays h5", I had no idea whether Garry was praising or accusing us. Right after the game itself, Clara Kasparova asked her son whether there was anything amiss. He replied that it was a typical computer game so there was certainly the possibility that he was praising us. In 1999, however, when interviewed by a chess journalist, he seemed to imply that his statement was an accusation. The chess journalist posted on the Internet what we understood to be Garry's assertion that no computer played h5, and therefore we had cheated. Within hours, someone on the Internet pointed out that at least one commercial chess program also played h5. The chess journalist happened to know that Garry had the very same commercial chess program on his own laptop a few feet away during the interview. So he not only wrongly accused us, but it appears he did not even bother to check whether any of the chess programs he owned played h5. I don't know why the commercial chess program played h5. It could be good programming, bad programming or just dumb luck.

When I saw the move h5 from Deep Blue, I knew precisely what hardware evaluation features prompted the move. During the last two months of chip design before the rematch, I added drastic changes to the hardware for king safety evaluation. Before the king castles, the hardware computes three sets of king safety evaluations, one for kingside castling, one for queenside castling, and one for staying in the center. The real king safety evaluation is the weighted linear combination of the three, with the weighting based on the relative ranking of the three, and difficulty of making the castling moves. Normal chess programs have a far simpler king safety evaluation. To avoid problems with king safety, chess programmers usually actively discourage their programs from playing moves like h5, because it damages the potential king safety for castling kingside, even though in reality, the programs might be able to castle queenside safely. Since Deep Blue could tell whether it could castle queenside safely on its own, we just allowed it to do whatever it wanted. In the game position, Deep Blue could always castle queenside safely, and therefore move h5 was perfectly playable from its point of view.

After Deep Blue's move twenty-two, it assessed that it had a slight edge. I was getting optimistic, "Could we possibly win this game?" Just when I was getting excited, I was called up to the pressroom to give interviews. Garry apparently thought he was in trouble as well. By the time I got back to the operations room, however, he had skillfully tiptoed around any potential problems. Around this time, Deep Blue played a move that led to some positional problems but Garry did not play the best continuation.

By move forty, Deep Blue assessed the position as being even. Garry later stated that he saw at this point how the game would end in nine more moves. The commentators on the auditorium stage did not see the game finish until the very end. The game finish was quite pretty. At first glance, Garry had a passed pawn that seemed very difficult to stop. Deep Blue, instead of trying to stop

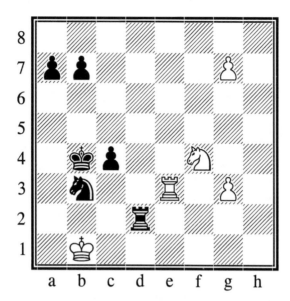

The final position in game 5. White to move.

the passed pawn, threatened to checkmate. After Garry fended off the mating threat, Deep Blue just marched its king forward, ignoring the passed pawn. The final game position had Garry ready to promote his passed pawn to a queen, but it was all to no avail. Deep Blue was about to initiate a drawing sequence based on repetition checks.

Garry stayed at the chess table after the draw was agreed, and began talking to his mother in Russian. Soon the game room was filled with people. Several of Garry's people were there as well as Ken and C J. In the operations room, we were at a loss as to what was happening. We were told not to go over to the game room yet. Word soon came that Garry wanted all the game logs to be printed, sealed, and placed in the possession of the match arbiter, Carol Jarecki. The day before, he had made a formal request that all the game logs be printed and placed in sealed envelopes. The appeals committee had voted against *requiring* IBM to do so, but had also suggested that IBM should *consider* doing it. Garry was told about the decision of the committee. Just prior to the game, an internal IBM decision was made that we would honor his request, reversing an earlier decision. So the problem was quickly resolved, although not without some hiccups. The computer printer had a paper jam that took a while to fix, and there was not enough paper nor enough time to print all the game logs. Only the log for game five was printed. The next day, two complete sets of game logs were printed and given to Carol Jarecki and Ken Thompson.

After Carol got the seventy-two pages of game five's log safely in her briefcase, she went up to the pressroom and briefed the press about what happened. Carol had the distinction of also being the match arbiter for the 1995 Kasparov vs. Anand World Championship match. Concluding her briefing, Carol made a comparison between the two matches, "I'll tell you one thing. This match is a lot more exciting than the World Championship."

She did not mean just the games.

A $300,000 Gamble

After five games, the match was tied at 2.5 points each. Deep Blue had White in the last game. Unless Garry could somehow manage to win the last game from the Black side, history would be made. Deep Blue would be either the first computer to tie the World Chess Champion in a regulation match, or better still, the first computer to beat the World Chess Champion in a regulation match.

The scalpers were out in full force, reselling the $25 tickets for as much as $500. If you had bought one of the $500 tickets, you would have paid about $10 for every minute of game time, as game six lasted less than an hour.

Personally, before game six, I felt a sense of calm. Murray, Joe, and I had worked long and hard to reach this stage. The match was tied. Deep Blue had White, so our chance of at least drawing the match was quite good. We had, however, no real control over what would happen next. "What will be will be," I told myself. Yes, my twelve-year endeavor might finally be over, but I could only watch at this point. The only thing I wanted was just a good—preferably great—game by both sides, and that the historians would say about the match, "Neither side deserved to lose." I did not care whether the anti-computer Garry or the normal Garry showed up. I just wanted a great fight as befitting the potentially historic occasion after such a closely contested match.

Most of the IBMers were also in great spirits, with the exception of the PR people. They were bracing for a firestorm should Deep Blue draw or win the match. Garry had been dissatisfied when the match was still tied. What might he say if he lost a match for the first time in his life? Yes, you read it right. Garry had never lost a single chess match in his professional life before the 1997 rematch. He had come close to losing to Anatoly Karpov in their first world title match, but that match was cancelled when Anatoly's health seemed to be failing. Some were concerned that Garry would react angrily to losing a match. I was surprised at this notion. The rematch was in many ways bigger than even the World Chess Championship matches. The PR people were making preparations for a volcanic eruption. The IBM team was asked to dress up for the occasion, and also asked specifically not to smile during the closing ceremony, especially if Deep Blue won the match. The PR people did not want to fan the fire should a firestorm erupt.

The atmosphere in the auditorium before the start of the game was festive. Video clips from the TV shows '*Late Night with David Letterman*' and '*The Tonight Show with Jay Leno*' about the rematch were shown, to laughter and applause from the audience.

Joe was the operator for the last game, with Murray as the backup. I had decided positively and definitively that I would not work on this particular day after twelve years. This was going to be my day as just a spectator.

The game began the same way as game four, with a Caro Kann defense. Instead of playing a weird sideline as he did in Game four, this time Garry played the main line. Deep Blue also played the main line for White; in fact, the main line that Garry as White used against Anatoly. Garry was in a familiar territory, albeit from the opposite side of the chessboard.

On Garry's seventh move, after spending nearly two minutes, he played 7. ... h6. Deep Blue instantly replied Nxe6, giving up a knight for a pawn. Garry acted a little bit surprised, but then played the next few moves very fast, as did Deep Blue. Both sides were still in book.

In the auditorium, Yasser was saying that Garry had blundered and transposed the move. He also said that Garry was in terror and distress. None of us in the operations room, including Ken, believed this. It was inconceivable that Garry, with his legendary memory, could have forgotten an opening line that he had played many times, albeit usually from the White side. Garry's expression was also more one of surprise rather than terror and distress. Those emotions would come later.

So what did happen? An International Master in Kasparov's camp was quoted the next day in the newspaper that the 7. ... h6

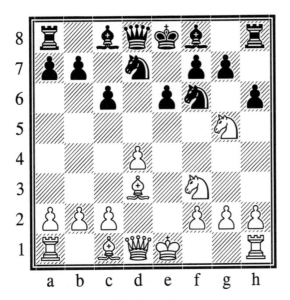

The position after Kasparov's 7. ... h6.

move was one agreed upon earlier. Garry himself stated months later in an interview that he regretted the decision to play 7. ... h6. So the move was never a slip of the finger as it was characterized in news articles immediately following the match. It was played by design.

So why did Garry play the move? Black's position was generally considered difficult at best after the knight sacrifice. This is true in games played by human players, but it is not true in games played between computers and human players. The commercial chess programs apparently had serious problems avoiding losing the game as White! Several Grandmasters had tried playing the Black side of the game positions against the top commercial chess programs and were able to win every single game. This fact did not come out until well after the match, but by then the media had moved on to other stories. What Garry played in game six on move seven was a very risky anti-computer chess move.

How did Garry get the idea to play 7. ... h6? In the post-match news conference, he seemed to blame his helpers. There were other possible sources. Several of the top commercial chess programs at the time were explicitly prohibited in their opening books from playing the knight sacrifice that Deep Blue played. So, apparently, lots of the commercial chess programmers knew that their programs could not play the sacrificial line. There were some rumors during the match that Garry thought Deep Blue was using the opening book of one of the commercial chess programs, so it was conceivable that he was expecting Deep Blue to retreat its knight as the other programs did. This would have given Garry a much better position than he could have achieved in the normal lines. In the "unlikely" event that Deep Blue did play the knight sacrifice, well, there was this nice article written by Grandmaster Timoshchenko, one of Garry's former seconds, in the March 1997 issue of the *International Computer Chess Association Journal*. Timoshchenko played exactly the same line against none other than Fritz, the chess program distributed by Garry's computer chess consultant, Frederic Friedel. Timoshchenko gave the verdict, "After the knight sacrifice, Black has enough possibilities for defense."

So there were lots of potential reasons to select the move 7. ... h6. First, Deep Blue might just retreat the knight. In this case, Garry would have equalized very easily. Second, Deep Blue might not "understand" how to attack. Then, Garry would have won the game and become the toast of the human race. (Although Deep Blue, in my opinion, might be the more important human achievement when all was said and done.) Third—and this one a stretch—if Deep Blue did "understand" the position and beat him, a bystander could always say that the last game did not count and, given that game two could have been drawn (as game one could have), he was the actual winner of the match. Believe it or not, there were actually people who used this argument to suggest that Deep Blue was the loser of the match. It would be way too cynical to believe that Garry had planned this third scenario.

Deep Blue was out of its opening book on move 11. Bf4. Its first evaluation of the position was that it was close to a pawn up, even though it was really down about two pawns in material over the board. Deep Blue saw close to three pawns worth of positional compensation. At about this time, Miguel popped in and asked what was Deep Blue's evaluation of the position. After we told him, he smiled broadly. All of us knew that the match was effectively over. Once Deep Blue had the initiative, and knew that it had the initiative, there was no stopping it. The position on the playing board had actually shown up in our lab about a month earlier when the other Grandmasters were working on Deep Blue's opening book. At the time, the Grandmasters did not bother to play out the position either; they just looked at Deep Blue's evaluation of the position and moved on to other work. They all had been on

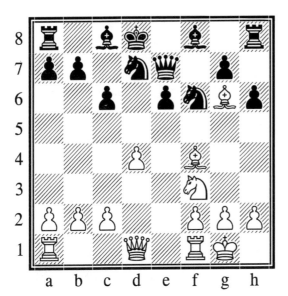

The position after Deep Blue's 11. ... Bf4.

the receiving end in similar positions. Miguel was not in the United States at the time of the discussion, so he had not yet seen Deep Blue's evaluation of the position. Maybe Black could draw the position, but probably no human player could hold the position against Deep Blue. It appeared that Garry's $300,000 gamble would backfire on him.

Garry's demeanor at the board quickly changed from surprised to distressed, as Deep Blue spurned a quick gain of small material and continued its attack. Near the end of the game, Garry started talking to Clara in Russian. It is against the rules of chess to talk to spectators while a game is still going on. It was not clear what he said to his mother. Perhaps he told Clara that there was no sense in playing on any more. After Joe played 19. c4 for Deep Blue, Garry looked at Joe in a questioning manner. Joe nodded slightly, confirming what he was suspecting. Deep Blue was winning major material. Garry then promptly resigned. The video segment of his resignation would be played many times, around the world, in the next few days. After his resignation, Garry shook hands with Joe and just walked straight out of the room with both arms up in the air the entire time he was walking out. It was a surreal scene. The game had lasted less than an hour.

At the moment of Garry's resignation, I suddenly felt very tired. The twelve years of work were finally over. I should have been exulting, but I was feeling empty inside. The game felt too easy, although in hindsight it wasn't. Without our hard work the year before, Garry might have won the game. A part of me also felt robbed. I am not a chess player, but the chess player in me was definitely disappointed. Win or lose, I had wanted the last game to be a real fight. I wanted the win to be another great game like game two, except without the final mistake. If it had to be another loss, I wanted it to be another hard-fought loss like game one, preferably without the bad moves from Deep Blue.

So, almost fifty years after Claude Shannon made the proposal on how to program a computer to play chess, the quest for the holy grail was finally over. It did not end with the greatest chess game ever, but how the match ended was not up to us.

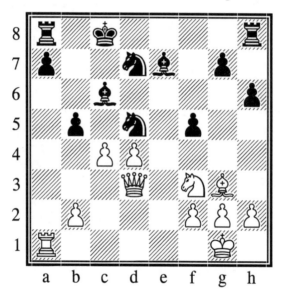

The final position of the match.

Epilogue

 CHAPTER 13

Life after Chess

The Press Conference

At the post-match press conference, Garry characterized the match as "lost by the world champion". He then lashed out at IBM and he seemed, to me at least, to be hinting at human intervention in game two. He also once again wrongly characterized the potential draw by repetition checks in game two as "simple". There was also some bravado. "I personally guarantee you, I'll tear it to pieces without question." "It will not help, because we know how the machines play." "I think the machine has too many weaknesses." One of the more surprising statements was "But it's not yet ready, in my opinion, to win a big contest." I don't know what he had been thinking, but in all media metrics, the rematch was a far bigger event than any other that he had played in. The number of "impressions" registered for the rematch alone, not counting post-match publicity, was 5 to 7 billion. This was probably 100 to 1000 times the number of impressions registered for any of his World Championship matches. If the rematch was not a big contest, I don't know what is.

On game six, Garry said, "Today's game doesn't even count as a game because probably it has been published before elsewhere. When the computer takes on e6 you can resign. I was not in the mood of playing at all, I have to tell you." I shook my head in my mind when I heard this. At the time, I was just appalled at the total absence of sportsmanship in the comment. I was not as certain as I am now that Garry had just made a $300,000 gamble and lost.

Going back to game two, Garry again stressed, "Forget today's game. I mean Deep Blue hasn't won a single game out of the five because again in game two, I resigned when I could have forced a

**Kasparov speaking in the press conference
after game 3.**
From left to right: *Mike Valvo, Garry Kasparov, Feng-hsiung Hsu, C J Tan,
Joel Benjamin, Murray Campbell, Joe Hoane, and Jerry Brody.
Kasparov was about to begin his public accusations.*

draw." He conveniently forgot to mention that he did not see the drawing continuations. By the same argument, we could have also said that he did not win a single game out of the five, as Deep Blue played a wrong move to lose game one, just as he made a wrong move, resignation, to lose game two.

On future matches, Garry wanted, "One condition, IBM as player, not a sponsor." I would not mind for myself getting the royal treatment that he was getting. To the best of my knowledge, the part of IBM that was the sponsor was attending to his every need, within reason. He was not getting the game logs from the IBM player while the match was going on, but this was simply a request for an unfair advantage. The match would have been a sham if he were given free access.

This was followed by another big surprise. I may have misinterpreted what Kasparov was saying, but it appeared he was accusing the Deep Blue team of cheating in game one, the one game we lost: "You know, it [the anti-computer strategy] was working, but suddenly it stopped working—suddenly Deep Blue found a way just to break the pawn chains and start a confrontation in a very, very convenient situation."

Garry eventually calmed down a little bit: "But obviously it's a historical achievement that the machine was even able to play on such a level with the World Champion."

More on future matches: "I think eight or ten games, a normal match." Later, he added, "I think we should play every second day. You should give a human being time to rest. You know, twenty days, ten games, a proper match."

Personally, I have some doubt whether a sponsor could be found for a match of the duration that he suggested. Excluding the prize fund, the extra length of the match would cost the sponsor in excess of one million dollars. The extra days could significantly reduce the media interest, especially with half being just rest days. There are good reasons why the NBA Championships and professional baseball's World Series are seven games each. It is difficult to keep the full attention of the media on a sports event for much longer than a week. His proposal would lead to an event lasting nearly three weeks and with nothing happening on half of the days.

The press conference lasted about thirty minutes. During the entire time, the Deep Blue team sat and listened to his monologue. We were asked not to smile to express our joy, nor could we voice our outrage at his implications. We had just accomplished what we had dreamt and worked for years: twelve years for me, about nine years for Murray and seven for Joe. And yet, we had to sit there and listen to these charges. It was one of the worst experiences of my life at a time that should have been my most joyous moment.

Afterwards, Joe said something that I remember to this day, "You know, he [Garry] ruined the joy of it."

The Old Gang

Two months later, we were at a more joyous occasion. On 29 July 1997, in Providence, Rhode Island, at the AAAI national conference, Murray, Joe and I received the Fredkin Prize for the first team to build or program a chess machine to defeat the World Chess Champion in a match. The $100,000 Fredkin Prize, which was one-seventh of the winner's prize for the rematch, was split evenly three ways, excluding the extra cent that was kept by the trustee of the Prize.

Right after the rematch, we did not believe that we would receive the Fredkin Prize. While satisfying the original intent of the Prize, the rematch did not conform to the Prize Committee's match conditions set a few years back, in particular the length of the match and the size of the prize fund. Shortly after Murray and I joined IBM, Dr Berliner, the chairman of the Fredkin Prize Committee, and our former royal opposition at Carnegie Mellon, issued a public statement specifying the required match conditions for claiming the Prize. At the end of his statement, Dr Berliner admitted that it was perfectly possible that his match conditions might not be to the liking of the World Champion and the match sponsor. For the Deep Blue matches, as far as I know, no one at IBM even bothered to look at Dr Berliner's list of match conditions when setting up the two matches.

The Fredkin Prize Committee did not make any announcement at the conclusion of the rematch; it appeared that the committee considered Deep Blue's match win inadequate. Winning the rematch was rewarding enough for us, so we did not pursue the possibility of claiming the Prize. It came as a pleasant surprise that, about a month after the rematch, Professor Raj Reddy informed us for AAAI that we had won it. What changed the mind of the committee? I have no idea. Maybe they realized that, for all intents and purposes to the world at large, the quest was over.

After the awarding of the Prize, I gave a presentation to the assembly on the contribution of Deep Blue. I was moved when I received a standing ovation before I started the presentation. In New York, after game five, one of the better games by Deep Blue, the partisan crowd booed us. This time, I was among friends, friends who understood that the match was never really "man versus machine", but rather "man as a performer versus man as a toolmaker". Whatever the outcome of the match, when we cheered the winner, we were cheering for a unique human achievement. When Garry won in 1996, the Deep Blue team cheered and applauded his outstanding personal performance. When Deep Blue won in 1997, society at large, not including Garry Kasparov, finally recognized Deep Blue for what it was, namely, the advancement of a powerful tool created by human beings.

Also present at the AAAI conference were several of our old friends from Deep Thought days, accepting the Allen Newell Award for Research Excellence for our joint work with Deep Thought. Thomas Anantharaman had left the Wall Street firm, and was working as an assistant professor at New York University, doing research related to the human genome project. Andreas Nowatzyk had left Sun Microsystems and joined Digital

Equipment Corp. When we had dinner together after the ceremony, Andreas mentioned the ambitious, personally-funded project he was working on in his spare time. He wanted to create a complete 3-D map of a frozen mouse down to 0.2-micron resolution, a resolution good enough to map most of the neural connections of the mouse's entire nervous system, including the brain. Mike Browne did not show up for the award ceremony. He had also left the Wall Street firm, had since worked at Sun Microsystems, and then joined Yago Systems, a successful startup working on smart switches for network connections.

Moving Pieces

What happened with the main characters after the rematch?

In early news articles, Deep Blue, the victor, was reported to have been disassembled and shipped to IBM customers, without the chess chips. Its death, however, was exaggerated. Due to its historical significance, as of this writing, Deep Blue is still alive and kicking in IBM Research. Early internal reports stated that only the outer frames of Deep Blue stayed in IBM. It turns out that only the RS/6000 nodes went back to the factory test floor, and have since been put back into the original frames. Deep Blue no longer has all the chess cards that it used in the rematch. Two cards went to IBM headquarters in Armonk, where a Deep Blue Jr was set up to give demos to visitors. Most of the cards are still in IBM Research. The 1997 Deep Blue now has half of its original chess cards. Some of the cards are placed in the old RS/6000 SP used in the 1996 match. A few are placed in standalone workstations. The rest are on shelves.

The Deep Blue RS/6000 SP is being used mainly for research projects unrelated to chess. It can still play chess—it serves as a web site that can play against up to one-thousand chess players simultaneously. The web-based program is, however, much weaker than even "Pico" Deep Blue Jr, the single chip and reduced speed version of Deep Blue Jr. The web-based program uses a single Deep Blue chess chip, at one second per move, including setup overhead. The actual computation time is probably less than half a second per move. The very short computation time means that the web-based program is comparatively weak tactically, more so than typical chess programs would be with shortened computation time. Most of the search extensions that are partially responsible for the tactical strength of Deep Blue Jr are effectively inactive, given the short computation time. This program also uses a simplified evaluation function, does not keep track of move repetition and does not "think" on the opponent's time. It is probably no stronger than about 2000 rating on the USCF scale. This is fine, normally, as the opponents for the web-based program are usually IBM customers, and it is perfectly acceptable to have happy IBM customers winning a few games against the program. In 1999, the International Computer Chess Association asked IBM to provide the web-based program to the spectators in a computer chess event. A commercial chess programmer took advantage of the poor defenseless web-based program by playing it against his own program, giving his own program a hefty time advantage of the order of 50 to 1. (To be fair to the programmer in question, he probably did not know what the actual time advantage was when he played the games.) The commercial chess programmer then posted the games that his program won on his own web site as evidence of the "superiority" of his program, which he is perfectly happy to sell to you.

As of this writing, Garry Kasparov has not played serious games publicly against any computer since the Deep Blue matches. His performance against human players has its dramatic ups and downs.

In a tournament right after the rematch, Garry punished the first human chess players he played and won the tournament fairly easily. For a short while after the rematch, his chess results were somewhat spotty; his match loss against Deep Blue probably provided an initial psychological boost to his human opponents. Then he had a phenomenal run of great chess performances, with his chess rating going up to the middle 2800s, well above any other human chess player. But the cracks in his armor that showed up in the Deep Blue matches eventually came back to haunt him.

By the year 2000, Garry had not defended his World Championship for over five years. The normal World Championship cycle was three years, and the recent trend is for even shorter cycles. In recent years, FIDE, the international chess federation, has held its own World Championship tournament once per year. While no one doubted that Garry was the strongest (human) chess player, there were people who considered the World Championship title vacant until he played a serious challenger. He had had three challengers since his 1995 title match against Vishwanathan Anand. The first was Alexei Shirov who won the right to challenge him by finishing second at the Linares tournament, ahead of Garry but behind Anand, whose written contract with FIDE prevented him from playing in 1998 for any non-FIDE world title. The match between Garry and Alexei never took place. In 1999, Garry designated Anand as the new challenger without a normal qualifying event, bypassing Alexei. Anand was ranked number two in the world, so there was some public support for the new choice, even though many people did not like the way that Alexei was treated nor the arbitrary way that the challenger was chosen. The scheduled new match with Anand also never took place. Early in 2000, Garry designated Vladimir Kramnik as the new challenger, replacing Anand. Anand had a dispute with the match organizer over contract conditions that he considered unacceptable, and was replaced as a result. The Kasparov vs. Kramnik match took place in October 2000, with the surprising result of Vladimir ending Garry's fifteen-year reign by beating him in fifteen games with the score of two wins and thirteen draws. Anand did not sit idle and became the FIDE World Champion himself. As of writing, Vladimir is the Braingames (the match organizer back in 2000)/Einstein (the acquirer of match rights from Braingames in 2002) World Champion, 18-year-old Ruslan Ponomariov is the surprise 2002 FIDE World Champion, and Garry is without a world title but still the top ranked player, with Vladimir closing in as the second ranked player in the world.

The Grandmasters who worked on Deep Blue have generally had good years since the rematch. None of the opening lines prepared for Deep Blue were really ever used, and the Grandmasters had very powerful secret opening weapons as a result of the cooperation with Deep Blue. Joel Benjamin and Nick DeFirmian became the 1997 and 1998 US Chess Champions respectively. Of course, they are strong Grandmasters in their own right, and had good chances to win the title with or without their work with Deep Blue. Miguel Illescas has the distinction of being Vladimir's match second in his successful title bid over Garry, and thus becoming the only person to be involved with the opposing teams in *both* of Garry's match losses.

The Deep Blue project had wound down in IBM. Murray and Joe moved on to financial modeling and data mining and had great success. Joe left IBM and joined a semiconductor startup in early 2001, while I left IBM earlier in late 1999. In his last computer chess work at IBM, Joe modified Deep Blue to provide a simple computation engine for the Deep Blue web server. Murray and Joe, as well as myself, have given presentations and written papers on Deep Blue. However, as far as I know, neither Murray nor Joe is working on computer chess any more.

Changing Landscape

In my opinion, it was Garry's own choice that he did not publicly play a computer match again.

From what I know, IBM had high hopes for a good post-match relationship with Garry. There were plans for possible commercial spots with him, whether Deep Blue won or not. His performance at the post-match press conference put those plans on hold. But as far as I can tell, to show good sportsmanship, IBM was still willing to grant him another match, at least initially.

For a short while after the rematch, I worked on a more powerful version of the chess chip. The possibility of a new match and the desire to remove any doubt from the Kasparov camp that he lost fair and square, drove me on. Then, one day, it dawned upon me. "Get a life. You are free." In the twelve years of my life I had dedicated to the project I forgot there was a world out there.

I knew that I wanted to do something else; the team had many public engagements after the rematch, and I did not have much time to think about what I really wanted to do for many months. Some time during this period, it became clear that there would not be any further IBM matches with Garry. There was no official decision, but the never-ending machinations finally took their toll.

When I finally had some time to myself, I made three decisions.

First, I decided to write this book. While Deep Blue is now a household name, few know about the real people behind Deep Blue. At least Murray and I are well known in computer chess circles. Joe has the worst of it. Even computer chess people don't know much about him. As the person who instigated the project, I believe that it is my responsibility to set the record straight. Besides, I do have stories to tell.

Second, I decided to get legal clearance from IBM to pursue the possibility of further developing the chess chip outside of IBM. Given that there would not be any IBM match with Garry, the only way a new match could take place would be for me to leave IBM, and build a new machine. If Garry really wanted a new match, I would do what I could to give him one. If he did not really want a new match, well, I would make an honest attempt to answer his challenges.

Third, I would leave IBM once I regained control of the chess chip. I wanted to pursue some off-the-wall interests on my own. Seeing what Andreas was doing in his spare time reminded me how much fun it was trying to do things out of the ordinary. Maybe it is a character flaw of mine, but every once in a while I like to poke my head into research areas in which I have no known expertise. At Carnegie Mellon, I had to take remedials for two of the core qualifier courses, in Computer Systems (hardware design) [1] and Artificial Intelligence. Based on my course results, I had no business to be the system architect of a machine like Deep Blue. But that was part of the fun. I did not know where my off-the-wall ideas would lead, but it would be an adventure. Anyway, this was the real reason behind my leaving IBM. Licensing the chess chip from IBM also required that I left IBM after signing the contract. (It was the precondition before any licensing negotiation.) But I would have left IBM, whether the licensing deal went through or not.

I left IBM in October 1999. After more than a year of contract negotiation, I finally had the legal clearance to do more or less whatever I wanted with the chess chips. I had saved up enough money [2] to build a PC-based chess machine that was more powerful than Deep Blue if I absolutely had to. Of course, if possible, I preferred to keep the fund in reserve for my other interests.

The Deep Blue chess chips were manufactured in 0.6 micron CMOS technology. It was possible to get 0.35-micron chips or even 0.25 micron chips at reasonable cost by then. By going to more advanced technology, and by refining the design of the chess chip, it would have been possible to create a single chess chip [3] that would be almost comparable to the entire Deep Blue in chess playing strength. I would have to work like a mad man, but it could be

---

[1] Well, I was not that bad. I took the exam for the Computer Systems course directly without taking the course itself or studying for the exam.

[2] IBM would not have allowed me to license the chess chip if I did not have enough resources to build a new chess chip.

[3] The chip should run at 30–100 million positions/sec, depending on the technology used and how many chess processors per chip.

done. With a few such chips, a PC costing less than one tenth of Garry's one day appearance fee of $30,000, should be more than adequate to beat him in a match, assuming that the fixed engineering cost associated with fabricating the chip is ignored.

Garry was still publicly making challenges for a new match and even went as far as suggesting that he would be willing to make the match a World Championship match. Personally, I didn't believe that machines should be allowed to play for the World Championship, but if Garry was willing, I was not going to argue with him. After all, his willingness would have made potential match sponsors far more interested.

My first action was to gauge the interests of a few potential match sponsors. The responses I got were that there would be some interests especially if Garry was indeed willing to make it a World Championship match. The match would then be an historic first. However, despite Garry's public challenges, the potential sponsors expressed serious doubts that he would really agree to a match. It was clear to anybody with some knowledge of the situation that IBM would no longer agree to a new match. He must have known perfectly well that he did not have to worry about his challenges being answered, that is, until I left IBM. The other problem was that he could always say that the machine yet to be built was not Deep Blue, even though the new machine would have represented the only chance that he would ever have to play again against Deep Blue, or something close to it. I could not find any argument to refute the sponsors' reasoning. Deep down, I had some doubts of my own. The sponsors would not do anything until they were sure that he was willing to play. This went on for about two months. At this point, I promised myself that if he did not seem interested, I would begin to pursue my other interests. After all, the only reason I was going through the motion of trying to set up the match was to answer his challenges. If he would not take his own challenges seriously, why should I bother?

Over the next month or so I made several contacts with Garry's manager, Owen Williams. Owen immediately ruled out any possibility of a World Championship match. This was fine by me. I was not comfortable with the idea of playing for the title. He was non-committal about the match; I could not even get him to say that, in principle, Garry was willing to play if a sponsor could be found. After a month of running around, I got final confirmation that Garry was not interested. I then sent out an open letter to a few widely read chess web sites and a copy to Owen. In the letter, I said my goodbyes, and thanks to the chess world, including Garry himself. I included information to say that Garry's challenge for a new match would be unanswered, since the challenge no longer existed. I did not say anything about why Garry was no longer interested in the match as Owen had not given me any hint as to what they were.

A few days after my open letter, Owen published his response that listed several reasons why Garry was not interested in playing a match. Among the reasons was that I had no credibility, no money, and I was not serious. Anyway, it was a no-win situation for me to get involved any further. I posted a short reply, pointing out that I went to the trouble to secure the right to the chess chip and I had enough personal funds to build a new machine if I absolutely had to. I did not bother to mention that I began with no computer chess credentials in 1985 and we built our first machine (ChipTest) with no budget whatsoever, which did not stop Deep Blue from beating Garry in 1997. It was all a matter of will. Maybe there were genuine misunderstandings in the whole process and Garry was sincerely interested in a match. Anyway, the issue was no longer of concern to me. I had fulfilled my obligation to try to answer the challenge.

There is nothing for Garry to gain by playing a new match, and it is very likely that he would be crushed. Computers can get better much faster than he can. In 1997, it took a multi-million-dollar supercomputer to beat him. In late 1999, a cheap PC in a college dorm with a few chess chips, fabricated in say 0.35 micron CMOS, should be able to do the job. During the 2001 Superbowl television broadcast, Pepsi ran a spot with Garry. In the commercial, he was seen beating a computer that looked like Hal (the insane computer in the novel/movie "2001") and then losing to a Pepsi vending machine. The reality in 2001 is that a palmtop computer like a Compaq iPaq, equipped with a 0.13 micron CMOS chess chip would have a decent chance to beat him. If you want to get fancy, you can even fit the entire machine into a cola can. It would be one very expensive can, but it can be done.

With Garry presently titleless, who might be an interesting opponent for computers? My gut feeling is that Vladimir could be a tougher opponent for computers. Garry's playing strength resides to a great extent in his tactical play, which happens to be

At a 1997 public exhibition in Taipei, Taiwan.

the forte of chess computers. The way Vladimir neutralized Garry's tactical play in their match means that he probably can do the same thing to a computer, which will make him a very dangerous opponent indeed.

A ten-game match between Vladimir and the program Deep Fritz was due to be played in October 2001 but was postponed. At the time of this writing, the match was rescheduled for October 2002. In case you are wondering, no, Deep Fritz has nothing whatsoever to do with Deep Blue. Ever since Deep Blue's win over Garry, several commercial programs have adopted the name Deep "whatever" for their multiple-processor versions. Deep Fritz is supposedly able to search over a million positions/sec. The base program Fritz, has an evaluation function that is probably worse than Deep Thought's. This means that an alert human opponent will be able to exploit Fritz's positional weaknesses. Vladimir should win the match easily, unless he gets careless.

What will be the next research area of interest in computer games? After chess, there is no clear choice. Among games with perfect information (games that do not depend on chance events like coin flips, die rolls or card shuffling), "Go" is generally recognized as the most difficult game. It is probably sufficiently difficult that it will not be "solved" within the next 20 years. Of the other games, two are of particular interest: Chinese chess and shogi (Japanese chess).

Technically, Chinese chess is not very interesting, since its characteristics are very similar to chess. The number of Chinese chess players is possibly comparable to the number of chess players. If computers had been developed in China first, then this book might very well have been about a Chinese chess computer. To me, Chinese chess holds some allure—it was the first board game I learned as a kid. But I doubt that I would spend time on it. It is just not sufficiently interesting technically. Shogi is an interesting case. It has a complexity between Go and chess, mainly from the rule that allows captured pieces to be dropped back onto the board. I have some ideas about how to tackle the computation complexity of shogi. Some day, I might build a shogi machine just to see how hard it is. It would not be a full-time effort like the Deep Blue project was—I want to do something practical for a change, and a full-time effort on another computer game is just not on the cards. I used to play Go passionately, but I don't believe I will ever work on it. The game is too hard for a computer at the moment.

As far as I am concerned, computer chess is no longer a part of my life. Would I agree to build a new machine to play against Vladimir Kramnik or Vishwanathan Anand? I seriously doubt it, unless someone makes me an offer that I cannot refuse, as I am having too much fun with new projects. At this point in my life, it is far more important for me to do new and exciting things, rather than going back to an old conquest, exciting though it may be. Do I miss the thrill of competition? Sometimes. But it is time for me to get on with the rest of my life. The world is full of interesting things to do.

Appendixes

 APPENDIX A

A Lad from Taiwan

This is background material, mostly about my life in Taiwan. It should give you a sense of what kind of person I am at the core, and what kind of bias may exist in telling my stories. *The Creatures in the Box* describes my first contacts with chess. *Learning Board Games* details how I learned Chinese chess, Go, and chess. It also provides a short primer on computer chess history up to the 1970s. *An Early Riser* is a short story about my early education, and an incident that I need to come clean about. *Sidestepping Authorities* provides some instances of my early tendency to ignore authority figures. This tendency has a bearing on what happened at Carnegie Mellon. *The Case for Carnegie Mellon* goes over the reasons why I ended up at Carnegie Mellon.

The Creatures in the Box

I was born in Keelung, Taiwan in 1959. Keelung is one of the major seaports of Taiwan, and at the time it had a population of around 200,000. In Taiwan, Keelung is known as the "Rainy Port" because typically it rains for more than 200 days a year. It is a bustling city, but not a glamorous city by any stretch of the imagination. It is not a gloomy city either; I probably saw rainbows more often in Keelung than anywhere else in the world.

When I was in kindergarten, our next-door neighbor bought the first television set in the neighborhood. It was a black and white set, as there was no color television broadcast in Taiwan yet. Every afternoon, the kids in the neighborhood would gather around to watch cartoons. I wondered how the creatures got into the box. There were a few small holes behind the box but they were too small for the creatures to get through. After a few weeks, the novelty wore off, and we got back to our normal games.

A few years later, my dad bought a television set for the family. At the time, there was only one television station, and the local production of television shows was close to nonexistent. The station broadcast only on afternoons and evenings, but to fill the time slot, it ended up rebroadcasting American TV series, with Chinese captions.

Chess was not big in the United States at the time. The boom resulting from Bobby Fischer winning the world title came a little bit later. But, occasionally, some of the foreign TV series carried episodes with chess themes. The first time I saw chess being played was in an episode of the "Family Affair" series. To me, it was a strange game played with beautifully sculptured pieces.

In the early days, most of these imported TV shows were family sitcoms. As new stations began broadcasting, a wider variety of shows were introduced. Spy shows became quite popular. *"Mission Impossible"*, *"The Avengers"*, *"Wild, Wild West"*, *"It Takes a Thief"*, *"The Man from U.N.C.L.E"*, *"Get Smart"*, and so on. The political symbolism of the 1972 Fischer (USA) versus Spassky (USSR) World Chess Championship Match caught the attention of scriptwriters, and chess was incorporated into some of the story lines.

One of the recurring TV themes went something like this. The bad guy is a Grandmaster chess player, usually of East European extraction, and very smart. Our hero has to play a chess match against the bad guy for some reason, perhaps to gain access to the bad guy, rescue another Grandmaster who is defecting, or stop something sinister at a chess competition. Obviously, it is preferable that our hero beat the bad guy, and thus upset him into making careless mistakes. There is one big problem. Even though our hero normally comes from the same country as Bobby Fischer, he is no chess Grandmaster. Of course, the USA is also known for its computer technology. So our hero is equipped with a well-hidden remote hookup to a chess computer. The game against the bad guy usually starts off fine for our hero. For dramatic effect, something typically goes wrong in the middle of the game. In the end, either the computer gets back on line and finishes off the bad guy, or our hero stumbles onto a move that checkmates the bad guy. The camera zooms into the face of the bad guy, who is in total disbelief. The now chastened bad guy then storms out of the hall, and before he can set off the bomb or do something else nefarious, our hero catches up with him, and stops him cold, just in the nick of time.

What is the moral of this story line? Well, computers are great tools for playing the game of chess against bad guys, especially if you are a handsome and debonair spy[1].

Learning Board Games

Chess is not popular in Taiwan. Both Chinese chess and Wei-chi, which is better known as Go in the West from its Japanese name, are far more popular. Of the three, Chinese chess is the most popular. It was also the first board game I learned as a kid.

Now, if this book was about the life of some famous chess player, I would be telling you about how I learned by watching my dad and older brother play, and one day surprised them by pointing out their mistakes in the game that they just finished. That would be a blatant lie. It was nothing like that. I learned the rules for Chinese chess on the street.

There were very few cars in Keelung when I was little, and the kids in the neighborhood played all sorts of games on the streets. You might wonder how we could have played outside when it rained over half of the year. Well, the commercial buildings in Taiwan, especially in Keelung, were usually built two or three storeys high. The storefront was usually about ten feet from the street. The upper floor(s), supported by pillars next to the street, formed an overhang in front of the store. The overhang provided a nice shelter for the customers and the passers-by. You could walk from one end of a block of buildings to the other end without being rained on. The space under the overhang became our playground when it rained.

I first learned what the pieces for Chinese chess were by watching older kids play the simpler variants of the game. Every once in a while, some of them decided to play "real" Chinese chess. Whenever they did, there was a sense of awe among us younger kids. The pieces move differently in the real game, and it took some time before I had an inkling of how the real game was played. My classmates in primary school were my earliest opponents and my dad played some games with me when I got a little bit older. I became somewhat competitive with my dad after about

---

1 Actually, they work well even if you are only an ordinary looking computer scientist and the opponent is a perfectly fine gentleman.

two weeks or so. One of my uncles visited and played some games with us. My uncle was far better than either of us, and afterwards graciously gave a pointer or two on how to start the game, and general playing principles. That was about the extent of my "formal" Chinese chess education.

The playing strength of most of the Chinese chess players in Taiwanese schools apparently was quite weak. I was above average in playing strength when I was in junior high. One day after class, a friend introduced me to another Chinese chess player. I played a few games, and was completely outclassed. I was so discouraged that I played very few games thereafter.

I did learn to play Western chess, or rather a bastardized form of chess, before I learned to play Go. My first game of "chess" was played against my elder brother, Feng-Lung. It was played on a homemade chess set that he put together. My brother won, of course, partly because of the fact he was telling me the rules as the game progressed. I learned the rule of pawn promotion[2] near the end of the game, when my brother promoted his pawn. This game was probably played when I was still in primary school. In junior high, some of my classmates would bring their magnetic chess sets to school once in a while, and we did play "chess" a little bit. None of us knew the rules well. In particular, our castling moves were all wrong. In Chinese, the castling move is translated as "swapping the castle", and we literally executed the move as a swap of the king with the rook.

I started to get interested in Go when I was in junior high. As part of the school's after-school recreational programs, a local amateur 3-dan[3] player came in from time to time to teach us. We did not get much beyond the etiquette, rules and some basic patterns.

---

[2] A pawn reaching the 8th rank is promoted to a more powerful piece, usually a queen, the most powerful piece in the game.

[3] The ranking system in Go is a three-tiered system. Within each tier, players are ranked either by the number of *kyu's* or the number of *dan's* they have. At the lowest tier, the players are ranked by the number of kyu's, with stronger players having fewer kyu's. The one-kyu players are the strongest kyu-level players. Above the kyu-level, we have the *amateur* dan-level players, and the *professional* dan-level players. At dan-level, a player with more dan's is the better player. One-dan players, also known as shodans, are the weakest dan-level players. For both amateur and professional dan levels, the highest ranked players are 9-dans. The amateur 9-dans are usually no stronger than professional shodans. An amateur 3-dan player roughly corresponds to a master level player in chess.

When I got into Cheng-Kuo Senior High in Taipei, the capital, one of my elder sisters, Jing-Feng, bought me a Go set as a gift [4]. Professional 9-dan Lin Hi-Fong (Rin Kaihou in Japanese), the Go pro who hailed from Taiwan, was winning major Go titles in Japan, and Taiwanese newspapers were covering his title matches extensively. It was at this time that I discovered Go books. Keelung was not a backward city, but it was not as cultured as Taipei. There were few bookstores in Keelung, and none near our home. In Taipei, within walking distance from Cheng-Kuo Senior High, there was an entire street of bookstores. The Go books changed how I approached technical problems later on in life. Whenever I encounter a new problem, my first reaction is usually to dig up everything in the literature I can find about the problem. In the old days, this meant going to the library or bookstores. Of course, today I would have to add Internet searches to the mix. Sometimes, it is better to think about the problem first before looking it up in the literature, but old habits die hard.

Studying Go was quite important in my early education. In the Far East, Go is more than just a game. It is an integral part of the culture. In Japan, businessmen sometimes would use Go proverbs to describe their business strategies. My Go study greatly influenced how I approached life. One of the most important lessons I learned from Go was to pick my spot. In Go, it is frequently unwise to react to every single provocation from your opponent; sometimes, it is far more profitable to judiciously ignore the provocation and move to a new area. In other words, be yourself, and don't always follow the crowd. This attitude sometimes backfires very badly, but it serves me well overall, in Go games and in real life.

Learning Go probably helped me understand some of the deeper concepts in chess. Sometimes when I asked good chess players about a specific formal concept that I learned from the Go literature, the answer frequently was "yes, that is an interesting idea, and I do use the concept intuitively". The concept, however, is usually not named in the chess literature. Go is a complicated game, but it has very simple rules. Perhaps the simplicity of Go rules makes it easier to describe the abstract concepts explicitly.

I learned the proper rules for chess during my freshman year

---

4 Cheng-Kuo is said to be the best public high school for boys in Taiwan and quite difficult to get in. Hence the gift for achieving entrance.

in National Taiwan University. One day, I decided to look through the catalogue of the school library for books on chess and was surprised to find a computer chess book listed. I was in the Electrical Engineering Department, so computers were of some interest to me. Finding a computer chess book listed was quite exciting, especially with the catalogue listing the author as none other than the World Chess Champion Mikhail Botvinnik. I was very annoyed when I could not locate his book.

With hindsight, not finding the book might have been a blessing in disguise. The approach he advocated appeared to go nowhere. For twenty years or so, he wrote many articles on how well his program performed in test positions. But, even to this day, no outside researcher has seen his program playing a single move, let alone competing against other programs. Some researchers even accused him of falsifying his results in the test positions. He had some good ideas, at least according to the chess players to whom I have spoken, but the ideas were difficult to work with even on the more powerful Western computers. Behind the iron curtain, they were likely impossible to implement. He died in the early 1990s, right around the time when the personal computer became widely available in the former USSR.

Anyway, with my interest piqued, I went through all the journal articles that I could find on computer chess. I learned the rules of chess, not from a book, but from one of the computer chess articles that happened to give a detailed description of the rules.

I continued to check the library catalogue from time to time. During my sophomore year, a new computer chess book arrived in the school library. The book, a collection of papers from a computer chess workshop, was *Chess Skill in Man and Machine*, which is now considered a classic by computer chess researchers. The most important chapter in the book is on the chess program *Chess 4.5* by David Slate and Lawrence Atkin. (Most of the modern chess programs are in one way or another clones of the Chess 4.5 program.) At the time I read the book, I had no idea how influential it was to become. I was mostly surprised by its pessimistic tone, especially given the usually rosy reports in the press but the pessimism turned out to be far more realistic.

The computer chess literature generally regards Claude Shannon's 1949 lecture as the beginning of modern computer chess history. Some of the early researchers were quite optimistic. In 1957, Herbert Simon, a Nobel laureate in Economics, and renowned computer scientist, went as far as stating "within 10 years a digital computer will be the world's chess champion, unless the rules bar it from competition". Ten years later, the best program was authored by Richard Greenblatt, an MIT student. His program played at the low end of Class C level which, on the chess rating scale, would be 1400 to 1600 rating points. World Champions are typically at around 2800 to 2900 rating points on the same scale. A 1400 player is better than a beginner, but would lose to more than half of the weekend tournament players, let alone the World Champion. A player one class stronger (200 rating points higher) than their opponent should win about three games out of every four. The best computer chess program in 1967 was playing at 1400 points, or seven classes, below the World Champion. Herbert Simon's prediction was way off the mark.

In 1975, when most of the material in *Chess Skill in Man and Machine* was written, Chess 4.5 was the best program. Its programmers, however, were consistently maintaining that the program was still at Class C level, or no more than 200 points higher than Richard Greenblatt's. In other words, the best chess programs gained less than 200 points after almost 10 years of development. At this rate of progress, it would have taken 60 more years, or around the year 2035, before a computer could challenge the World Champion. No wonder the general tone of the book was pessimistic. Some optimism came back a few years later when Chess 4.9, running on a supercomputer, was shown to play at close to 2000 rating points. But I did not know about the renewed optimism until I was studying for my PhD degree at Carnegie Mellon University many years later.

Chess books were difficult to find in Taiwan. The ones available were in English and I had to go to specialty bookstores to find them. Those that I found were either game collections or introductory books. The introductory books were too elementary—they did not go much beyond the game rules, and the game collections did not explain things at my level. My first contacts with chess positional concepts were from the computer chess literature. It was only when I was in the United States that I read my first book on chess positional concepts. I was a very weak chess player when I moved to the United States.

During my college years, I continued to play Go from time to time. I also played a few games of chess, mostly because of my interest in computer chess. I hardly ever played Chinese chess, although I do remember winning one casual game when I tried to "think like a computer", by imagining how a program would "reason" about the position. My thought process in that Chinese chess game, however, had no bearing whatsoever on how Deep Blue actually played chess decades later.

After college, I spent two years in mandatory military service, and then went to Carnegie Mellon University in the United States. I quit playing Go when I was in the US. I was about shodan (one dan) on the American scale when I quit. I started my own computer chess project at Carnegie Mellon about a year after quitting Go, but the two decisions were totally unrelated. I was never really a chess player, and played few games even after I began working full time on computer chess. I became better at chess because of the computer chess work, but I have never had a formal chess rating. I am pretty certain that I was, at best, no better than an 1800 on the chess rating scale. What I really learned from the Deep Blue project is a stronger appreciation of the beauty of the art practiced by the Grandmasters.

An Early Riser

The following story has nothing to do with chess or computer chess, but it does tell you something about me. The reason why I include it here is to come clean. My parents, my teacher and my classmates in junior high deserve to know the truth.

The education system in Taiwan can be traced back to the Tang Dynasty in China. During this period, an Empress took over the reign of China after the death of her Emperor husband, becoming the first and only Empress to directly rule over the country. While traditionalists might not look upon her reign favorably, one of her edicts had profound effects on the Chinese psyche, and the family tradition of the entire Far East. She established a system for selecting government officials based on public exams. The public exams became the main social migration paths as there was no restriction on who could take part. Potentially, the son of the poorest peasant could become the Prime Minister. Education of children became the most important thing in family life for many parents in the Far East as other rulers in the region copied the system. In time, the education system itself began to revolve around examinations of various sorts. This thousand-year-old education system was designed to produce obedient civil officials for the imperial government. Creativity was, of course, not necessarily a desirable trait for obedient civil officials.

At the time when I was enrolled in primary school, a Taiwanese youngster needed to go through three entrance exams before reaching college. The first entrance exam was for junior high (after six years of primary school), the second was for senior high, and the last was the college entrance exam. The first two were regional, but the college entrance exam was nationwide. During my third grade, the Taiwanese government decided that all children should have at least nine years of education, and the junior high entrance exam was abolished. So I did have a little bit of childhood without the immediate pressure of the entrance exams.

The entrance exams placed a premium on memorization, and the whole education system in Taiwan was seriously skewed as a result. Many students in Taiwan would spend time in private tutoring classes after regular school, studying for the entrance exams at considerable expense to their parents. To tell the truth, I have no idea what or how they studied in those private classes, as I never attended one myself. I managed to avoid taking private classes because I developed a peculiar method of "studying" while I was in primary school. My way of "studying" was only good for memorization, and not for truly understanding the subject. A few subjects, such as math and physics, still required regular study, but I pretty much got by with the other subjects that only required memorization.

My brother was in junior high while I was still in primary school. Occasionally, he would get up very early on the day of school exam because he had not finished studying from the day before. But when I thought about it, it made perfect sense to do the studying on the very day of the exam, assuming that it could be done. There were several good reasons.

First, my memory would still be fresh, without the decay from a night of sleep. Second, the short time available for studying would force me to focus, and thus less studying time was actually needed. Third, given Taiwan's subtropical weather, it was far more pleasant to study in the early morning. Of course, my true motivation was that if the scheme worked, I would not need to spend a lot of time studying. I am a lazy person, and my laziness started very early in life.

By the time I was in junior high, early morning cramming had become a ritual for me. On the day of a school exam, I would get up at, say 1.00 am, and study until daybreak. After taking the exam, I crashed and forgot all the silly tidbits that I force-fed into my brain in the early morning. I was getting fairly good grades, constantly at or near the top of the class. My teacher started to take notice, as I was the only student at the top of the class not taking private classes.

One morning, my teacher gave a speech to the entire school. That morning I was on duty to clean up the classroom, and thankfully was not present for the speech. I was shocked to find out later that I was the subject of part of the speech. Apparently, my teacher got wind of the fact that I was studying in the wee hours of the morning, and gave a glowing account of how the other students should follow my example. He was assuming that I did it every day, and was using me as an example on how the other students should study as *hard* as I supposedly did.

My teacher never did realize the real reasons for my early morning studying. I was even more embarrassed when my mother proudly repeated what my teacher said after hearing it from my classmates' mothers. I never did tell my mother or my teacher what really transpired. Well, now they know.

Sidestepping Authorities

Teenagers are known to be rebellious. I was reasonably well behaved, but I did have a rebellious streak. I respected the authorities when they proved to my satisfaction that they deserved respect, but respecting the authorities did not mean that I would not try to sidestep them. This attitude towards authoritative figures had some bearing on some of the later events at Carnegie Mellon, during the early years of the chess project

My brother was studying Chemical Engineering in college when I enrolled in senior high, and I picked up some of his college textbooks that he was no longer using. My first math teacher at the senior high was a fairly irresponsible person, who spent more than half of the time in class complaining about this and that instead of doing real teaching. After listening to him a few times, I decided that my time in class would be better spent doing my own reading, so I started going through my brother's math textbooks. The math teacher was so busy complaining about his life that he never realized that I was reading my own books, or maybe he just did not care. My second math teacher was a good teacher, but since I had already gone through some of the material, I continued my own extracurricular math study in the class from time to time. One day the teacher noticed that I was not paying attention to him and came down on me. When he found out what I was reading, he backed off but gave me a warning not to do it again. Not surprisingly, he began to pick on me, frequently asking me to go up to the blackboard and demonstrate that I knew the subject. This went on for a while until he came up with a problem that he thought I could not possibly solve.

It turned out to be solving a second order finite difference equation [5] resulting from a random walk problem. Of course, finite difference equations are not really part of the high school curriculum. As a matter of fact, they were not in my college curriculum either. But I got lucky. They were in my brother's college curriculum, and I happened to have read about them a few months earlier in his books. I went up to the blackboard and solved the equation in about 30 seconds, using notations none of the other students knew anything about. It was priceless to see the teacher's face. I knew that he could not possibly have expected me to solve the equation using the method that I used. I was curious about how he was going to explain things to the class, and what his alternative solution was.

"Well, that was called a finite difference equation, but we are not going to solve it that way." So he did have an alternative way to solve the equation. This was going to be interesting. For the next ten minutes or so, he filled up half of the blackboard with complicated algebraic equations, and eventually obtained the same solution as I had earlier. I checked the supplementary books afterwards, and found out that was indeed the solution recommended in them.

The teacher eased up on me after the incident. I made quite an impression on some of my high school classmates, and they gave me the nickname "Crazy Bird [6]." Later on, when I came to the United States, people who had problems pronouncing my name knew me as CB.

After I enrolled in the National Taiwan University, I had a few small incidents with some professors, but nothing serious. One

---

5 If you don't know what a finite difference equation is, don't worry about it. I found the knowledge useful, but you certainly can read the rest of the book without knowing what it is.

6 In Chinese, the word "crazy" has the same sound as "feng", the Chinese character for "peak" and the first character of my given name.

incident took place in the physics class and was somewhat similar to what happened in my high school math class, but not as dramatic. Afterwards, our physics professor had the strange notion that I would make a good physicist. I got good grades, so I had no reason to complain. I did something more daring in my Chinese class. We were supposed to write a Chinese essay on what we read in Chuan-Tzu, a Chinese literary classic. Chuan-Tzu happened to rhyme with the Chinese translation for "atomic". The title for the essay was something like "On Reading Chuan-Tzu". I changed the title to "Experiments on Chuan-Tzu Collisions" and wrote the essay as a satire in the form of a report on atomic collisions experiments. In my essay, I made fun of our Chinese professor extensively. He was not too happy with my portrayal of him, but was sufficiently amused to give me my highest ever grade for an essay. As I suspected, he did have a strong sense of humor.

In Taiwan, boys were required to serve two years in the military after college. In my opinion, the net effect was that college boys became dumber; I certainly felt dumber. My reaction time was slower, and I definitely lost an edge along the way. The military environment was designed to produce obedient soldiers, not free thinking souls. The lack of intellectual stimulation led to mental atrophy. The fact that many of us were placed in high-pressure environments also did not help. I was luckier than most, in that my service was mainly teaching new soldiers and junior officers, the subjects of basic electricity and English, at the Missile Command Training Center. The hours were long, and it was frustrating that the majority of the soldier students were from the bottom of the barrel. Most of the students either could not or would not learn the English alphabet. In the end, I just concentrated on the few that had some chance of making it. Anyhow, I was not happy, and I wanted to change things.

The Missile Command had a few simulators for training officers in charge of firing the missiles. The simulators were expensive, and they were all broken. Before I became an instructor, I went through maintenance training for the command module, and was somewhat familiar with its internal structure. The simulator was based on a modified command module, and was effectively a glorified video game that used the radar screen as the display. The Center had the schematics for both the simulator and the command module. They were based on ancient technologies: relay-based logic, analog potentiometers for waveform generation, and so on. Typical military stuff, ten to twenty years out of date. The video stream for the command module was easily accessible, and modifying it was trivial. To be able to turn a command module into a simulator was clearly desirable—there were many working command modules. I made a proposal to the Commander of the Training Center, and got the go-ahead to do a demonstration. I went to the electronic-component stores in Taipei and acquired a few parts. It took about a day to put things together, and I was able to inject my own video signal onto the radar screen. The Commander was thrilled and I was asked to write a formal proposal. It was turned down in the end, as I had absolutely no intention of staying on beyond my regular service.

Military service was a traumatic experience for me. Physically, I was fine. Psychologically, the long period of mental suppression took its toll. It was probably close to two years after military service before my mental acumen fully recovered. I managed to do a few things out of the ordinary while in the military, but being subject to two years of unconditional authority was simply too much for me. Looking back, I wonder whether my early escapades in graduate school were a result of long deprivation of free will during my military service.

My last year of military service was 1982. Early in that year I received notification from Carnegie Mellon University that I was accepted into their Computer Science Department. So, that August, a couple of weeks after leaving military service, I got on the plane and left for the United States.

The Case for Carnegie Mellon

How did I end up at Carnegie Mellon? Well, it was kind of convoluted.

The Taiwanese information technology (IT) industry was virtually nonexistent when I was an undergraduate in the Electrical Engineering (EE) Department of National Taiwan University. The microprocessor revolution had just begun. Seeing that the microprocessor might provide a way for the Taiwanese IT industry to leapfrog, the National Science Council in Taiwan funded microprocessor research projects in universities. As a result, in my sophomore year I began to work for our department head on a microprocessor research project.

I joined the project after a classmate of mine, Chia-Min Hwang, asked whether I was interested in partnering him to work on the project. For this project, opposite to what happened in the chess project, I was the software guy and Hwang was the hardware guy. Our project was to do vibration analysis of tooling machines. The project lasted until my graduation. In retrospect, my work was not much in terms of real research, but I developed some useful computer skills. This experience played a role in my choice of graduate school.

The university-based microprocessor research projects were almost all software projects. Research in IT hardware was effectively out of the reach of Taiwanese universities. To handle hardware research, the government set up industrial research agencies, one of which was the Electronics Research and Services Organization (ERSO). In my senior year, a representative from ERSO gave a talk to students in the EE Department. He stressed that silicon chips would be critical in every aspect of our lives and, given the lack of natural resources in Taiwan, developing an IC industry would be vital for the future growth of the economy. The speaker from ERSO, Chintay Shih, is today the President of the Industrial Technology Research Institute, which includes ERSO itself. The talk must have been a good one, because afterwards I decided that I wanted to study how to design chips [7].

At the time the best place to study chip design was the United States, so I sent several applications to US universities. Most of my applications were sent to EE Departments. However, I did send one to the Computer Science (CS) Department at Carnegie Mellon University in Pittsburgh. There were two reasons that I sent my application there.

The first reason was that my microprocessor experience made the idea of a CS department palatable, as long as I got to work on chip design. The fact that the CS Department at Carnegie Mellon was ranked among the top three did not hurt either.

The second reason had something to do with my faculty advisor at Carnegie Mellon, Professor H T Kung, but not in the way you might think. I did not choose Carnegie Mellon because of Professor Kung's presence there; it was a bit more complicated. In the late 1970s and early 1980s, Professor Kung did what he could to help the budding IC industry in Taiwan to get on its feet. One of the

[7] Well, I am exaggerating a little bit. I had an existing interest in learning how integrated circuits work. A personal project of mine forced me to learn about the subject.

things that he did was to introduce the book *Introduction to VLSI Systems* by Carver Mead and Lynn Conway, to Taiwanese researchers. This book was the bible for VLSI classes in the early 1980s. In the book, there was a chapter by Charles Leiserson (then a student of Professor Kung's) and Professor Kung himself. Charles, by the way, is now a professor at MIT. Anyway, from this chapter it was obvious that there was an active and well-respected VLSI group at the CS Department of Carnegie Mellon. This was the second reason for my sending in the application.

I received two admissions from schools that I was really interested in. One was for the EE Department at Stanford University, in the heart of the Silicon Valley. The other one was for the CS Department at Carnegie Mellon University. With my electrical engineering background, Stanford would have been my first choice, but the research assistantship offered by Carnegie Mellon tipped the scale, and I went to Pittsburgh

![rook icon] APPENDIX B

Selected Game Scores

Chiptest-Recom, 1986 ACM Championship, Dallas, Round 5

1. f4 d5 2. e3 c5 3. Bb5+ Bd7 4. Be2 g6 5. Nf3 Bg7 6. c4 dxc4 7. Bxc4 b5 8. Be2 Bc6 9. O-O c4 10. a4 a6 11. axb5 axb5 12. Rxa8 Bxa8 13. Na3 Bxf3 14. Rxf3 Qd5 15. b3 cxb3 16. Bxb5+ Nd7 17. Bc4 Qb7 18. Bxb3 Ngf6 19. Rf1 O-O 20. Nc4 Ra8 21. Ne5 e6 22. Nd3 Ne4 23. Nf2 Nxf2 24. Kxf2 Nc5 25. Bc4 Na4 26. Qc2 Nb6 27. Bb2 Nxc4 28. Bxg7 Nxd2 29. Qxd2 Kxg7 30. Kg1 Ra4 31. Qc3+ f6 32. Rc1 Qe4 33. Qb3 Ra7 34. Rc8 e5 35. Rc4 Qa8 36. Kf2 exf4 37. exf4 Ra2+ 38. Rc2 Qa7+ 39. Kf1 Ra1+ 40. Ke2 Qe7+ 41. Kd2 Qd6+ 42. Ke2 Qxf4 43. h3 Qe4+ 44. Kf2 Qh4+ 45. g3 Qxh3 46. Rc7+ Kh6 47. Qe3+ g5 48. Rxh7+ Kxh7 49. Qe7+ Kg6 1/2-1/2.

Bent Larsen-Deep Thought, 1988 Software Toolworks Chess Championship, Long Beach, Round 3

1. c4 e5 2. g3 Nf6 3. Bg2 c6 4. Nf3 e4 5. Nd4 d5 6. cxd5 Qxd5 7. Nc2 Qh5 8. h4 Bf5 9. Ne3 Bc5 10. Qb3 b6 11. Qa4 O-O 12. Nc3 b5 13. Qc2 Bxe3 14. dxe3 Re8 15. a4 b4 16. Nb1 Nbd7 17. Nd2 Re6? (Ne5!, with the idea of Nf3 giving up the c pawn for a strong attack, possibly with Bd3 later) 18. b3 Rd8 19. Bb2 Bg6 20. Nc4 Nd5 21. O-O-O N7f6 22. Bh3 Bf5 23. Bxf5 Qxf5 24. f3 h5 25. Bd4 Rd7 26. Kb2 Rc7 27. g4 hxg4 28. Rhg1 c5 29. fxg4 Nxg4 30. Bxg7 Rg6 31. Qd2 Rd7 32. Rxg4 Rxg4 33. Ne5 Nxe3 34. Qxd7 Nxd1 35. Qxd1 Rg3 36. Qd6 Kxg7 37. Nd7 Re3 38. Qh2 Kh7 39. Nf8 Kh8 40. h5 Qd5 41. Ng6 fxg6 42. hxg6 Kg7 43. Qh7 Kf6 0-1

Deep Blue-Garry Kasparov, 1996 ACM Chess Challenge, Philadelphia, Game 1

1.e4 c5 2.c3 d5 3.exd5 Qxd5 4.d4 Nf6 5.Nf3 Bg4 6.Be2 e6 7.h3 Bh5 8.0-0 Nc6 9.Be3 cxd4 10.cxd4 Bb4 11.a3 Ba5 12.Nc3 Qd6 13.Nb5 Qe7 14.Ne5 Bxe2 15.Qxe2 0-0 16.Rac1 Rac8 17.Bg5 Bb6 18.Bxf6 gxf6 19.Nc4 Rfd8 20.Nxb6 axb6 21.Rfd1 f5 22.Qe3 Qf6 23.d5 Rxd5 24.Rxd5 exd5 25.b3 Kh8 26.Qxb6 Rg8 27.Qc5 d4 28.Nd6 f4 29.Nxb7 Ne5 30.Qd5 f3 31.g3 Nd3 32.Rc7 Re8 33.Nd6 Re1+ 34.Kh2 Nxf2 35.Nxf7+ Kg7 36.Ng5+ Kh6 37.Rxh7+ 1-0

Garry Kasparov-Deep Blue, 1996 ACM Chess Challenge, Philadelphia, Game 2

1.Nf3 d5 2.d4 e6 3.g3 c5 4.Bg2 Nc6 5.0-0 Nf6 6.c4 dxc4 7.Ne5 Bd7 8.Na3 cxd4 9.Naxc4 Bc5 10.Qb3 0-0 11.Qxb7 Nxe5 12.Nxe5 Rb8 13.Qf3 Bd6 14.Nc6 Bxc6 15.Qxc6 e5 16.Rb1 Rb6 17.Qa4 Qb8 18.Bg5 Be7 19.b4 Bxb4 20.Bxf6 gxf6 21.Qd7 Qc8 22.Qxa7 Rb8 23.Qa4 Bc3 24.Rxb8 Qxb8 25.Be4 Qc7 26.Qa6 Kg7 27.Qd3 Rb8 28.Bxh7 Rb2 29.Be4 Rxa2 30.h4 Qc8 31.Qf3 Ra1 32.Rxa1 Bxa1 33.Qh5 Qh8 34.Qg4+ Kf8 35.Qc8+ Kg7 36.Qg4+ Kf8 37.Bd5 Ke7 38.Bc6 Kf8 39.Bd5 Ke7 40.Qf3 Bc3 41.Bc4 Qc8 42.Qd5 Qe6 43.Qb5 Qd7 44.Qc5+ Qd6 45.Qa7+ Qd7 46.Qa8 Qc7 47.Qa3+ Qd6 48.Qa2 f5 49.Bxf7 e4 50.Bh5 Qf6 51.Qa3+ Kd7 52.Qa7+ Kd8 53.Qb8+ Kd7 54.Be8+ Ke7 55.Bb5 Bd2 56.Qc7+ Kf8 57.Bc4 Bc3 58.Kg2 Be1 59.Kf1 Bc3 60.f4 exf3 61.exf3 Bd2 62.f4 Ke8 63.Qc8+ Ke7 64.Qc5+ Kd8 65.Bd3 Be3 66.Qxf5 Qc6 67.Qf8+ Kc7 68.Qe7+ Kc8 69.Bf5+ Kb8 70.Qd8+ Kb7 71.Qd7+ Qxd7 72.Bxd7 Kc7 73.Bb5 Kd6 1-0

Deep Blue-Garry Kasparov, 1996 ACM Chess Challenge, Philadelphia, Game 3

1.e4 c5 2.c3 d5 3.exd5 Qxd5 4.d4 Nf6 5.Nf3 Bg4 6.Be2 e6 7.0-0 Nc6 8.Be3 cxd4 9.cxd4 Bb4 10.a3 Ba5 11.Nc3 Qd6 12.Ne5 Bxe2 13.Qxe2 Bxc3 14.bxc3 Nxe5 15.Bf4 Nf3+ 16.Qxf3 Qd5 17.Qd3 Rc8 18.Rfc1 Qc4 19.Qxc4 Rxc4 20.Rcb1 b6 21.Bb8 Ra4 22.Rb4 Ra5 23.Rc4 0-0 24.Bd6 Ra8 25.Rc6 b5 26.Kf1 Ra4 27.Rb1 a6 28.Ke2 h5 29.Kd3 Rd8 30.Be7 Rd7 31.Bxf6 gxf6 32.Rb3 Kg7 33.Ke3 e5 34.g3 exd4+ 35.cxd4 Re7+ 36.Kf3 Rd7 37.Rd3 Raxd4 38.Rxd4 Rxd4 39.Rxa6 1/2-1/2

Garry Kasparov-Deep Blue, 1996 ACM Chess Challenge, Philadelphia, Game 4

1.Nf3 d5 2.d4 c6 3.c4 e6 4.Nbd2 Nf6 5.e3 Nbd7 6.Bd3 Bd6 7.e4 dxe4 8.Nxe4 Nxe4 9.Bxe4 0-0 10.0-0 h6 11.Bc2 e5 12.Re1 exd4 13.Qxd4 Bc5 14.Qc3 a5 15.a3 Nf6 16.Be3 Bxe3 17.Rxe3 Bg4 18.Ne5 Re8 19.Rae1 Be6 20.f4 Qc8 21.h3 b5 22.f5 Bxc4 23.Nxc4 bxc4 24.Rxe8+ Nxe8 25.Re4 Nf6 26.Rxc4 Nd5 27.Qe5 Qd7 28.Rg4 f6 29.Qd4 Kh7 30.Re4 Rd8 31.Kh1 Qc7 32.Qf2 Qb8 33.Ba4 c5 34.Bc6 c4 35.Rxc4 Nb4 36.Bf3 Nd3 37.Qh4 Qxb2 38.Qg3 Qxa3 39.Rc7 Qf8 40.Ra7 Ne5 41.Rxa5 Qf7 42.Rxe5 fxe5 43.Qxe5 Re8 44.Qf4 Qf6 45.Bh5 Rf8 46.Bg6+ Kh8 47.Qc7 Qd4 48.Kh2 Ra8 49.Bh5 Qf6 50.Bg6 Rg8 1/2-1/2

Deep Blue-Garry Kasparov, 1996 ACM Chess Challenge, Philadelphia, Game 5

1.e4 e5 2.Nf3 Nf6 3.Nc3 Nc6 4.d4 exd4 5.Nxd4 Bb4 6.Nxc6 bxc6 7.Bd3 d5 8.exd5 cxd5 9.0-0 0-0 10.Bg5 c6 11.Qf3 Be7 12.Rae1 Re8 13.Ne2 h6 14.Bf4 Bd6 15.Nd4 Bg4 16.Qg3 Bxf4 17.Qxf4 Qb6 18.c4 Bd7 19.cxd5 cxd5 20.Rxe8+ Rxe8 21.Qd2 Ne4 22.Bxe4 dxe4 23.b3 Rd8 24.Qc3 f5 25.Rd1 Be6 26.Qe3 Bf7 27.Qc3 f4 28.Rd2 Qf6 29.g3 Rd5 30.a3 Kh7 31.Kg2 Qe5 32.f3 e3 33.Rd3 e2 34.gxf4 e1Q 35.fxe5 Qxc3 36.Rxc3 Rxd4 37.b4 Bc4 38.Kf2 g5 39.Re3 Rd2+ 40.Ke1 Rd3 41.Kf2 Kg6 42.Rxd3 Bxd3 43.Ke3 Bc2 44.Kd4 Kf5 45.Kd5 h5 0-1

Garry Kasparov-Deep Blue, 1996 ACM Chess Challenge, Philadelphia, Game 6

1.Nf3 d5 2.d4 c6 3.c4 e6 4.Nbd2 Nf6 5.e3 c5 6.b3 Nc6 7.Bb2 cxd4 8.exd4 Be7 9.Rc1 0-0 10.Bd3 Bd7 11.0-0 Nh5 12.Re1 Nf4 13.Bb1 Bd6 14.g3 Ng6 15.Ne5 Rc8 16.Nxd7 Qxd7 17.Nf3 Bb4 18.Re3 Rfd8 19.h4 Nge7 20.a3 Ba5 21.b4 Bc7 22.c5 Re8 23.Qd3 g6 24.Re2 Nf5 25.Bc3 h5 26.b5 Nce7 27.Bd2 Kg7 28.a4 Ra8 29.a5 a6 30.b6 Bb8 31.Bc2 Nc6 32.Ba4 Re7 33.Bc3 Ne5 34.dxe5 Qxa4 35.Nd4 Nxd4 36.Qxd4 Qd7 37.Bd2 Re8 38.Bg5 Rc8 39.Bf6+ Kh7 40.c6 bxc6 41.Qc5 Kh6 42.Rb2 Qb7 43.Rb4 1-0

Garry Kasparov-Deep Blue, IBM Kasparov vs. Deep Blue Rematch, Game 1

1.Nf3 d5 2.g3 Bg4 3.b3 Nd7 4.Bb2 e6 5.Bg2 Ngf6 6.O-O c6 7.d3 Bd6 8.Nbd2 O-O 9.h3 Bh5 10.e3 h6 11.Qe1 Qa5 12.a3 Bc7 13.Nh4 g5 14.Nhf3 e5 15.e4 Rfe8 16.Nh2 Qb6 17.Qc1 a5 18.Re1 Bd6 19.Ndf1 dxe4 20.dxe4 Bc5 21.Ne3 Rad8 22.Nhf1 g4 23.hxg4 Nxg4 24.f3 Nxe3 25.Nxe3 Be7 26.Kh1 Bg5 27.Re2 a4 28.b4 f5 29.exf5 e4 30.f4 Bxe2 31.fxg5 Ne5 32.g6 Bf3 33.Bc3 Qb5 34.Qf1 Qxf1+ 35.Rxf1 h5 36.Kg1 Kf8 37.Bh3 b5 38.Kf2 Kg7 39.g4 Kh6 40.Rg1 hxg4 41.Bxg4 Bxg4 42.Nxg4+ Nxg4+ 43.Rxg4 Rd5 44.f6 Rd1 45.g7 1-0

Deep Blue-Garry Kasparov, IBM Kasparov vs. Deep Blue Rematch, Game 2

1.e4 e5 2.Nf3 Nc6 3.Bb5 a6 4.Ba4 Nf6 5.O-O Be7 6.Re1 b5 7.Bb3 d6 8.c3 O-O 9.h3 h6 10.d4 Re8 11.Nbd2 Bf8 12.Nf1 Bd7 13.Ng3 Na5 14.Bc2 c5 15.b3 Nc6 16.d5 Ne7 17.Be3 Ng6 18.Qd2 Nh7 19.a4 Nh4 20.Nxh4 Qxh4 21.Qe2 Qd8 22.b4 Qc7 23.Rec1 c4 24.Ra3 Rec8 25.Rca1 Qd8 26.f4 Nf6 27.fxe5 dxe5 28.Qf1 Ne8 29.Qf2 Nd6 30.Bb6 Qe8 31.R3a2 Be7 32.Bc5 Bf8 33.Nf5 Bxf5 34.exf5 f6 35.Bxd6 Bxd6 36.axb5 axb5 37.Be4 Rxa2 38.Qxa2 Qd7 39.Qa7 Rc7 40.Qb6 Rb7 41.Ra8+ Kf7 42.Qa6 Qc7 43.Qc6 Qb6+ 44.Kf1 Rb8 45.Ra6 1-0

Garry Kasparov-Deep Blue, IBM Kasparov vs. Deep Blue Rematch, Game 3

1.d3 e5 2.Nf3 Nc6 3.c4 Nf6 4.a3 d6 5.Nc3 Be7 6.g3 O-O 7.Bg2 Be6 8.O-O Qd7 9.Ng5 Bf5 10.e4 Bg4 11.f3 Bh5 12.Nh3 Nd4 13.Nf2 h6 14.Be3 c5 15.b4 b6 16.Rb1 Kh8 17.Rb2 a6 18.bxc5 bxc5 19.Bh3 Qc7 20.Bg4 Bg6 21.f4 exf4 22.gxf4 Qa5 23.Bd2 Qxa3 24.Ra2 Qb3 25.f5 Qxd1 26.Bxd1 Bh7 27.Nh3 Rfb8 28.Nf4 Bd8 29.Nfd5 Nc6 30.Bf4 Ne5 31.Ba4 Nxd5 32.Nxd5 a5 33.Bb5 Ra7 34.Kg2 g5 35.Bxe5+ dxe5 36.f6 Bg6 37.h4 gxh4 38.Kh3 Kg8 39.Kxh4 Kh7 40.Kg4 Bc7 41.Nxc7 Rxc7 42.Rxa5 Rd8 43.Rf3 Kh8 44.Kh4 Kg8 45.Ra3 Kh8 46.Ra6 Kh7 47.Ra3 Kh8 48.Ra6 1/2-1/2

Deep Blue-Garry Kasparov, IBM Kasparov vs. Deep Blue Rematch, Game 4

1.e4 c6 2.d4 d6 3.Nf3 Nf6 4.Nc3 Bg4 5.h3 Bh5 6.Bd3 e6 7.Qe2 d5
8.Bg5 Be7 9.e5 Nfd7 10.Bxe7 Qxe7 11.g4 Bg6 12.Bxg6 hxg6 13.h4
Na6 14.O-O-O O-O-O 15.Rdg1 Nc7 16.Kb1 f6 17.exf6 Qxf6 18.Rg3
Rde8 19.Re1 Rhf8 20.Nd1 e5 21.dxe5 Qf4 22.a3 Ne6 23.Nc3 Ndc5
24.b4 Nd7 25.Qd3 Qf7 26.b5 Ndc5 27.Qe3 Qf4 28.bxc6 bxc6
29.Rd1 Kc7 30.Ka1 Qxe3 31.fxe3 Rf7 32.Rh3 Ref8 33.Nd4 Rf2
34.Rb1 Rg2 35.Nce2 Rxg4 36.Nxe6+ Nxe6 37.Nd4 Nxd4 38.exd4
Rxd4 39.Rg1 Rc4 40.Rxg6 Rxc2 41.Rxg7+ Kb6 42.Rb3+ Kc5 43.Rxa7
Rf1+ 44.Rb1 Rff2 45.Rb4 Rc1+ 46.Rb1 Rcc2 47.Rb4 Rc1+ 48.Rb1
Rxb1+ 49.Kxb1 Re2 50.Re7 Rh2 51.Rh7 Kc4 52.Rc7 c5 53.e6 Rxh4
54.e7 Re4 55.a4 Kb3 56.Kc1 1/2-1/2

Garry Kasparov-Deep Blue, IBM Kasparov vs. Deep Blue Rematch, Game 5

1.Nf3 d5 2.g3 Bg4 3.Bg2 Nd7 4.h3 Bxf3 5.Bxf3 c6 6.d3 e6 7.e4 Ne5
8.Bg2 dxe4 9.Bxe4 Nf6 10.Bg2 Bb4+ 11.Nd2 h5 12.Qe2 Qc7 13.c3
Be7 14.d4 Ng6 15.h4 e5 16.Nf3 exd4 17.Nxd4 O-O-O 18.Bg5 Ng4
19.O-O-O Rhe8 20.Qc2 Kb8 21.Kb1 Bxg5 22.hxg5 N6e5 23.Rhe1 c5
24.Nf3 Rxd1+ 25.Rxd1 Nc4 26.Qa4 Rd8 27.Re1 Nb6 28.Qc2 Qd6
29.c4 Qg6 30.Qxg6 fxg6 31.b3 Nxf2 32.Re6 Kc7 33.Rxg6 Rd7
34.Nh4 Nc8 35.Bd5 Nd6 36.Re6 Nb5 37.cxb5 Rxd5 38.Rg6 Rd7
39.Nf5 Ne4 40.Nxg7 Rd1+ 41.Kc2 Rd2+ 42.Kc1 Rxa2 43.Nxh5 Nd2
44.Nf4 Nxb3+ 45.Kb1 Rd2 46.Re6 c4 47.Re3 Kb6 48.g6 Kxb5 49.g7
Kb4 1/2-1/2

Deep Blue-Garry Kasparov, IBM Kasparov vs. Deep Blue Rematch, Game 6

1.e4 c6 2.d4 d5 3.Nc3 dxe4 4.Nxe4 Nd7 5.Ng5 Ngf6 6.Bd3 e6
7.N1f3 h6 8.Nxe6 Qe7 9.O-O fxe6 10.Bg6+ Kd8 11.Bf4 b5 12.a4
Bb7 13.Re1 Nd5 14.Bg3 Kc8 15.axb5 cxb5 16.Qd3 Bc6 17.Bf5 exf5
18.Rxe7 Bxe7 19.c4 1-0

APPENDIX C

Further Reading

On Deep Blue and Its Predecessors

Deep Blue, January 2002, Artificial Intelligence, vol. 134, pp. 57–83.
IBM's Deep Blue Chess Grandmaster Chips, Mar/Apr 1999, IEEE Micro
Magazine, pp. 71–81.
A Grandmaster Chess Machine, October 1990, Scientific American,
pp. 44–50.
Deep Thought, 1990, a chapter in the book *Computers, Chess, and
Cognition*, Springer-Verlag, pp. 55–78.
The web site http://www.chess.ibm.com is an archive of the 1997
Deep Blue match web broadcast. Deep Blue game logs from the
1997 rematch can be found on this web site as of this writing.

On Computer Chess in General

Chess Skills in Man and Machine, Springer-Verlag, is still a classic.
The chapter on *Chess 4.5*, while dated, is still an essential primer
on how to program a chess computer.
Computers, Chess, and Cognition, Springer-Verlag, is a book on more
recent developments up to the early 90s. It also contains some
material on computer go.
Journal of the International Computer Chess Association, is a source for
latest developments in computer chess. For subscription information, see http://www.dcs.qmw.ac.uk./~icca/. The web site also
contains interesting links.

On Other Games

One Jump Ahead: Challenging Human Supremacy in Checkers,
Springer-Verlag, is a book on the creation of Chinook, a World
Championship class checkers program. It also contains a different

perspective on the computer chess world in the 1980s and the early 1990s.

http://www.ff.iij4u.or.jp/~jun1/csa/index_e.html is the web site for the Computer Shogi Association.

http://www.usgo.org/computer/ is a web site maintained by American Go Association on computer Go.